SWEET LAND
of LIBERTY

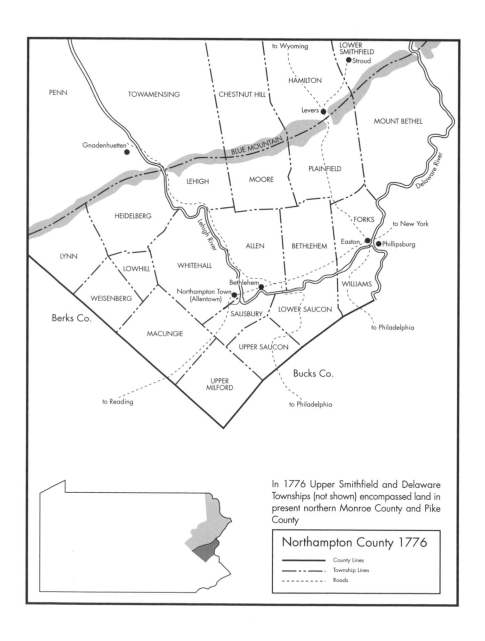

to Wyoming

LOWER
SMITHFIELD
●Stroud

HAMILTON

PENN

TOWAMENSING

CHESTNUT HILL

Levers●

MOUNT BETHEL

Gnadenhuetten●

BLUE MOUNTAIN

PLAINFIELD

Delaware River

LEHIGH

MOORE

HEIDELBERG

Lehigh River

FORKS

to New York

ALLEN

BETHLEHEM

Easton●
●Phillipsburg

LYNN

WHITEHALL

LOWHILL

Bethlehem●

WILLIAMS

WEISENBERG

Northampton Town●
(Allentown)

SALISBURY

LOWER SAUCON

Berks Co.

to Philadelphia

MACUNGIE

UPPER SAUCON

Bucks Co.

UPPER
MILFORD

to Reading

to Philadelphia

In 1776 Upper Smithfield and Delaware
Townships (not shown) encompassed land in
present northern Monroe County and Pike
County

Northampton County 1776

————————	County Lines
—·—·—·—·—	Township Lines
---------	Roads

SWEET LAND

of LIBERTY

. . . .

THE ORDEAL OF THE

AMERICAN REVOLUTION

IN NORTHAMPTON COUNTY,

PENNSYLVANIA

FRANCIS S. FOX

The Pennsylvania State University Press
University Park, Pennsylvania

Library of Congress Cataloging-in-Publication Data

Fox, Francis S., 1925–
    Sweet land of liberty : the ordeal of the American
Revolution in Northampton County, Pennsylvania /
Francis Fox.
        p.   cm.
    Includes bibliographical references and index.
    ISBN 0-271-02062-8 (cloth : alk. paper)
    ISBN 0-271-02063-6 (pbk. : alk. paper)
    1. Northampton County (Pa.)—History—18th
century. 2. Northampton County (Pa.)—
Biography. 3. United States—History—
Revolution, 1775–1783—Social aspects.
4. Pennsylvania—History—Revolution,
1775–1783—Social aspects. 5. United States—
History—Revolution, 1775–1783—Biography.
6. Pennsylvania— History—Revolution,
1775–1783—Biography. I. Title.

F157 .N7 F69   2000
974.82203—dc21   00-020695
                                                       CIP

It is the policy of The Pennsylvania State University
Press to use acid-free paper for the first printing of
all clothbound books. Publications on uncoated
stock satisfy the minimum requirements of
American National Standard for Information
Sciences—Permanence of Paper for Printed
Library Materials, ANSI Z39.48–1992.

. . . .

It is our indispensable duty to establish such
original principles of government, as will best
promote the general happiness of the people of
this State . . . and provide for future improve-
ments, without partiality for, or prejudice against
any particular class, sect, or denomination of
men whatever.

—From the preamble to the
Constitution of Pennsylvania, 1776

CONTENTS

. . . .

PREFACE

. . . .

I still wore short pants when my mother began to infuse me with facts and fiction about ancestors and kin. On long journeys she smoothed the way with dramatic monologues—voice-overs, really—about runaway horses, picnics, berry picking, natural disasters, festive dinners, sleigh rides, weddings, and funerals. These stories teemed with grandparents, aunts, uncles, cousins—and black sheep. Over time Mother's magical tales slipped away from me. But years later I discovered that the names of a few persons and places lodged in my memory.

Around 1970, while browsing in a library, I came across a collection of books on Pennsylvania history. *Annals of Buffalo Valley* caught my eye. Set in ornate, cursive type decked with simulated gold leaf, this title illuminated the spine of the book from top to bottom. What is more, Buffalo Valley had a familiar ring. I pulled the volume from the shelf, turned to the index, and found an entry for John Kleckner, who, according to my mother, had been the progenitor of her line in America. However, as I learned that day, the honor actually belonged to John's parents, who had emigrated to Pennsylvania in the eighteenth century. "Never heard of 'em," said Mother. I decided then and there to search for the lost generation.

Anthony and Elizabeth Kleckner, and their son, John, left Derschen—located in the Duchy of Wurttemberg, Germany—in 1753 and journeyed to Philadelphia, Pennsylvania.[2] Upon completing a seven-year indenture in Germantown, Anthony moved his family north and took up land in Northampton County.[3] In the search for my ancestor I discovered that Anthony had attended an auction in 1778 and purchased a set of blacksmith tools for £73.[4]

I pursued his lead and discovered that in 1778 a magistrate in Northampton County had ordered eleven Mennonite men to swear allegiance to the Commonwealth of Pennsylvania, an oath mandated by law. The Mennonites pleaded that they could not obey the order because their religion forbade swearing. But the magistrate ignored this supplication and directed the Mennonites to forfeit their personal property and leave the state within thirty days. The sheriff descended on the Mennonites, seized their cattle and the contents of their homes, and sold the lot at public auction. Thus eleven families were stripped of the necessities of life by a government that had proclaimed it would "promote the general happiness of the people without prejudice against any particular class, sect, or denomination of men whatsoever."[5]

This incident motivated me to investigate how the American Revolution unfolded in Northampton County. The findings altered my perception of that epic period in our nation's history. But repeated attempts to frame this insight in a conventional narrative fell short. Finally, I hit upon the notion of letting men and women caught up in the Revolution speak for themselves. I did not search for them. Over a span of fifteen years, they came to me.

Many librarians and archivists generously guided me through their collections. And when I found little or nothing on their shelves, they offered encouraging words and steered me to other places that, hopefully, might make my day. I am, therefore, grateful to the following institutions and their personnel: The Historical Society of Pennsylvania, Library Company of Philadelphia, American Philosophical Society, Pennsylvania State Historical and Museum Commission, Pennsylvania State Library, Lawmaking and Legislators in Pennsylvania Project, Bucks County Historical Society, David Library of the American Revolution, Easton Public Library, Northampton County Historical and Genealogical Society, Northampton County Courthouse, Archives of the Moravian Church, Bethlehem Public Library, Lehigh County Historical Society, Monroe County Historical Society, Bucks County Historical Society, American Antiquarian Society, Boston Public Library, New England Historic Genealogical Society, and Library of the Boston Athenaeum.

Early in the preparation of this book I sought the company of historians and found it at the McNeil Center for Early American Studies. There, through a dizzy succession of brown-bag lunches, seminars, and gatherings of the *salonistès*, I began to learn a new language. Additionally, I am grateful to numerous persons for valuable advice and criticism, a group that includes Geoffrey Austrian, Wayne Bodle, Richard S. Dunn, Mahlon Hellerich, Peter Charles Hoffer, Louise Jones, Molly Kalkstein, Karen Madsen, Dea

Mallin, Jerry Mathieu, William Pencak, Richard Ryerson, Linda Stanley, Jonathan Stayer, Hope Tompkins, Donald Winslow, Claudia Waszkis, Marianne Wokeck, and Stephanie Wolfe.

Then, there is Michael Zuckerman. For more than a decade Mike has inspired me to continue digging and writing. I dedicate this book to him with affection and thanks.

. . . .

INTRODUCTION

. . . .

Immigrants drifted into the northern part of Bucks County, Pennsylvania, around 1725. Twenty-five years later some 5,000 persons inhabited this region. Craving convenient access to county courts and officials, these settlers appealed to the governor to detach nine townships from Upper Bucks and treat them as the nucleus of a new county. This initiative resulted in the formation of Northampton County in 1752.[1]

Northampton encompassed the entire northeastern corner of the province, an area of more than 5,000 square miles. The county was bounded on the north by New York, on the east by the Delaware River, on the south by Bucks County, and on the west by Berks County. Kittatinny Mountain, commonly known as Blue Mountain, stretched across Northampton. South of the mountain lay the Lehigh Valley, which attracted the majority of settlers. Above the mountain, the land rolled northward in a seemingly endless succession of ridges and narrow valleys. Beyond the gap in Blue Mountain carved by the Delaware River, narrow strips of alluvial soil lined both sides of the waterway.

By 1774 the number of inhabitants in Northampton County had risen to 15,000, or about 5 percent of Pennsylvania's population.[2] Persons of German ancestry comprised close to 80 percent of the county's inhabitants. Scots-Irish, English, Huguenots, Dutch, and Welsh made up the balance. Half of the total population was twenty-one years of age or younger.[3]

Northampton boasted three towns, each situated about fifty miles north of Philadelphia: Allentown, Bethlehem, and Easton, the county seat. The second-largest of eleven Pennsylvania counties, Northampton contained twenty-five townships: eighteen in the Lehigh Valley and seven north of Blue Mountain.[4] Each township functioned as an outpost of law and order. Inhabitants elected a number of officials, of which the most important was a constable who served warrants issued by justices of the peace, presided over township elections, and enforced the law that forbade drinking in public houses on Sundays.[5]

A cash economy had begun to replace subsistence farming in Northampton. The grain harvest in 1774 would have filled 4,500 Conestoga wagons. Sixty gristmills and and thirty sawmills dotted the landscape. The inhabitants tended 3,000 horses and mares, 3,400 horned cattle, and more than 1,000 sheep.[6] Nearly 200 men engaged in a trade. Taverners, forty-six in number, headed the list. Inhabitants with financial means acquired indentured servants and Negro slaves. Scattered about the county were places of worship for Reformed, Lutherans, Presbyterians, Moravians, and Mennonites. Reformed, with twenty-three congregations, and Lutherans, with twenty, greatly outnumbered all other religious groups in Northampton.[7] Moravians and other sects comprised fewer than 10 percent of the inhabitants.[8]

Four times a year the population of Easton swelled as inhabitants and officials visited the town for quarter sessions courts. In 1772 a visitor described the Northampton seat as "a dog-hole of a place, remote from all the world."[9] Nonetheless, Easton, with its courthouse, seventy-five shops and houses, and a population of about 400, was the burgeoning center for business and politics in Northampton. Moreover, Easton straddled the primary inland highway of the colonial period. From this county town travelers ferried across the Delaware River and headed northeast to Morristown, Hackensack, Perth Amboy, New York City, and New England, or followed improved roads west and southwest to Bethlehem, Allentown, Reading, Lancaster, York, the Shenandoah Valley, and beyond.

Many Northampton inhabitants not only had risen above a marginal existence but also had tired of jousting with officials in Philadelphia. For more than two decades, the legislative and executive branches of the provincial government had ignored their grievances. To begin with, the Pennsylvania Assembly and the proprietaries logrolled the bill that established Northampton. Eager to preserve their controlling majority, the old-guard faction in the Assembly agreed in 1752 to place the county seat at Easton— a new town to be erected on land owned by the Penn family—in return for a provision that limited to one the number of representatives in the new county.[10] Subsequently, the Assembly not only tabled petitions to move the seat to a location more central for the majority of the people, but it also sidetracked repeated attempts to increase the size of the county's delegation in the Assembly.[11]

. . . .

Machinations of this sort bred contempt for government, which surfaced in 1765 when Northampton's inhabitants defied the Stamp Act.[12] Long-term proprietary land policies that favored speculators at the expense of Northampton settlers also helped erode respect for authorities in Philadelphia. On the eve of the Revolution, Northampton's inhabitants had become restive. By chance, however, Parliament, not the provincial government in Philadelphia, touched off the rebellion in this frontier county.

On June 21, 1774, the doors of the courthouse opened for a mass meeting, the first ever held in the county. Fired up by a prominent local leader, the crowd voted to support a radical faction in Philadelphia. These reformers had been angered by Parliament's harsh response to the Boston Tea Party and called for a Continental Congress to negotiate American grievances with Great Britain. Consequently, at the request of Congress, the people of Northampton elected a committee of observation and inspection to help enforce an American boycott of British goods.

In April 1775, when news of the Battle of Lexington and Concord reached Northampton, the Committee seized the initiative and ordered the inhabitants to mobilize for self-defense. More than 2,300 men, most of the county's male population between the ages of sixteen and sixty, joined township military associations and elected officers. When Congress offered a bonus to volunteers who would serve in the Continental Army under General George Washington, a company of Northampton men marched to Boston, their pockets "ringing with the musical jingle of solid clink."[13]

War fever gripped Northampton. Inhabitants who refused to join the militia were ostracized and denounced as enemies of the county. Congress paid the Committee more than $3,000 to offset the cost of raising the troops. The provincial government contracted to pay the master of Durham Ironworks £700 for cannonballs. Blacksmiths received £600 as a down payment for rifles. Smaller amounts of cash trickled down to farmers and artisans for saltpeter, bayonets, and scabbards.

In early spring 1776, the Committee of Privates, a radical group in Philadelphia who professed to fight for the rights of the common soldier, contacted Northampton militiamen. This committee had pressed the Assembly to stiffen the penalty against men who refused to bear arms. Northampton's militia joined the argument and complained to the Assembly that sectarians in their county shunned military service. Then, in May, heeding a signal from radical leaders in Philadelphia, 900 militiamen assembled near Allentown and pledged to support the overthrow of Pennsylvania's provincial government. In Northampton, the Revolution had begun.[14]

The framers of Pennsylvania's Constitution of 1776 promised to establish a government that would promote the "happiness of the people." This goal is reflected in a charter generally regarded as the most democratic of those put forward during the Revolutionary period. But even before the convention completed its work, Constitutionalists, who defended the new frame of government, and Republicans, who opposed it, locked horns. These adversaries voiced their ideological differences in the court of public opinion and in the Assembly. Meanwhile, a confrontation with a different bent jolted Northampton. Hate and revenge fueled this contest. In a rerun of an age-old scenario, the avengers destroyed lives and property, mocked the new constitution, and challenged the authority of the elected state government.

Northampton's radicals silenced inhabitants who hoped Congress would negotiate with Great Britain. Are you for or against freedom? barked the intimidators. What is more, when the rebels closed Pennsylvania's courts, the Northampton Committee vowed to maintain law and order in the county. Hearsay and anecdotal evidence marked these proceedings. The Committee arrested and jailed persons whom zealous patriots had fingered as suspected Tories. It issued summonses and dispatched squads of armed militiamen to apprehend persons who disregarded its authority. It extracted confessions, levied fines, and published the names and offences of the guilty in Philadelphia newspapers. In short, frontier justice thrived in Northampton.

In December 1776, some 600 Northampton militiamen marched to help defend Philadelphia from the British Army. But when these sometime soldiers experienced the hardship and danger of military life, they threatened to revolt unless the government took action against those who "remained at home with their families enjoying in peace . . . all the benefits arising from the virtuous efforts of those who have ventured their lives in the defense of liberty and their country."[15]

Officeholders in Pennsylvania's fledgling Revolutionary government were beholden to militia rank and file who had pulled down the provincial government, raised a new state, and elected them. As a result, the Assembly legislated the Militia Act (March 17, 1777) and the Test Act (June 13, 1777). The first statute compelled men between the ages of eighteen and fifty-three to serve in the militia or pay heavy fines. The second ordered all men to swear allegiance to the state or lose their rights as citizens. Consequently, the radicals' imperial vision of promoting the happiness of the people survived only as a rhetorical flourish in the Constitution of the new state.

Waving the Militia Act and the Test Act or, more often than not, self-serving interpretations of them, extremists in Northampton whipsawed Moravians and Mennonites who refused to bear arms or swear allegiance because of their religious beliefs. Wrapped in the newly consecrated American flag, these opportunists set out to bankrupt sectarians, force them out of the county, and seize their land. Their success on the first count dealt a blow to Northampton's Moravian communities from which they never recovered.

Most Northampton men took the Test. However, this compact with the state did not give them immunity from prosecution under the Militia Act. Many of them risked courts-martial and fines rather than muster for active duty. Even when the enemy threatened to overrun their homes, they could not overcome their fear of bullets and arrows and the scalping knife. Protect us, they hollered to the president and the Supreme Executive Council. Send more money, cried battalion colonels.

Despite amendments to the Militia Act, Pennsylvania's Revolutionary government failed to win the hearts of Northampton's militiamen. The farmers had grown weary of their role as soldiers. Moreover, a byzantine relationship between Northampton's county lieutenant, a civilian commander of the militia who had been appointed by the president, and battalion officers, who had been elected by their men, foiled the dictates of the law. Isolated by natural boundaries, hampered by poor communications, red tape, and intramural disputes, each Northampton battalion became a fiefdom whose leaders distanced themselves from the county lieutenant, county officials, the president, and the Council.

Apprized of mutinous rumblings in Northampton, the president pleaded with the militia: "Let there be one dispute: who shall serve his country best?"[16] But pep talks and patriotic slogans had lost their sizzle in Northampton. Fearing for his life, the sheriff refused to collect fines from 300 delinquent militiamen. "They wont suffer no sheriff, constable, or any other fit person to serve any executions on them," he reported.[17] Later, when Indians and Tories threatened to clear settlers from the frontier, the president promised battalion commanders ammunition and money for scouting parties and scalps, but he warned them that the militia could not be useful if "they meet at taverns and spend their time in amusement and frolick."[18] In the months ahead, the mutiny escalated.

By 1784 most Northampton inhabitants wished to put the war behind them and get on with their lives. A revitalized citizenry pounced on the Test Act, but Constitutionalists defeated all attempts to amend one of the cornerstones of Pennsylvania's Revolutionary government. Despite the Constitutionalists' effort, in March 1786 the Assembly passed a Republican-sponsored bill that substantially amended the statute. Republicans achieved this victory with help from the entire five-man Northampton delegation, which, a year earlier, had voted unanimously to preserve the Test Act. To effect this turnabout, the electorate replaced two legislators who had voted in favor of the Test. The three remaining legislators retained their seats, but they doubtless had heard the drumbeat.[19]

The noise in Northampton over the Test Act was muted in contrast to the clamor to amend the Militia Act. With each passing year, more and more men refused to serve in the militia, or send a substitute, or pay a fine. In 1784, for example, when the state ordered units of Northampton's militia to put down a disturbance caused by the presence of illegal settlers in the northern part of the county, "not more than one-third of the number called appeared at the place of rendezvous, and among these, but very few declare themselves to be perfectly willing to go farther."[20] Northampton citizens did not oppose a well-regulated militia, but they insisted that the "present mode of conducting it is, in fact, one of the greatest nuisances in the state. . . . Battalion days . . . subserve only the purposes of idleness, disorder, and vice, depraving the morals of the rising generation so that many of us, otherwise not averse to militia duty, have withdrawn ourselves and grown sons from such musterings." The inhabitants also protested delinquent fines and special collectors who abused their power to serve their own "vicious and sinister purposes."[21] Finally, in 1788 the Republican-controlled Assembly suspended the collection of militia fines levied under earlier versions of the law. This maneuver gutted the Militia Act and, with it, the Constitutionalist Party.[22]

In brief, the Revolution in Northampton burst forth overnight. The Committee ruled the county with courts of inquiry and armed guards. Extremists marched to their own drummer. Undeclared martial law spread fear in the county and caused revulsion from the Constitutionalists. After the war a majority of Northampton's citizens embraced the Republican Party, which advocated the repeal of the Test Act and the Militia Act, the ratification of the Federal Constitution, and, in 1790, the adoption of a new state constitution. Constitutionalists failed to bring happiness to the people of Pennsylvania. To deliver that promise, Northampton turned to a new generation of silver-tongued orators.

. . . .

Sweet Land of Liberty brings the Revolution alive with sketches of men and women caught up in it. These sketches range from the quasi-biographical to lean cuttings. Robert Levers, whose dream of rising in the world had been shattered, embraced the cause of freedom and started a new career as a powerful county official. Lewis Gordon, who was a longtime servant of the king, could not find his way in the storm. Elias Long spoke out against the radicals, but his independence came at a steep price. Henry Geiger, an old soldier, unsheathed his sword and wielded it like a scythe. Michael Ohl started off on the right path, but he changed his mind and twice landed in jail. John Wetzel and John Ettwein engaged in a struggle that exhausted both men and left them and their followers worse off for it. Elizabeth Kurtz sang her own song, and what a song it was. Joseph Romig stood up to local tyrants, only to be denounced as a traitor. Notwithstanding elected county and state officials, Jacob Stroud set the pace in the sparsely settled area north of Blue Mountain. George Taylor understood the what, why, and how of colonial politics and initiated the rebellion in Northampton, but severe illness and the failure of his business cut short a promising future in the Revolutionary government. Phillis, a slave, told her secret, but to what end? Mathew and Mary Myler numbered among the thousands of wartime transients whose presence in Northampton drew the county into a much larger world. Isaac Klinkerfuss, a Hessian soldier, found a bride and a home in hostile territory. A dead mercenary named Henry Legel became the focus of a mischievous contest between two men who had more urgent business at hand. Finally, Eve Yoder and Esther Bachman, who refused to be evicted from their homes, seized the initiative and sent Constitutionalists in the Assembly hurrying for political cover.

. . . .

I

. . . .

ROBERT LEVERS

On October 4, 1723, Robert and Elizabeth Levers christened their son, Robert, at St. Mary Whitechapel in Stepney Parish, an Anglican vicariate that skirted the Thames River in the east end of London, England.[1] The boy came of age in the heart of the city's shipping industry. On any given day some 2,000 seagoing vessels vied for space at quays along the Pool, a four-mile serpentine stretch of the Thames extending from Limehouse Reach, off Stepney, to the Custom House, just east of London Bridge.[2] Upon completion of his formal education, the fourteen-year-old honors student apprenticed with a merchant. After nearly ten years of tracking and tallying goods around the world, Robert Levers looked abroad himself, and boarded a schooner bound for Philadelphia and the West Indies.

A solitary belfry atop the courthouse greeted travelers who arrived at Pennsylvania's capital city by way of the Delaware River. The sight of this homely landmark probably gave Levers a turn. Compared with London, where the spire of St. Paul's Cathedral towered over a population of some 675,000 people, Philadelphia, with about 10,000 inhabitants, resembled an English market town.[3] Nonetheless, the adventurer canceled plans to sail on to the West Indies, and cast his lot in the fastest-growing city in North America.[4]

Levers taught school, kept books for an ironmaster, copied documents for a notary, and clerked for Charles Brockden, recorder of deeds for the City of Philadelphia. None of these positions held much promise. But Brockden, a member of the colonial elite who had united with the Moravian Church, took Levers under his wing and recommended the talented clerk to Moravian authorities at Bethlehem, and to a longtime colleague named Richard Peters.[5] Peters, who simultaneously juggled posts as head of the land office, proprietary secretary, and member of the provincial council, probably knew the business of governing Pennsylvania better than anyone. Some contemporaries believed that had it not been for Peters's nearly undecipherable handwriting, the lawyer and Anglican minister might have been an even more effective administrator. In fact, Benjamin Franklin once sent Peters a handwriting expert, claiming that if the man could teach the provincial secretary to write legibly, his reputation would be made.[6] In Robert Levers, Richard Peters found not only a person who wrote with a clear hand but also someone to whom he could entrust his personal affairs. The aspiring man from Stepney and Pennsylvania's secretary forged a close relationship. Until his death in 1776, Peters favored Levers with advice, loans, and spiritual guidance.

While Levers learned the inner workings of the land office, he acted as a proxy for Peters's land speculations. In this enterprise Levers scouted the backcountry until he located acreage likely to appreciate in value. Next, he applied to the land office for a warrant, or permission to survey the land. No money changed hands. Levers merely laid claim to a tract of land situated, say, on the north side of Conedogawinet [sic] Creek in Pennsboro Township in Cumberland County. When Levers received the warrant some months later he sold it to Peters for £5. Peters then decided whether to bear the cost of surveying the land or to hold the warrant and perhaps sell it at a profit.[7] Like Richard Peters, many politically connected men of the better sort employed proxies to conceal their land speculations.

Know the territory. Be bold. Attend to details. Pay nothing down. Hold here. Sell there. Maneuvers of this kind had become second nature to Levers in the back rooms of the warehouses along the Thames. Moreover, it was Levers's good fortune to have arrived in Pennsylvania at the beginning of a period of unprecedented growth. From 1745 to 1765 the population of Philadelphia grew from 10,000 to 25,000. At the same time, thousands of immigrants passed through the city to take up land in the backcountry.[8] Levers set out to make a fortune as a speculator and move up in the world.

The organization of Northampton County in 1752 officially opened more than 3 million acres for settlers and speculators. Not content with information gleaned from land office transactions and an earful of politics—Richard Peters was a notorious gossip—Levers made numerous trips to Northampton. Capitalizing on his connections with the Moravians, Levers followed the church's missionaries and their Indian converts across uncharted land north of Blue Mountain. Levers searched out prime stands of timber, studied the watershed, and marked the site of beaver dams, which

. . . .

collected the spring runoff and turned arable land into swamps. He memorized the landmarks and pathways that honeycombed this vast undulating landscape. In brief, the boy raised in the dirt, stink, and noise of plague-ridden London became an expert on the pristine wilderness north of Blue Mountain.[9]

Levers paraded his knowledge in Bethlehem and in Philadelphia's coffee houses.[10] Wealthy merchants and government officials invited him to broker their land speculations. Levers parlayed these connections and his relationship with Richard Peters into the ability to borrow money, which enabled him to speculate for his own account. About 1753, for example, Levers acquired several tracts of land north of Blue Mountain, including one tract on Brodhead Creek, which lay opposite the Moravian Mission Church at Dansbury (present Stroudsburg, Pennsylvania).[11] He also traveled west across the Susquehanna River and acquired warrants in Cumberland County. The industrious land agent was off to a fast start; however, the French and Indian War (1753–63) temporarily crushed the land boom in Pennsylvania. War parties torched the frontier, including the settlement at Dansbury. Thousands of settlers fled for their lives. In Northampton 216 adults and children were killed or captured in the early years of the war,[12] a nightmare memorialized by an inscription—"This is the year in which raged the Indian war parties"—engraved on a stove plate cast in 1756.[13] Immigration slowed to a trickle. Land prices plunged. Moravians at Bethlehem who had planned to purchase 5,000 acres from Levers terminated negotiations. "The land is now not worth a groat. Hard fate, indeed," moaned Levers.[14]

With business in the land office at a standstill, Levers struck out on his own.[15] First, however, on January 3, 1756, at Christ Episcopal Church, a place of worship favored by Philadelphia's Anglican elite, with Reverend Peters officiating, thirty-three-year-old Robert Levers married Mary Church, who had just celebrated her twentieth birthday. The groom described his bride as "a young woman of sober character but with little fortune."[16] Why, given his financial woes—debts contracted by Levers in the 1750s followed him to the grave—did Levers not marry into a wealthy family? Perhaps he tried that path, and failed. On the other hand, Robert Levers did so value rectitude that he likely asked Mr. Church for his daughter's hand because he held her in great esteem. Perhaps, even, because he loved her.

In March 1756, Levers announced in the *Pennsylvania Gazette* that he would draw mortgages, bonds, wills, and deeds, and copy writing at the Post Office in Third Street, where he had found employment as an assistant to postmaster William Franklin.[17] Levers assured customers that he would handle their work with "utmost care, secrecy, and dispatch."[18] Nonetheless, Levers's income fell short of his needs, so he sold three properties in Northampton at bargain rates.[19]

Although Levers and his wife managed to live in reduced circumstances for the good part of a year, the birth of a daughter named Mary in December 1756 changed the equation. (Over the next twenty years Mary Levers bore six boys and two girls, of whom only one failed to reach adulthood.)[20] Desperately in need of money, Levers signed on as clerk to the captain of a privateer. Within days of Mary's birth Levers left home and sailed the high seas for seven months. Upon his return to Philadelphia, Levers refused to sign for a second cruise because, he wrote to a friend, "at best I think it is little better than piracy."[21] Even in difficult circumstances, Levers hewed to his principles. Fortunately, Richard Peters rescued his protégé and found him a post as a clerk with the governor's secretary.[22] In the meantime Levers also secured a loan and rented a store situated on Third Street, "Three [doors] below the Harp and Crown."[23] Here he continued to draw mortgages, bonds, deeds, wills, and other instruments of writing, and sold an assortment of dry and wet goods that he had acquired from the previous owner of the store.

On September 20, 1759, less than a year after he had opened his business, Levers announced that he had just received from London and Bristol a huge assortment of "European and Indian goods suitable for the season." One week later he placed an advertisement in the *Gazette* in which he listed his inventory and promised to sell it "at the very lowest prices." (He also continued to offer his services as a scrivener.) Here are some of the goods Philadelphia shoppers found at Levers's store.

> Neatest patterns of printed cottons, calicoes and linens, cambricks [cambrics] and lawns [fine open texture]; Irish linens and Russia sheeting, cotton and linen checks, damasks and diaper [pattern] tablecloths, napkins, English silk damasks, satins, peelings [thin cloth], mantuas; grograms [coarse ribbon made of silk and mohair]; striped lutestrings [plain and lustrous silk for ribbons]; taffetam [taffeta], persians, paduasoys [heavy silk]; hats, black, white and cloth colour silk mittens; plain and figured ribbons, Irish poplins silverets, dicklenets [under petticoat]; Rum, Jamaica Spirits, loaf and muscovado sugar [unrefined brown sugar]; green and bohea tea [inferior Chinese black tea]; and a great variety of other dry and wet goods.[24]

. . . .

Levers's business prospered, and he branched out. In May 1760, in addition to advertising goods sold at this store and his services as a scrivener, Levers offered to act as a broker for persons who wished to borrow or lend money. Such transactions, he assured his clients, would be carried out with the "utmost diligence and circumspection." Later the same year Levers expanded his inventory to include Mary McGlaughlin, "an Irish servant girl with about three years to serve," whom he had purchased for £16, a Dutch [German] boy with eleven years to serve, and a servant girl with three and a half years to serve. In 1762, Levers rented larger quarters at the Three Nuns on Third Street.

Levers not only sold his wares to the general public but he also acted as a supplier of these goods to the provincial government. To get his foot in this door Levers had help from Governor James Hamilton and officials whom Levers had represented in land speculations. In June 1762, for example, Levers sent "sundries by wagon to Easton for the use of [Governor Hamilton] and his company." To ease the Governor's hardship while negotiating with Indians, Levers supplied the Governor and his staff with "1 Quarter Cask Madeira Wine, 10 Gallons Jamaica Spirit, 1 bag Hyson tea [Chinese green tea], 4 loaves doub:refind [*sic*] sugar, 4 lb Ground Coffee, 1 Box Lemons." The shipment also included 22,850 grains of wampum.[25]

Although he enjoyed the good offices of men like Richard Peters and Governor Hamilton, Levers's income as a storekeeper and scrivener did not generate enough profit to meet the needs of his growing family. In fact, Levers had overextended himself. As a result, in November 1762 Levers offered his stock for sale at special prices and announced that he was "intending for the West Indies." But before he could settle his affairs and leave Philadelphia, the French and Indian War spawned one final assault on the Pennsylvania frontier. When the provincial government sent soldiers to the backcountry, Levers revived his connections with members of the provincial commission responsible for the recruitment, maintenance, and disposition of troops on the frontier, and canceled his departure for the Caribbean. The commissioners, among them Speaker of the Assembly Joseph Galloway and Benjamin Franklin, awarded Levers a contract to supply food for three companies garrisoned between Fort Augusta (present Sunbury, Pennsylvania) and Fort Hamilton, which adjoined Levers's tract of land at Dansbury. This business generated more than £4,000 in billings.[26]

When the war ended in 1763, settlers swarmed into Pennsylvania's back counties. As the price of land rose, speculators dusted off their files. Even as

. . . .

Levers delivered provisions to the provincial troops, he smelled prosperity. Ten years earlier he had explored the region north of Blue Mountain and had accumulated warrants for numerous tracts of land. Levers used windfall profits from the war and eased out of his store, certain that he would now succeed as a land speculator.[27]

As new settlers began to work the land north of Blue Mountain, Levers erected two mills on his property at Dansbury. The mill place at Hermon— so named by Levers after Mount Hermon, a site traditionally considered as the place of Jesus' transfiguration—enabled Mary and the children to escape the summer heat and humidity of Philadelphia. Although neither Levers nor his wife had united with the Brethren, they opened their house at Hermon to Moravian missionaries whose religious services attracted as many as sixty settlers at a time.[28] This gesture enabled Levers not only to strengthen his ties with the Brethren but also to ingratiate himself with newcomers to the territory. Having established Hermon as a base of operation, Levers plunged into land speculation for his own account and in combination with others.[29] In one partnership Levers teamed with Joseph Galloway and William Franklin, the statesman's son. Through Levers's efforts this trio "discovered and took up fifteen thousand two hundred acres in Northampton."[30] Acting for Galloway alone, Levers acquired twenty-two tracts of 300 acres each in Northampton County and registered them under straw names.[31] As he had more than a decade earlier, Levers also acted as an agent for wealthy individuals who hoped to compound their money in land speculations.[32]

Levers became such a trusted and reliable fixture in Northampton that Governor John Penn, doubtless on the recommendation of Richard Peters, appointed him a justice of the peace. The governor did not really need another magistrate in Northampton, but he did require a discreet person to help him finesse a thorny problem. In 1764 the people of Northampton had, for the first time, elected a German to the office of sheriff; however, the sheriff-elect owned and operated a tavern, which, by law, posed a clear conflict of interest. Angry supporters of the man who lost the contest for sheriff petitioned the governor and demanded that the recent election be set aside, and a new election be called immediately. To calm both sides in this dispute, the governor first ordered the sheriff to step down until such time as he could divest himself of the tavern. Then he appointed Robert Levers to act as sheriff from February until the annual elections in October 1765. (Levers's appointments as magistrate and acting sheriff occurred the same

. . . .

day.) This maneuver, as the governor and Peters had doubtless foreseen, gave the sheriff in limbo time to divest his tavern. Hence, on election day in 1765, the German sheriff elected the previous year stepped forward to claim the remainder of his three-year term of office. (After a three-year hiatus required by law, the people elected the same sheriff to another three-year term.) Robert Levers had been at the right place at the right time. Being a party to a behind-the-scenes political maneuver at the highest level of government would prove to be an invaluable experience for the ambitious promoter. But, as later events will bear out, of even greater value to Levers would be his chance appointment as magistrate.[33]

Although land speculation attracted chiselers from all walks of life, Levers held himself to a higher standard. In fact he may have been too forthright to succeed in this business. Bringing into play his keen memory, Levers's correspondence in this period is an amalgam of who said what, when, and where, together with a litany of promises kept and broken, confidences shared and betrayed, blame assigned and the blamed unrepentant, as if recitations could have solved the problems at hand. At times Levers pouted like a schoolboy, as in this letter to a business associate: "I never can be so certain of anything as I am that the [surveyor] never mentioned Mr. [Lewis] Gordon's name to me respecting those lands. . . . The fact is . . . I repeatedly told [the surveyor] I had six 300 acre applications to [survey] there, and he would almost as frequently forget what I had said, and repeatedly ask me and say—What, have you six hundred acres more to survey here? I replied I had 12,000 more, and I propose two of them to adjoin the H and A survey, and the other two to lay over yonder pine swamp."[34] This disagreement followed Gordon to his grave, as did Levers's debt of five-and-a-half shillings owed Gordon for filing a warrant.[35]

Levers had facts at his fingertips: creeks, brooks, runs, waterfalls, rocks, trees, stumps, natural wonders—boundary markers, a land speculator's stock in trade. Levers remembered; they did not. And when some person dared question his integrity, Levers roared. Intent on protecting his relationship with Richard Peters, Levers skewered a highly placed merchant in Philadelphia who had complained to Peters that Levers had reneged on a promise to sell him a desirable piece of land. "With respect to character, I am as delicate of throwing out the least insinuation as any man existing," Levers advised Peters.

If Mr. [Abel] James has any just pretense of claim I wish that he would

. . . .

set it forth under his own hand, that it might be duly weighed and considered by those concerned; it would undoubtedly be rather better than uncharitably endeavoring by all undue means to destroy [my] family, root and branch. Poor man, God bless him. He is intended for a voyage. And may the Great God meet him in mercy in the wide deep. . . . Upon the whole, were I conscious of having made Mr. James the most distant promise of the lands in question, I would abide by it, tho it would prove my ruin. But on the contrary, I at night, laying on my pillow, frequently call upon the great searcher of hearts to bear witness to my integrity in this matter. Doubtless he will, either soon or late.[36]

Levers cultivated an air of invincibility, but he lived on the cusp. Perennially short of cash, Levers flashed each pound as many times as possible before parting with it, a practice that sometimes backfired. For example, when Margaret Smith paid Levers £40 to purchase a tract of land for her, Levers held the money too long before attempting to complete the transaction, and Smith hauled him into court to recover her advance.[37] Because of his lack of capital, Levers skated on thin ice, and some of his creditors set out to corner him. "I am now in these hard times obliged to sell at an undervalue to pay debts which if I could get in would save my own estate," said Levers in full retreat.[38] "My affairs being something embarrassed, I proposed to two of my creditors to sell them some lands on moderate terms in payment of [my] debt."[39] Although unforgiving creditors chased him like a pack of wolves, Levers put up a brave front. In late summer, 1769, he wrote to his principal creditor. "I lost your first letter. . . . The children must have gotten to it, though I have told them not to touch my papers. . . . Mrs. Levers, myself, and our young child struck with all the marks of death . . . better days lie ahead. . . . I am again launched in the world of business [Levers had reopened his store in Philadelphia]. Still my best Hyson tea is all gone and the present confusion between England and America will prevent more coming in unless it is smuggled. I trust Providence will be propitious and smile on my labors."[40] Despite his optimism, Levers's speculations had brought him to the brink of bankruptcy.

Could Levers escape to the West Indies? Not at age forty-two with six children, another on the way, and no capital. Levers turned for advice to his aging mentor, Richard Peters, who suggested that Levers make a fresh start as a farmer and offered him easy terms on 1,000 acres in the vicinity of Mount Hermon. Overwhelmed by Peters's kindness and generosity, Levers

. . . .

experienced a spiritual rebirth. He renewed his vows to God and sought the blessing of His infinite wisdom and mercy. In June 1770, Levers and his family left Philadelphia and settled on a place near the trail which passed through the Wind Gap in Blue Mountain (present Saylorsburg, Pennsylvania).[41]

The Leverses occupied a new house built by William Tidd, who charged £8 for labor and materials, which included 2,000 hand-cut shingles. For an advance of £1 John Smith delivered some of the 2,000 split rails with which Levers intended to fence his meadow.[42] After just ten days on his farm, Levers informed Peters of his safe arrival in the wilderness, the nearest neighbor being more than a mile distant. "Here we have been ten or eleven days, pretty unsettled as we must expect to be for sometime; but the season of the year is healthy and pleasant and my family all well. Mrs. Levers, I have reason to hope, will be contented here which will greatly assist all things to go right. It is a pleasant place I am settling on and I hope in a year or two to make it look like a pleasant farm.... I hope our children will ever retain my sense of obligation to you."[43]

The heart of summer passed. Brimming with enthusiasm and purpose, Levers cleared eight acres of land and sowed it with wheat and rye. He had also cleared four acres of meadow with much more to come. This place, which Levers named Pleasant Valley, was capable of great improvement. "I hope to make [the farm] of sufficient value in itself to secure [your loan to me]," he told Peters. His family had been healthy. Levers also declared that through the blessing of God "his mind was in great composure," and that he had made the education of his children the principal part of his duty. In closing, Levers prostrated himself before Peters. "May the God of Peace and Love reward you for all your kindness to me and mine," he said, "and make me mindful that these mercies to me should lead me to sincere repentance and a practical holy life."[44] Levers had found the Promised Land, or so he professed. In fact Levers must have been terribly depressed at having been consigned to a fate that would forever force a rake and scythe into his hands.

In October 1770, less than six months after he had settled in as a farmer, Levers told Peters that, although he could not yet purchase a horse to work his place, everyone agreed he had done great things. Levers had also observed that Indians passed his place on their way to Bethlehem and Nazareth. The opportunity to "open a trade with them" was too great to ignore, he said. "There is no risk because the Indians pay in skins which could be used as credit." Moreover, Levers went on, there would be far more profit in such a business than the money from the farm, "which after maintaining my family for some years to come, cannot amount to much."[45] Dreams of genuine prosperity, no matter how remote, got Levers moving again.

A few months later Levers confided to Peters that several county magistrates had informed him that it was his duty to become an active magistrate. Ever one to hold himself above the fray, Levers confessed to Peters that he had "studiously endeavored not to interfere in the unhappy tumults" in Northampton. (The "tumults" occurred after Connecticut speculators laid claim in 1753 to the upper third of Pennsylvania and began to colonize the Wyoming Valley, a region that included present Wilkes-Barre. When Pennsylvania sought to dislodge the newcomers, they fought back and won support from many inhabitants north of Blue Mountain who viewed the provincial government with contempt.) Nonetheless, Levers promised Peters that he would act consistently with his duty when called upon.[46] Levers might have added that he could use the fees earned as a magistrate.

As it turned out, Levers was pressed into action as a justice of the peace on the spur of the moment. Driven by moral certitude, Robert Levers allowed himself to be drawn into a controversy that began to unfold in March 1771. Justice Daniel Brodhead, one of the veteran magistrates who had urged Levers to resume the magistracy, had sentenced one John Wickhiser to jail "on suspicion of his being a person of lewd life and conversation, and a coiner of money." As Wickhiser passed Levers's place on his way to jail in Easton, the prisoner asked the constable, in whose custody he had been remanded, for permission to speak with Justice Levers. Wickhiser pleaded with Levers to review his case. Levers replied that he would not interfere with a warrant issued by another magistrate. Wickhiser persisted. "Look at my papers," he said, "and you will see that Justice Brodhead was drunk when he ordered me to jail." This accusation caught Levers's attention. Upon examining the papers he concluded that Justice Brodhead had indeed "been in liquor" when he wrote the warrant for Wickhiser's arrest, a fact confirmed by the attending constable.

According to Wickhiser, his trouble with Justice Brodhead began when he, Wickhiser, had the magistrate's brother arrested for the nonpayment of a debt. Justice Brodhead intervened and guaranteed the bond for his brother's release. When the brother disappeared, Wickhiser called on Justice Brodhead to pay up. This move so angered Brodhead that he arrested Wickhiser on trumped-up charges.

"Wickhiser had with him a good many papers," Levers told Peters,

. . . .

"which showed he was a man of some business. He also had with him three good horses, and a pass . . . purporting he came honestly by them." On these considerations "fluctuating between doubt and compassion," Levers discharged Wickhiser. At the same time Levers did not doubt that he could vindicate his conduct to Justice Brodhead. In fact, by freeing Wickhiser he "rather thought he did [Brodhead] a service than an injury."

But Brodhead did not see it that way and complained to Pennsylvania's chief justice about Levers's intervention. The chief justice ordered three Northampton magistrates to hold a hearing on the matter with both Brodhead and Levers in attendance. The official finding is missing, but Levers did not believe the panel found him so very culpable. The master apologist shored up his flank and stole away. "I declare," he wrote to Peters, "I was moved by no peak, resentment or dislike to Mr. Brodhead; I was sorry for the man [Wickhiser] whom I had no reason to think guilty of any crime. . . . And I really thought Mr. Brodhead would have judged [it] best to let the matter pass over, [and] speak to me in private of it."[47] Right and wrong: Robert Levers came down on one side or the other.

As for the farm, Levers complained that "having hands is so expensive that I cannot make much of this favorable season for clearing meadow . . . indeed hiring eats me up." He also reckoned that he had put in more labor at Pleasant Valley than all the labor in his life put together. "It is too much for me," he cried, "it has brought a fixed pain in my breast."[48] Nonetheless, Levers plunged ahead. In addition to working the farm, he had opened a store, which, no matter its ideal location near the Wind Gap Trail, failed to measure up to his expectations. Levers cataloged his woes to a supplier in Philadelphia who had pressed him for payment of outstanding bills.

A hogshead of New England rum had arrived with a small leak. Upon opening the bunghole, Levers found the container "not full by five inches." Levers suspected foul play among the wagoners because the rum was far below common proof, a clear indication to him that it had been watered. Besides, he added, "New England rum is not so well-liked here as Philadelphia rum." Levers also complained that he was losing customers to a competitor named Jacob Stroud, located some ten miles to the north [on the site of Dansbury], who sold goods at lower prices.[49] At the end of this long letter Levers addressed the matter of his outstanding debt. "If the bills do not raise your spirits," Levers quipped, "they depress mine. God forbid that I should be the means of leading my greatest enemy, much less a person I esteem, to destruction." Levers then demonstrated his ability to stretch money. Having

. . . .

sold £30 worth of skins, he paid £9 to a creditor who had camped on his doorstep, reserved £6 for wagoners who were to pick up new supplies in Philadelphia, and enclosed the remaining £15 in his letter to his Philadelphia creditor.[50]

Adrift in the mountains some twenty hard miles north of Easton, Levers despaired. The farm drained his energy, the store generated little profit, and the provincial surveyor-general demanded payment for warrants Levers had applied for years earlier. Levers threw himself on the mercy of the surveyor-general. "Unless favored and assisted by you respecting my applications [for warrants]," he begged, "I must sustain a very heavy loss."[51] Moreover, although Levers had indentured his eldest daughter to a Philadelphia merchant, not an uncommon practice for a person in the Leverses' station, the arrival of a new child kept six young mouths at his table.[52] No amount of good weather could lift Levers's gloom. Life's fiber had been ripped from him. Each day seemed worse than the one before. Vows made shortly after his arrival at Pleasant Valley weighed on his conscience. "I have seen the mercy of God so clearly in bringing me here and snatching me from impending destruction," he had told Peters, "I trust I shall be enabled to devote my whole future life to him [*sic*] in such a manner, as I shall be able to receive the summons of Death with Joy and in that time look with confidence for the mercy of God unto eternal life thru Jesus Christ our Savior."[53]

In June 1774, Levers learned that George Taylor, a magistrate, ironmaster, and former assemblyman, had urged the people of Northampton to gather at the courthouse in Easton on the third Tuesday of the month prior to the opening of quarter sessions courts. Taylor had called this meeting at the behest of radical leaders in Philadelphia who implored each of Pennsylvania's eleven counties to discuss and approve its plan to resist Parliament's crackdown on the North American Colonies that followed in the wake of the Boston Tea Party.[54] Having resumed the magistracy, Levers had intended to be present at court to earn his fees. However, he had no desire to participate in a seditious assemblage. Perhaps he simply hovered in the doorway.

Several hundred persons gathered at the courthouse to hear Taylor lay out the plan proposed by the radicals. In the end the crowd took it upon themselves to speak for the entire county, and they approved the radicals' plan unanimously. At the heart of this scheme was a proposal that delegates from the thirteen colonies would convene in Philadelphia to discuss the crisis concerning Great Britain. The crowd also named five Northampton

. . . .

magistrates and the county's elected assemblyman to serve on a committee to initiate contact with committees in other counties. Prothonotary Lewis Gordon, the provincial government's key appointee in Northampton, agreed to chair this illegal committee. Lewis Gordon's betrayal of his oath to the king stunned Levers, who decided to keep close watch on the budding resistance movement and to hold his tongue.

In July 1774, delegates from the county committees convened at Carpenters' Hall in Philadelphia.[55] They urged the Assembly to take aggressive action against British imperialism at the upcoming Continental Congress. But the moderate-dominated Assembly resisted pressure from the radicals and instructed its congressional delegation to take a neutral stand and "to avoid everything indecent or disrespectful to the Mother State."[56] The outcome of this confrontation between radicals and the duly elected representatives of the people doubtless gratified Levers. But Levers's satisfaction was short-lived. On September 5, 1774, the Continental Congress assembled in Carpenters' Hall. To pressure Parliament to negotiate American grievances, Congress suspended trade with Great Britain. More important, Congress requested that every city, town, and county in the North American colonies elect a committee of observation and inspection to enforce the boycott. When Levers learned of Congress's bold action against Great Britain, he retreated to consider his options. If he distanced himself from the resistance movement and the movement failed, he would be on safe ground. On the other hand, if the radicals succeeded, he might be ostracized or, worse, suffer physical harm. Levers chose to forgo his fees rather than to go to Easton for September quarter sessions courts.

Soon after the Continental Congress adjourned on October 26, 1774, Levers traveled to Bucks County to visit Joseph Galloway, with whom he had done business over a period of twenty years. Galloway, an archconservative, had attempted to mediate the United Colonies' dispute with Great Britain, but Congress rejected his proposal and expunged his remarks from the record. Levers's purpose in visiting Galloway is unknown. Galloway, a Tory who later fled to England, had probably requested Levers to assist him in disposing of his land holdings. In the course of this visit, Galloway doubtless attempted to convince Levers that it would be in the best interest of all parties to negotiate their differences rather than go to war. Curiously, had it not been for a horse thief named Francis McCue, the meeting between Levers and Galloway would have gone unnoticed. While Levers was engaged with Galloway, McCue entered Galloway's stable and stole Levers's horse. Levers placed an ad in the *Gazette* and offered a reward for the apprehension of the thief and the return of the horse. In the ad Levers described McCue with the attention to detail he customarily lavished on an application for a land warrant: "[McCue] is of a fresh complexion, very red nose, about 5 feet 6 inches high, an Irishman; had on a grey surtout coat, a lincey [*sic*] jacket, grey yarn stockings, a red under jacket without sleeves, an old ragged shirt and tow trousers, and a pair of old shoes, a buckle in one, and a string in the other."[57]

On December 21, 1774, before the opening of quarter sessions courts, Northampton's inhabitants responded to Congress and elected twenty-nine men to serve on a committee of observation and inspection.[58] Four months later, on April 19, 1775, minutemen and British soldiers clashed at the Battle of Lexington and Concord. The Northampton Committee mobilized the county for self-defense.[59] The Committee ordered each township to take up arms, to form companies, and to elect officers. With muskets, fowling pieces, rifles, axes, hayforks, and homemade pikes at the ready, men in every township mustered and drilled. War fever gripped the county. From Charleston, South Carolina, and Baltimore, Maryland, came news of patriots who had seized arms and gunpowder. Ethan Allen captured Fort Ticonderoga. A Continental Army had been organized under the command of General George Washington.[60]

The undeclared state of war between the United Colonies and Great Britain so disturbed Levers that once again he did not appear for court in June 1775. But as the political winds shifted that summer, Robert Levers experienced a conversion no less rapid and profound than his rediscovery of Christ some five years earlier. As a result, in September the inhabitants of Hamilton Township elected Levers to fill the place on the Committee vacated by Captain Abraham Miller, a veteran of the French and Indian War, who had gone off to fight at Boston. Beginning with the day he vowed to support the resistance movement, Levers placed all citizens in one of two categories: persons who supported the common cause of freedom and persons who did not. For Robert Levers, friend or foe had the same kind of uncompromising, back-straightening moral definition as right or wrong.

In the early spring of 1776, radical leaders pressured the Pennsylvania Assembly to reverse its stand against independence, but the Assembly refused. As a result radicals decided that the political balance of the Assembly must be changed. With an infusion of new members of a more liberal stripe, radicals argued, the balance of power in the Assembly would shift in their

. . . .

favor. But the tactic backfired. At a special by-election on May 1, 1776, radicals failed by a narrow margin to win control of the Assembly. So long as moderates and conservatives controlled the Pennsylvania Assembly, the provincial congressional delegation would refuse to vote for independence.

Anxious congressmen and radical leaders conferred behind closed doors. On May 15 Congress recommended that new governments be established throughout the United Colonies under the "authority of the people."[61] Pennsylvania's radical leaders argued that because provincial authorities had restricted the right to vote, the men who sat in the Assembly did not represent all of the people. Hence, there was no alternative but to hold new elections, and overthrow the provincial government.

On May 20, radical leaders presented their message at a mass meeting in the State House Yard. In the end the crowd rejected the authority of the Assembly and called for a new government to be organized at a constitutional convention with delegates elected by the people.[62] Hard on this victory, radicals attempted to win support in Northampton and other back counties. "To rid yourselves forever of [a tyrannical government] is now in your power," the Philadelphia Committee reminded its rural counterparts. "If you embrace it, your descendants will glory in their ancestors; if you neglect it, you will entail a slavery on your posterity, and they will justly execrate your memory as unworthy of a parent's name."[63] The Philadelphia Committee also invited all county committees to send delegates to a conference where rules would be established for the election of the men who would frame Pennsylvania's new constitution.

On May 27, just one week after the mass meeting in the State House Yard, 900 militiamen from Northampton's Second Battalion gathered in a meadow near Allentown. Broadsides in English and German were distributed to the crowd. One placard stated, in part: "The question is short and easy—you are called upon to declare whether you will support the union of the colonies or whether you will support the [Pennsylvania] Assembly [which has voted] against the union of the colonies."[64] The Second Battalion voted unanimously to create a new government in Pennsylvania and support the union of the colonies. Two days later 400 militiamen from the Fourth Battalion mustered at a farm just north of the landmark gap in the Delaware River and clamored for a government "under the authority of the people."[65]

On May 30, the Northampton Committee met in Easton to decide whether or not the county would participate in the overthrow of Pennsylvania's colonial government. When Chairman Lewis Gordon sent word that he was "indisposed," the Committee promptly elected Robert Levers to take the chair.[66] Line by line, the former schoolmaster led the assemblage through the documents sent to Easton from Philadelphia by both radical and conservative leaders. At one point an impatient emissary from the Philadelphia Committee interrupted the proceedings and shouted: "Whoever still presses himself as favoring the King should be hanged on the nearest tree."[67] At the conclusion of this fractious meeting, the Committee unanimously endorsed a resolution in favor of a constitutional convention "for the express purpose of forming and establishing a new government in Pennsylvania under the Authority of the people only."[68] Committeemen also named Levers one of six delegates to represent Northampton at the upcoming conference of county committees. The preface to the proceedings of the meeting struts with Levers's rhetoric: "Animated by that good spirit, which, in a very remarkable manner, has hitherto smiled on the laudable endeavors of the United Colonies for the preservation of valuable liberty, the free gift of God, our business was carried on without the LEAST opposition, and in full confidence of the continued protection and assistance of Him, in whose sovereignty is the disposal of all things."[69]

When the Provincial Conference of County Committees convened at Carpenters' Hall on June 18, 1776, two radical factions vied for control: ultraradicals, who had won the support of the common soldier, and radicals of a more moderate cast.[70] As the first order of business, the conferees agreed that each of eleven counties and the city of Philadelphia would have one vote. With that resolution on June 19, 1776, the balance of political power in the province shifted from the capital city and the three counties formed in 1682—which, together, held about one-third of Pennsylvania's population—to the eight back counties. Men intent on setting things right in Pennsylvania had taken charge of the convention.[71]

The ultraradical faction made certain that militiamen would control the state's Revolutionary government. They did so by liberalizing the franchise to give nearly all militiamen the right to vote for delegates to the Constitutional Convention. With the same stroke, the conferees required that all other inhabitants who wished to vote must disavow allegiance to King George III, a rule designed to disenfranchise a substantial block of voters. Moreover, to enable newly enfranchised voters to cast ballots closer to home, the conference increased the total number of electoral districts in Chester, Lancaster, York, Cumberland, Northampton, and Westmoreland Counties from six to twenty-three. Most important, these new electoral districts had

. . . .

been gerrymandered to coincide with the jurisdictions of thirty-one of the state's fifty-three militia battalions.[72] With a series of astute moves, the ultraradical faction had transformed farmer-soldiers into a brotherhood tied to the ballot box, and thereby laid the groundwork for a paramilitary political organization in Pennsylvania. Thus did the authority of the people become cradled in the arms of the militia.

On July 8, 1776, Northampton's inhabitants gathered in Easton to celebrate the Declaration of Independence and to choose delegates for Pennsylvania's Constitutional Convention.[73] At the courthouse the crowd called on Levers to read the Declaration. A spectator gave an account of the festivities in Easton: "The Colonel, and all other Field-Officers of the First Battalion, repaired to the Court-House, the Light-Infantry company marching there with drums beating, fifes playing, and the Standard (the device for which is the Thirteen United Colonies), which was ordered to be displayed; and after that the Declaration was read aloud to a great number of spectators, who gave their hearty assent with three loud huzzas, and cried out, 'May *God* long preserve and unite the Free and Independent States of *America*.'"[74] At the special election held the same day—the date had been set by a convention committee of which Levers had been a member—militia officers won all of Northampton's eight seats at the Constitutional Convention. In fact, militia officers comprised a majority of the delegates who met at the State House from July 15 to September 28 to draw up Pennsylvania's new charter.[75]

While framers of the Constitution battled Philadelphia's sultry heat and each other, British troops overran General Washington's forces at the Battle of Long Island. Even as remnants of Washington's army retreated west across the Delaware, Pennsylvania's Council of Safety began to recruit and organize twelve regiments, about 8,000 men in all, for the Continental Line. Of the eight companies that comprised the Twelfth Pennsylvania Regiment, Northampton supplied one company of ninety men, as well as the regiment's second-in-command, a former member of the Northampton Committee and a delegate to the Constitutional Convention.[76] By mid-October all officers of the Twelfth Regiment had been named, except for the regimental paymaster, a post reserved for a civilian appointee.[77]

Levers applied to the Council of Safety for the job. Previously, he had met five council members at the Convention of County Committees. One of them, Frederick Kuhl, had been present three months earlier in Easton when Levers distinguished himself as chairman pro tempore of the Northampton Committee. On November 13, 1776, council president Thomas Wharton Jr.

. . . .

appointed Robert Levers paymaster of the Twelfth Regiment of the Continental Line.[78] Levers was a perfect match for the post that required him to handle large sums of money, track the number of men in the field, pay each man only once, hold money due to prisoners of war, and deduct the cost of uniforms from the amount owed each soldier. The post not only paid Levers $12 a month but also presented him with an opportunity to restart his career as an appointee of Pennsylvania's Revolutionary government.[79]

General Sir William Howe capitalized on his victory at New York and turned his troops toward Philadelphia. Pandemonium gripped Pennsylvania. The state's political factions, which had locked horns over the Constitution, declared a truce in order to defend the commonwealth. Congress fled to Baltimore. Howe exploited the panic by offering to pardon any person who would lay down his arms and take an oath of loyalty to the king within sixty days. Lewis Gordon, who had been a man of two minds for at least a decade, welcomed the amnesty and informed the Committee "that he would no longer attend."[80] The Committee ordered him to appear "to answer such matters as shall be objected against you." Gordon, however, citing his "low and weak" condition, refused; nonetheless, he invited the Committee to visit him at his home, an offer the Committee declined. The standoff between Gordon and the Committee continued for six months, at which time state authorities placed Gordon under house arrest.[81]

When Levers learned of Gordon's defection, he set his sights on becoming Northampton's next prothonotary, even though he had just taken on the job of regimental paymaster. Because of General Howe's threatened invasion of Pennsylvania, however, the new state government had been unable to collect itself, let alone consider a replacement for Lewis Gordon. But in February 1777, while Levers was at General Washington's winter quarters in Morristown, New Jersey, where he had gone to prepare a payroll for the Twelfth Regiment, the paymaster learned that the Pennsylvania Assembly had not only achieved a quorum but also had begun to take steps to create a working government. The pace had quickened. Levers returned to Pleasant Valley on March 1, 1777, where "he found his house as it were an hospital, my family being sick." In fact, Mary had been "brought to bed and was very ill" in the final month of a pregnancy that resulted in the birth of Sarah, the couple's eighth child.[82] Despite these dreadful conditions, Levers remained at home only six days before setting out for Philadelphia to resign as paymaster for the Twelfth Regiment, and to apply for the prothonotaryship of Northampton County.

. . . .

The paymaster general, however, refused to accept Levers's resignation because he had not prepared his final accounts in the proper format. While Levers restated his numbers, regimental officers badgered him for money they had advanced to him to pay their troops. His honesty challenged, Levers wrote directly to Congress to set the record straight. It would reflect on "my credit and reputation," he said, to leave town without paying the officers. Moreover, Levers intended to discharge his responsibility to the Twelfth Regiment with "great faithfulness, integrity, and punctuality."[83] Several months later Levers received an honorable discharge from the paymaster corps. In the meantime, however, President Thomas Wharton Jr. had appointed him Northampton prothonotary, and in this, Levers, for a change, may have experienced a stroke of good luck.

In March, when he left his sick family and headed for the capital, Levers chanced to meet President Wharton on the road outside Philadelphia. Levers doubtless took this opportunity to inform Wharton of his desire to replace Gordon as prothonotary.[84] Wharton, who needed every good man he could find to turn the wheels of government, probably encouraged Levers to apply immediately. Within days of this roadside encounter, Levers's application arrived on Wharton's desk. Like many men who held high posts in Pennsylvania's Revolutionary government, Levers had no formal training in law; however, his masterful letter to President Wharton and the Supreme Executive Council won the appointment he coveted. Who on the Council could have read Levers's petition and not believed that this zealous patriot exemplified the sort of common man who should inherit the new state?

> That your Petitioner, from a Natural love of Knowledge, and a Desire of becoming serviceable to that Part of the Community among whom his Lot is cast, as far as his attendance on his Family would permit, has applied himself to the Study of the Laws of the Country in which he lives, and by which he is to govern himself; so that he humbly apprehends himself in some Degree qualified for the said office. . . .
>
> That at the Time the Committee of Northampton County had in Consideration the Resolve of Congress of the 15th May 1776, recommending a Declaration of Independency, your Petitioner had the Honor to preside in the Chair, and took a very active Part in Support of the said Resolve, was afterward on the Committee Conference, and in every Instance has been Zealously affected toward the Glorious Cause in which

. . . .

America is engaged, and is a true Friend to the Constitution of this State.[85]

On March 26, 1776, the Council conferred on Levers, in his words, "the honor of being the First Prothonotary of Northampton County in the free and independent state of America."[86]

Upon his return from Philadelphia, Levers called on Lewis Gordon.[87] The two men had become acquainted nearly thirty years earlier in Philadelphia when they clerked for Richard Peters: Gordon in law, Levers in the land office. Cut from different cloth, Gordon and Levers did not patronize the same taverns and clubs. During Peters's lifetime, however, they publicly maintained a cordial relationship. Then, Gordon, who had first betrayed the king, turned against the new state. Radicals spat on the traitor in their midst. Levers took the high road and used the power of his new office to level the former prothonotary and his family.

When the two antagonists met in May 1777, Levers displayed his commission as prothonotary and requested Gordon to hand over records pertaining to the office. Gordon delivered some papers but "declined delivering up the remainder through one evasion or the other."[88] Levers put his request in writing, but Gordon informed the jailer, who delivered Levers's letter, that he had no idea what Levers meant, that he had no papers in his possession.[89] Stymied by Gordon's noncompliance, Levers requested the court to intercede. Gordon, however, defended his position by telling the court that he had withheld certain papers because "all indictments and bills found by the grand jury were lodged with him by the king's attorney,"[90] but Levers argued: "Indictments of grand juries were papers of record and ought to be lodged with the court or the proper officer of the court."[91] Unraveled by Gordon's logic and his authoritative demeanor, the court failed to reach a decision on this matter, and thus the former prothonotary retained possession of the papers.

For the time being Levers ignored the lie and turned his attention to reopening Northampton's courts, which had been closed for a year. As a boon for citizens of the new state, some 140 cases dating back to 1765 were stricken from the docket.[92] This move pleased most persons, but it infuriated Easton's major storekeeper who had many actions pending for nonpayment of bills. But even as Levers began to restore some semblance of law and order in Northampton, Lord Howe's army captured Philadelphia. The state government fled to Lancaster. Congress hurried west, first to Lancaster, then across the Susquehanna River to York.[93] Authorities in Philadelphia

. . . .

impressed two Northampton farmers who had delivered a load of produce to the city and directed them to haul the State House [Liberty] bell to Allentown, where it was hidden in the cellar of Zion Church.[94] Other bells were sunk in the Delaware River to avoid capture and the blast furnace. Nine hundred wagons loaded with ammunition and equipment were driven north and parked in the fields outside Bethlehem. Papers and more than £13,000 from the state's General Loan Office were packed in "a large iron chest, a case, and a barrel" and, along with the books from the state library, dispatched to Robert Levers for safekeeping.[95]

Many blamed General Washington and his field commanders for Howe's victory. But had the militia "risen as one man, attacked the foe at a distance from his fleet, and speedily inclosed the enemy like a lion in the toils," as President Wharton had urged, Howe's offensive might have been stopped in its tracks.[96] On the other hand, radicals blamed the state's woes on Tories, the disaffected, and sectarians. They argued that the government should intensify the war against internal enemies, seize their property, and drive them from the state.

Fearing that the British invasion of Pennsylvania would spread beyond Philadelphia, Levers wrote to President Wharton. "As a member of the commonwealth, and sincere friend to the cause of the United States of America," he said, "I conceive it my duty to inform your excellency that the county of Northampton now contains a great body of stores, which if lost may prove our ruin."[97] Levers also expressed his belief that Lewis Gordon, although under house arrest, might still open the gates for the enemy. While he could not say with certainty that Gordon was a spy, Levers observed that prisoners of war who lodged with Gordon "always possessed the earliest and best intelligence."[98] Levers reported that Gordon had twice-weekly communications from his seventeen-year-old son, William, who lived in Philadelphia with his sister, Mrs. Thomas Affleck, whose father-in-law, a Quaker, had been banished from the state. Levers also pointed out that Gordon's eldest son, twenty-two-year-old John Gordon, had slipped into Philadelphia just ahead of Lord Howe and had probably taken letters with him. Also, John had not returned to Easton. "Whether Lewis Gordon is friendly [to the cause] or no," Levers confided to President Wharton, "I will not take upon me to say. One thing I know, that whilst the affairs of America wore a blooming aspect, he was sick, languid, and dejected; but now, on the late unfavorable change in American affairs he is brisk and lively, and in his countenance expresses the highest satisfaction."[99]

. . . .

Levers reminded the president that although Gordon had been placed under house arrest, he retained the lease on the Easton ferry. "Persons of all characters are passing and repassing [the river] and as the ferriage is constantly paid to Mr. Gordon, or some of his family, it affords an opportunity of conveying and insinuating backwards and forwards . . . a dislike to the American cause."[100] Levers also argued that anyone employed by the state in public offices of trust should immediately conform to the law and take the Test. Moreover, he insisted that such persons should be suspended until they had taken the "oath of fidelity and allegiance to this state." (Levers himself did not take the oath until March 1779.)[101]

Levers's report on the activities of the Gordon family reached Lancaster just as the Pennsylvania Assembly convened for a brief session. Levers's letter may have helped persuade beleaguered legislators to amend the so-called Test Act to lower to sixteen the age at which any person who had been observed traveling [in and] out of Philadelphia, or the county in which he resided, must swear allegiance to the state or be jailed. Even if they did not plan to travel outside their county, the amended law stipulated that persons sixteen and older "suspected of being unfriendly to the freedom and independence of the United States" must take the oath or "be forthwith committed to jail, there to remain without bail" until they swore allegiance to the state.[102] The Assembly also placed the state's government under the temporary jurisdiction of a twenty-one member Council of Safety with dictatorial powers.[103]

The Council of Safety took a hard line against "evil-minded persons encouraged by open or secret practices to assist the common enemy, and further to distress the good people of this commonwealth."[104] Between October and December 1777, the Council appointed commissioners to purchase arms, blankets, and clothing from persons who had not taken the Test. Should reasonable measures fail, the Council authorized taking such goods by force. In each county the Council appointed a committee to seize the personal assets of traitors. (Levers was named one of four Northampton commissioners who, for their work, received expenses plus 5 percent of the value of the seized assets.) The Council set a ceiling on the price of whiskey and cracked down on hoarders and forestallers. Most important, the Council demanded that county lieutenants not only collect money advanced by the state for substitutes but also seize and sell a delinquent's goods and chattels if he refused to pay. The Council also authorized lieutenants to employ squads of militia to enforce the ordinance.[105]

. . . .

By the time annual elections rolled around in October 1777, many Northampton inhabitants had lost their zest for war and independence. Before the election, according to Levers, the people showed little interest in forming a ticket. On election day only 154 persons, about one-tenth of the eligible voters, cast ballots. Levers reported that just five ballots were cast in Easton, "four votes besides myself, and these I called upon at the last hour." Levers conceded that through the confusion of the times regular notice of the election was not given. (It was Levers's duty to give such notice.) "This, however," he said, "could not be a principal cause" for the low turnout.[106] In fact Levers suspected that traitors may have been responsible, the "Germans generally at this time being so inactive, rather unfriendly if not inimical [to the cause of freedom]."[107]

As the year 1777 came to a close, Levers not only had lost some of his zeal for the cause but also was broke again. "Because of the unhappy crisis [brought about by the British occupation of Philadelphia]," Levers complained, "the profits of the offices [prothonotary, clerk of orphan's court, magistrate] would not procure to my family even the means of purchasing firewood." In desperation Levers took on additional work as assistant commissary and deputy barrack major. Levers assured the Council that "acceptance of these appointments will in no wise prevent my executing the trust reposed in me granted me by Council."[108] A few days later, however, Levers advised the Council that he had resigned his position as assistant commissary because he found it to be so troublesome and "to interfere so much with the duty I owe the public, in the office I hold under the state as a magistrate."[109]

Because of his crusade to ensure that every man, especially those in public service, took the Test, Levers made numerous enemies. "I am sorry for it," he told the Council, "but my attachment to my country leads me to sacrifice every consideration to what I believe to be the public good."[110] Seizing on Levers's loyalty to the cause, Vice-President George Bryan asked him to investigate whether there might be persons in the county appointed to office by Congress "who have not taken the oath of allegiance to [Pennsylvania] or any other [state]." Levers's response confirmed what Bryan and other officials already feared: "When men speak against or object to taking the Test . . . they do not consider the almost irreparable injury done to the American cause. It is such a stumbling block to the ignorant as hardly can be conceived. This county is a manifest proof thereof. The Test is the cry, but the truth is, tho it dare not be spoken, supporting glorious independency is the great offence." Levers proceeded to identify six prominent Northampton men employed by

Congress "who are under no solemn tie of allegiance to the states, unless an oath . . . has been taken very recently."[111] Shortly thereafter these officials took the oath. But even if backcountry men like Michael and Jacob Messinger had taken the Test, their pledge would have been meaningless.[112] "The Whigs at Easton began the war," an informer had heard the two men say, "and the people had better rise and hang them than protect them." The Messingers had also asserted that the leading men in the county were Whigs for the sake of personal gain, and that the King had good reason to hang every one. "We had as good a right to be against the cause as we had for it," the men said, adding, that the "Council of Safety were robbers and them that put their laws in force were the same."[113]

In February 1778, John Gordon slipped into Easton, took the oath before a magistrate, and returned to Philadelphia. A month later, when the young man returned to Easton from the capital, Levers decided that even though John Gordon had taken the oath, he had since visited Philadelphia and must, therefore, certify allegiance to the state by posting a cash bond or signing a parole. Levers cautiously turned to the Council for advice. "I do not see," he said, "by what authority I can legally demand [John Gordon to enter] into security, unless something be alleged against him, either in proof, or on probable grounds of suspicion."[114] Besides, Levers said, the one person in Easton who could actually swear that Gordon had been in Philadelphia refused to do so, on grounds that he would jeopardize his contacts in the city. Nonetheless, John Gordon's return to Easton so agitated Levers that he decided not to wait on the Council and confronted Gordon at once.

Levers questioned the loyalty of the local constable, so he requested the militia to arrest John Gordon and bring him to his office; however, the Northampton militia colonel dodged the assignment and handed the task to a lieutenant in the Continental Army who arrived at Levers's place with "four men from Massachusetts with fixed bayonets." Levers deemed the colonel's conduct to "be such an indignity shown to the natural strength of [Pennsylvania], and reproach on himself and his fellow citizens," that he dismissed the Continentals and sent the constable by himself to find Gordon.[115] Levers informed young Gordon that "there was too much ground for suspicion that he had been in Philadelphia since he had taken the oath" and required that in order for him to remain at large he must sign a parole. Levers advised Council that he had been in this matter more circumstantial than was necessary "because my whole conduct herein might be seen."[116] Council brushed aside Levers's concerns that he had exceeded his authority and informed him that in the matter of John Gordon, "the laws should be put into immediate execution."[117]

As for Lewis Gordon, Levers informed Council that the former prothonotary was "a fixed, determined enemy of the American state; but then [he] is wearing away, lately lost his wife, and peevish at times to childishness; and tho' he is capable of being a dangerous man, yet I sincerely pity him." Nonetheless, Levers continued to press Gordon to take the Test. Finally, in May 1778, as the former chairman of the county's Revolutionary Committee lay on his deathbed, he summoned Levers and swore allegiance to the Commonwealth of Pennsylvania.[118] Justice had been served. However, as Gordon's coffin slid into the earth, some at the burial ground stared at Levers with vengeance in their hearts.

On July 3, 1778, a large force of Tories and Indians massacred several hundred soldiers at Wyoming, about sixty-five miles northwest of Easton. News of the atrocity reached Easton three days later. Levers advised the Council "that upwards of two hundred people had been scalped" and suggested that "our town" might be the next target. On the other hand, Levers speculated that since the British had left Philadelphia and headed back to New York it would be more likely that the Indians would roam the frontier and do "incredible mischief, before a check can be given to them."[119] Frightened settlers north of Blue Mountain joined the stream of refugees who headed south for the relative safety of Lehigh Valley.[120] North of the mountain, Colonel Jacob Stroud, popular leader of Northampton's Fourth Battalion, confronted a painful dilemma. "Shall we retreat with the inhabitants, or stand with a handful of men to be destroyed, or whether I can depend on relief," he pleaded with his superior. "I beg your instructions as I have had none yet from you. . . . I assure you I cannot stand nor keep my men here without more assistance."[121] If the enemy wiped out Stroud's men, they could easily attack the Lehigh Valley, Bucks County, and Philadelphia itself, a fact not lost on the state's leaders.

The Council consulted with Congress who dispatched a detachment of Continental troops to the frontier, along with a troop of cavalry from Count Casimir Pulaski's Legion under the command of Colonel Michael de Kowatz.[122] "But it is necessary to add to these troops a considerable body of militia," the Council said, and ordered Northampton to call out 300 men to go over the mountain and defend the frontier.[123] Despite the gravity of the situation, no one consulted Robert Levers, who knew the settlers and territory north of Blue Mountain as well as any man in the county. The Council conducted the state's business along strict political and bureaucratic lines, and Levers had no responsibility for the militia. Nonetheless, Levers stuck his neck out and informed the council that "as an individual of the county, from the consideration of the services I owe the public, and a regard to the distressed inhabitants in the upper part of the Delaware, I have thought it my duty to delay no time but to give your honor . . . necessary information."

Levers complained that Colonel de Kowatz was "totally inadequate to the important task of conducting military operations in an Indian country . . . he being as perfectly unacquainted with the country . . . as he is to the nature of the Indian manner of fighting."[124] Levers also advised the Council that he was not "without apprehensions that the upper part of the Delaware will soon receive a severe stroke, unless we shall be so fortunate as to repel the enemy."[125] Two months later, Levers reported that "Tories and Indians are burning and destroying all before them" in the upper Delaware. The men at Stroud's have "neither military stores or provisions so that if [the enemy] should suddenly attack . . . that part of the county must fly before them." To underscore the danger of life on the frontier, Levers warned the Council that "three persons were killed near Wyoming and another was sent in with his life, scalped to his eyebrows almost. . . . You may be convinced that this account is to be depended on."[126]

One week later the Council received a salty letter from Stroud himself. The Council had promised to send help, but none had arrived. "Between me and the great swamp," Stroud told the Council, "there is no settlement but the bare woods. Now if it can be thought best not to have the frontier here, I could wish the Council in their wisdom would point out the place. . . . Hoping you will do at this distressing time something for us . . . as we have our eyes on you, as we have no other place to apply to for relief."[127] But the onset of winter brought a respite from Indian raids on the Northampton frontier, and the Council turned its attention to more pressing business. Levers pouted. There had been no response to his criticism of efforts to stem the war on the frontier. A self-described spectator, Levers focused on managing the court docket, deposing witnesses, and issuing marriage and tavern licenses.[128]

In the spring of 1779, Tories and Indians resumed their raids on the Northampton frontier. Congress stepped in and directed Major General John Sullivan to secure the region. In June, Sullivan mobilized several thousand men at Easton and struck north to drive the enemy back to their base at Niagara, New York. This expedition inflicted much damage on the enemy, but

. . . .

within months Tories and Indians resumed their attacks on both sides of the upper part of the Delaware River. The following year the enemy forays resumed with even greater intensity. Northampton's militia colonels argued among themselves. With few exceptions militiamen south of Blue Mountain refused to travel beyond it, even at the risk of endangering their own homes and family members. President Joseph Reed, a staunch defender of the militia law who had presided over the Council since December 1778, did not mince words. In a letter to Northampton's colonels and field officers he directed them to "bestir yourself, support your [superior officers] with your utmost weight and influence . . . let there be but one dispute [among you]— who shall serve his country best . . . support each other, and be assured we shall support you with every necessary."[129] To spur bounty hunters to attack the enemy, Reed authorized rewards of $1,500 for every Indian or Tory prisoner taken and $1,000 for every Indian scalp. The bounties were quickly raised to $3,000 and $2,500. Even so, there were few takers.

When enemy incursions on the Northampton frontier resumed in 1781, inhabitants again begged for help. Reed promised money and supplies, but as for sending reinforcements, Pennsylvania's president had lost patience with the commanders of the Northampton militia. "We recommend you to your own exertion and the blessing of Providence which will help those who are earnest to help themselves, and which Council doubts not you will do," he said.[130]

Although the Militia Act rendered it almost impossible for President Reed to replace militia officers who had been elected by their own men, the president had the authority to appoint the county lieutenant, a civilian who commanded the militia in each county. In June 1781, when the Northampton lieutenant submitted his resignation after only one year on the job, President Reed appointed Robert Levers to take charge of the county's militia, which numbered about 6,000 men. "We shall much depend on your activity, firmness, and zeal," Reed told his newest county lieutenant. "Pay strict adherence to the Militia Law on all occasions," he said, "and as the serving militia are to be paid out of the fines of the delinquents, you cannot be too expeditious in collecting them."[131]

For three years Levers had closed his eyes and remained silent while two county lieutenants permitted militia officers to abide by their own rules. Levers assured Reed that he was "well convinced of the real service to be effected by a steady and firm adherence to the Militia Law, and your excellency and the Supreme Executive Council may be fully persuaded that I shall on all occasions resolutely make it my rule of conduct."[132] Moreover, "no exertions of mine shall be wanting in the duties of the office I am entrusted with."[133] To serve simultaneously as county prothonotary and county lieutenant would have overwhelmed most men, but Levers, at age fifty-eight, tackled his new job like a man who had spent a lifetime preparing for this mission.

From July to September 1781, express riders churned the Easton/ Philadelphia road carrying messages between Levers and Reed.

LEVERS: I have advised commanding officers on the outer edge of the frontier to post the militia house to house and thus create one continuous picket line. If the militia do their duty in scouting, this disposition will effectually guard the interior parts and thus prevent the militiamen from injuring themselves rather than protecting others. . . . Provisions are greatly wanted. Farmers demand hard cash for their beef and produce.[134]

REED: We request you to make suitable dispositions of the militia in the future without any regard to the murmurs of individuals who are actually led to seek their own safety. . . . We are very sorry that it is not in our power to give you the necessary financial aid for want of hard money in the treasury.[135]

LEVERS: The want of provisions is great. This morning I wrote to the sub-lieutenants and asked them to entreat with the ablest patriots and friends among them to provision the militia until money is obtained from the new tax law. . . . The situation on the frontier is really distressing. Out of sixty men called up, only eight have marched. I have ordered the fines of every delinquent to be immediately levied. Moreover, it appears necessary for the safety and protection of the frontier to call out more men, otherwise I fear the frontier will be on the south side of Blue Mountain. . . . Such is the disposition of the people that scarcely no provisions can be had without hard money, and had I not been so fortunate to have obtained the loan of the trifling sum of £27, the militia, who had been five days without any other provision than flour, would have returned home. . . . On my own I suggested that farmers who supplied provisions at reasonable cost to the militia should be credited with having paid an equivalent sum in hard money on their

. . . .

tax bill. . . . The common people speak plainly, and the truth is, all confidence [in the government] is lost.[136]

REED: We are pleased with the alacrity with which you have attended to the business of your appointment. We hope farmers will not take advantage of the public distress to make up extravagant charges to be paid in hard money.[137]

LEVERS: The wretched situation of a few troops of the Third Pennsylvania Regiment stationed here [Easton] prompts me to comment on a subject *entirely out of my line* in any other way than as bearing a proportion of each man's burden thro this life of woe. The troops have had no flesh meat for the last fifteen or sixteen days and their officers have had no money to assist them. I will lend them some money and propose to repay myself by a small collection from among the local inhabitants. In justice to these suffering men, there has been no injury to local inhabitants except a goose now and then and an attempt to kill a sheep. . . . I find myself in the necessity of troubling you and the Supreme Executive Council more than I would wish, but it is my desire to proceed aright.[138] [emphasis added]

REED: We are always glad the gentlemen in office would apply for direction in case of difficulty rather than hazard measures which may involve them and us in embarrassments. . . . It will be a source of great discontent if other counties learn that Northampton inhabitants have paid their taxes in produce. As an alternative, we enclose an order that will permit you to withdraw £100 from the county treasury payable out of the first money received for taxes. . . . If the people of the county will not give their assistance to feed the troops employed for the defense of themselves and their fellow inhabitants we can only regret the misfortunes that will unavoidably follow.[139]

On September 10, 1781, Levers advised Reed, "Some militia from the second battalion marched for the frontier today," and continued, "I flatter myself that in a little time the militia of this county will see the necessity, use, and advantage of a due subordination and strictness of discipline."[140] This letter, however, elicited no response from Reed, who, as he neared the

. . . .

end of the three-year statutory limit on his term in office, had begun to dis-
engage from his responsibilities as president.

Although his hand in glove relationship with Pennsylvania's president
had come to an abrupt close, Levers, who had mastered the nuances of the
professional bureaucrat, did not let up on his efforts to bring the Northampton militia under control. He lashed out at his sublieutenants: "It is vain for
me to endeavor to regulate the militia agreeable to law," he said, "unless you
will be guided by that law and pay attention to instructions" from the Council and him. And when he discovered that illegal substitutes, including a deserter from the British Army, had been accepted for duty, Levers threw the
book at his officers: "I refer battalion commanders to the 48th and 51st sections of the Militia Act for your consideration and guide." He continued,
"Captains should pay attention to the 41st section of the law."[141]

This outburst suggests that the staggering complexity of the job had begun to take a toll on Levers. Better than any other person in Northampton,
he knew that only a handful of militia officers possessed the ability to read
and comprehend the state's militia law. Had he embarked on a fool's mission?
Self-doubt aside, Levers continued to press commanders to collect fines. In
May 1782, however, Levers admitted to the Council that fines collected in
Northampton would be insufficient to pay the militia who had turned out for
duty: "The country seems to labor under so many difficulties through scarcity
of money . . . that in the Second Battalion, which is now on the frontiers, out
of more than £1,000 in fines, not more than £40 has yet come into my
hands."[142] On a more hopeful note, Levers advised President Moore that although there had been "continual alarms and real appearances of Indians"
they perpetrated no mischief except to kill and scalp one lad that spring.[143]

Indians may have reduced their attacks on the frontier, but the militia
demanded their pay. In January 1783, Levers wrote to newly elected President John Dickinson, "who knows me well," and got right to the point: "A
sum not less than £10,000 will be required to discharge the pay due the militia." Then Levers backed and filled—"my predecessor had given certain orders" and "from the sheriff I learn the scarcity of money occasions the fines
to come in slowly"—before dropping the other shoe: "the fines in this county
will fall short of £10,000 by about £8,000."[144] Levers realized that he had no
hope of balancing his accounts. Indeed, in this letter his frustration and
weariness begin to surface when he absently refers to himself as "the present
lieutenant of the county."

Levers closed this dispirited letter with a long paragraph that must have

. . . .

astonished the Council. Motivated by the "public trust he held" and doubtless his own self-interest, Levers shifted his ground and unleashed a rambling protest about "great trespasses and waste committed by divers persons upon vacant and unappropriated lands on the north side of Blue Mountain." This was not the first time that Levers had spoken out of his line. Someone, according to Levers, had been cutting white pine to be made into boards and shingles, not so much for neighboring inhabitants, but "for sale far and wide." Although some of this timber had been cut in areas that would not be suitable for farming, Levers believed that these places would "handsomely suit a craftsman, and the destruction of the timber thereby becomes a public injury." Levers also looked forward to a time when "a means would be found to bring that timber down the Lehigh [River] to great public advantage." In fact the Assembly had passed a law in 1780 designed to prevent the waste of public land, but Levers reminded the Council that the law had expired after one year: "Your excellency will I am persuaded be convinced that it is from the integrity of my heart [that] I have given this information." Levers, of course, held land warrants in the region being lumbered by unauthorized persons.

President Dickinson and the Council did not question Levers's integrity; however, they were persuaded that the time had come to relieve him of his job as county lieutenant. In June 1783, the Council advised Levers that they intended to fill as many of the [county lieutenant] appointments as possible with those "who had served their country with honor and fidelity in the field" and they hoped that the nomination of such a person for the office he now held "would not be unacceptable to you."[145] Levers did not mind giving up the county lieutenancy; however, the tone of the letter (had *he* not served with honor and fidelity?) and the fact that the letter requesting his resignation (or was it a dismissal?) came from the Council secretary rather than President Dickinson rubbed Levers the wrong way. In his letter of resignation, Levers minimized the Council's action and subtly jabbed them for tossing him aside like an old sock:

> Had it not been for sometime past the full purpose of my mind to have applied to the Supreme Executive Council for leave to resign the office of lieutenancy, with great pleasure and satisfaction I would have given way for a gentleman so perfectly well qualified to fill the station as I know Colonel Thomas Craig to be. At first, it was perfectly out of respect to the Council that I undertook [the appointment as county lieutenant], and as far as my abilities enabled me and my attention to the

civil offices I hold (which, indeed, are three in number) would permit, I have done my duty, and feel myself extremely happy that the Council have been satisfied with my services. They have been honest exertions, however they may have been wanting.[146]

With the end of the war, the state bureaucracy expanded; it also began to grind at an exceedingly slow pace. A 1784 law plucked the magistracy from the bowl of political plums and required that each township, or pair of townships, elect magistrates annually. Because all local elections had to be certified by the prothonotary, the new law created an avalanche of paperwork for Levers. Another new law also governed the issuance of certain peddlers' licenses. Levers found a loophole in the statute and tossed it to the Council. "Application has been made [at Easton] for a license as a pedlar with one horse," said Levers. "As I know not whether the appliers are to come down to [Philadelphia] to receive their licenses, or to be issued out in the county as in tavern licences, I beg you will take the trouble to inform me by a line."[147] (Levers's by-the-book approach, which must have become tiresome to local inhabitants as well as to officials in Philadelphia, may have led some persons to question his continued usefulness as a public servant.) All in all, however, in the postwar years Levers had begun to achieve some personal financial stability. But his good fortune came to an abrupt end on the night of July 28, 1785.

On that fateful evening Lewis Gordon's sons, Alexander, age twenty-three, and William, twenty-five; Gordon's grandson, James Taylor, about seventeen; and two other young men gathered in front of Robert Levers's house with stones, tomahawks, and axes. They then proceeded to break down the front door. Once inside the house they terrified Levers's family and "injuriously and insultingly treated his house and his office of justice of the peace."[148] The men may have been drunk, but the Gordons had doubtless planned and carried out this attack on Levers and his family in retaliation for the abuse and humiliation suffered by their father and other family members during the Revolution. A magistrate ordered the arrest of Levers's attackers and directed them to appear at September quarter sessions courts; however, the case never came to trial. All but one of the men fled to Virginia where they melded into the populace.

Of the many letters written by Robert Levers—more than 130, containing

. . . .

about 70,000 words have surfaced thus far—among the most interesting is one in which he welcomes Benjamin Franklin home from France:

> I congratulate you on your safe arrival to America, and particularly into that country and city which has received so many favors from you, and oftentimes has been so highly honored by your past labors and exertions for her welfare and benefits. When I look back so long ago as the year 1754, and reflect on your great care and interests and happiness of America generally, in the wise plan proposed for the Union of the Colonies at the Treaty of Albany; and advance forward to the year 1776 and contemplate the great share you had in establishing the Virtuous Independency of America; and go on to consider your abundant fatigues in an advanced life . . . at the Court of France, and indeed throughout Europe, it may with exactness of truth be said: you went about doing Good. Every good man must feel an uncommon satisfaction of mind at your return; how much more at your condescension to preside in this state. May your efforts be blessed and rewarded with success.[149]

Levers communicated with Franklin not only to praise the man but also, it would appear, to lay the groundwork to protect himself from certain persons in Northampton who had launched an effort to remove him from office. Franklin had returned to Pennsylvania just in time to calm troubled political waters and to win the state's presidential election. That Franklin took office under the banner of the Constitutionalist Party, whose constituents supported the state's Revolutionary government, doubtless gave Levers heart, because Levers held his appointment as prothonotary at the pleasure of the president. At issue, and this is inferred from Levers's correspondence, was a land deal executed by Levers about 1765 that had come back to haunt him. The details are sketchy, but they suggest that Levers found himself at odds over this old transaction with a man who happened to be Northampton's current elected representative on the Supreme Executive Council. In short, Levers found himself confronted with enemies who wanted him out of office. Levers turned to Franklin for help. In this letter he immediately pulled out all stops:

> It is said there is a disposition in the Supreme Executive Council to make a change of officer in the prothonotaryship of this county. At the beginning of the late Revolution I took an early and decided part in fa-

. . . .

vor of the independency of America, and in 1777 was appointed prothonotary of the County of Northampton, and which office I have had
the honor to hold until this time, and have had a large and dependent
family to support. I have now advanced in life to the age of sixty-three
and upwards, and have strenuously devoted myself at all times to the duties of the office, and the public weal in general. The profits of the office
are but a support, and to the Honorable Robert Traill, Esq., our present
member of Council, I beg leave to ask your excellency to condescend to
enquire into my conduct therein generally; and should it appear such as
may be thought worthy your countenance, I humbly hope for your excellency's patronage and interest to continue me in the office I hold; the
substance I profess being insufficient to maintain my family, and too far
spent in life to bristle thru it for the support of a wife and six children
dependent on me. Through a long tract of time your excellency may not
immediately recollect my name; I had the honor to be intimately acquainted with Governor Franklin your son, and served under him and
conducted the post office in Philadelphia. Mrs. Becke and the late Mrs.
Franklin honored Mrs. Levers with their acquaintance and the latter
also expressed a tender regard towards [Mrs. Franklin].[150]

A response to Levers's anguished plea has not been found, but Franklin
doubtless intervened on his behalf and quieted moves to remove Northampton's aging prothonotary. Levers now worked at a much slower pace. In his
last years he certified elections, argued softly with Richard Peters (son of
Levers's mentor) over a tract of land, informed another client that "Mr. Bel-
lows, who has usually cut grass on your meadow, wishes to have the liberty
of continuing to do so," issued a peddler's license to one William Miller, and
processed an election return from Bethlehem Township "which, together
with the list of electors, I have carefully copied and filed in my office, agreeable to law."[151]

On the evening of May 20, 1788, Robert Levers, age sixty-four, "departed this life leaving a distressed family."[152] His place of burial is unknown.
Although Levers had written many wills, he never got around to drafting
one for himself. As a result, Mary Levers had to secure a letter of administration from probate court in order to process her husband's estate. An ap-
praiser made quick work of Levers's unremarkable assortment of household
goods, which were valued at £46.6.3. To unravel Levers's land holdings and
balance his books required more time. Not until 1809, twenty-one years af-

. . . .

ter his death, did the court rule that the adjusted value of Levers's estate amounted to £833.[153] Given this glad tiding in his lifetime, the man from Stepney probably would have danced a jig. He was well prepared. After all, the receipt book he carried for more than twenty years contained fourteen carefully autographed pages of dance music. Levers may have played flute, or violin, or perhaps he had a friend lay down a tune while he himself kicked up his heels now and again.

. . . .

2

. . . .

*L*EWIS GORDON

Around 1742, Lewis Gordon settled in Philadelphia.¹ His name appears first in Pennsylvania's public records in 1745, when he registered the purchase of land warrants in Bucks County.² After a stint as a conveyancer, the young Scotsman secured an appointment as a clerk in the law office of Richard Peters.³ Peters served the Penn family as a private councillor, secretary of the land office, and secretary of the Provincial Council, the executive branch of Pennsylvania's colonial government.⁴ The most influential men in the colony crossed Peters's threshold, and Lewis Gordon had the opportunity to brush shoulders with all of them.

In 1749 Gordon won admittance to the bar in Philadelphia, Chester, and Bucks Counties. That same year he married Mary Jenkins, daughter of a prominent merchant, in Christ Church, a house of worship attended by the city's Anglican elite.⁵ In the same year, Gordon became a charter member of the St. Andrew's Society, a group of twenty-five Scotsmen who aimed to improve the lot of poor Scottish immigrants.⁶ With the formation of Northampton County in 1752, Peters urged Gordon to sacrifice the comforts of Philadelphia and move to Easton, the seat of the new county, and apply for admission to the bar. Gordon's relocation would serve the interests of both men. The Scotsman would benefit as the first resident attorney in the county. Richard Peters would have a trusted ally in place to succeed his longtime friend, William Parsons, the incumbent prothonotary of Northampton County.⁷ Since Gordon had no family connections with the elite men who ran colonial Pennsylvania, the prospect of securing a lifetime appointment as a county prothonotary presented him with a rare opportunity, even though it meant that he and his family would have to move to the frontier and take up residence at a ferry landing on the Delaware River.

The prothonotary was "the most considerable personage" in the county.⁸

He served as clerk of common pleas court, quarter sessions court, and orphan's court, as well as county recorder and deputy register of deeds. In addition, he held a commission as justice of the peace, and served as a judge in common pleas court.[9]

The prothonotary drew up trial lists, maintained dockets, minutes, and related files, recorded the name of plaintiffs and defendants, and kept track of the amount of judgments rendered, fines and costs paid, and appeals to higher courts. He also maintained a list of jurors and a register of persons to whom he had granted marriage, burial, tavern, and peddler's licenses. When the prothonotary put pen or seal to paper to execute one of nearly 100 registry transactions, money changed hands. Fees set by the Assembly ranged from a high of four shillings and six pence for issuing a summons to a penny for recording a civil action; however, the volume of work generally enabled the "clerk," as local inhabitants knew him, to amass a sizable estate. In addition to official duties, the prothonotary provided the Provincial Council with timely information about conditions in his county, and acted as a troubleshooter and personal emissary for his superiors.

In June 1752, Lewis Gordon presented himself at the first quarter sessions court in Northampton and gained admittance to the bar. Of twenty-seven civil actions registered that day, Gordon filed nine. In the next two meetings of quarter sessions courts, Gordon appeared as attorney in 108 of 160 civil actions. From the beginning, then, many Northampton inhabitants turned to their resident attorney for legal assistance.[10]

Although it would be 1764 before the Northampton court moved from a tavern to a courthouse, ten years earlier county commissioners had constructed a jail and erected a pillory and whipping post in Easton's town square—a conspicuous reminder that law and order would prevail in Northampton. James Egelson and his son, John, numbered among the first to be tied to the post and whipped. Convicted of horse stealing, James Egelson received twenty-one lashes, and his son, nineteen, a sentence so severe that the *Pennsylvania Gazette* carried a report of the whipping. "As it seldom happens that parents draw in their children to be accomplices with them in their wickedness," reads the unsigned account, "the novelty of the occasion drew great numbers of people to be spectators of the punishment. Many of the spectators were affected with pity towards the son, and some showed a good deal of concern for the present circumstances of the father."[11]

Lewis Gordon's practice thrived, but the French and Indian War (1753–63) interrupted his career. In November 1755, word reached Easton that In-

. . . .

dians planned to attack a Moravian mission at a place named Gnadenhuetten. Men from both sides of the Delaware, Gordon among them, formed a
relief party and set off for the village, but they arrived too late.[12] Horrified by
the sight of dead and dismembered bodies, Gordon moved with his wife and
children across the Delaware River to the safety of Bordentown, a village
south of Trenton, New Jersey. Gordon gained admittance to the New Jersey
bar and, for the next three years, practiced law on both sides of the river.[13]

William Parsons died in 1757, but the governor passed over Gordon and
handed the prothonotaryship of Northampton County to a man named
Charles Swaine. The governor, it seems, owed Swaine a favor.[14] The governor
admired Swaine, who had commanded, in 1753 and 1754, two voyages to
Hudson Bay and the coast of Labrador and had written a book about his ad-
ventures.[15] More to the point, the governor admired one of Swaine's female
relatives who had accompanied the governor from England to America. To
the relief of Richard Peters, who, along with many Philadelphians, had in-
vested in Swaine's Arctic explorations, the explorer soon resigned the post
and departed for places unknown. Governor James Hamilton, with whom
Gordon had dined monthly while a member of the St. Andrew's Society,
promptly named Lewis Gordon prothonotary of Northampton County.

No sooner had Gordon resettled his family in Easton than the proprietaries requested him to help them with the Connecticut problem, a territo-
rial dispute that originated in the court of Charles II. The king had first
granted, in 1662, all land within the present boundaries of Pennsylvania
north of the forty-first parallel of latitude to Connecticut. Then, in 1681,
nearly twenty years later, the king included some of the same land in a grant
to William Penn. In 1753, Connecticut entrepreneurs noticed the discrepancy in the charters. They asserted Connecticut's right to the upper two-
fifths of Pennsylvania, organized a land speculation named the Susquehanna
Company, and announced their intention to settle the region.

The Susquehanna Company sparked a boundary dispute that plagued
scores of Pennsylvania officials. From 1753 to 1810, provincial and state
leaders resorted to threats, legal appeals, political skullduggery, and armed
force to throw out the intruders from Connecticut. The so-called New England men and their sympathizers were arrested, tried, and jailed. They encountered hostile Indians. They fought posses and bounty hunters in three
bloody skirmishes dubbed the Pennamite Wars.[16] Yet neither these ordeals
nor the Revolution halted the advance of the Susquehanna Company in
Pennsylvania.

. . . .

In the summer of 1753, the Company sent a committee to survey the Wyoming Valley, a fertile region watered by the Susquehanna and its tributaries near present Wilkes-Barre. This valley lay within the boundaries of Northampton County. As the committee traveled through the upper part of Northampton, they informed the inhabitants about their land company and offered to sell shares of it. Disgruntled by proprietary land policies and title disputes with Philadelphia speculators, some settlers purchased shares on the spot.[17]

William Parsons was not surprised by the warm welcome the Connecticut men received. "We have too many malcontents amongst us who would cheerfully embrace so favorable an opportunity [to buy land from the Susquehanna Company]," he advised Richard Peters, and added, darkly, "You too well know the disposition of the people in general towards the Proprietaries."[18] A few months later Parsons warned Governor James Hamilton that "this affair may not only be very injurious to the interests of the Proprietaries but it may also be the means of occasioning very great disorders in the back parts of this province."[19]

Governor Hamilton ordered Northampton's magistrates to apprehend the intruders and commit them to jail at a high bail; however, when one magistrate arrested a local man on his way to Connecticut with money collected from his neighbors who hoped to acquire land in the Wyoming Valley, the constable in whose custody the prisoner had been remanded freed him. "This appears to be a sort of anarchy," the magistrate warned the governor, "which if not soon stopped will prove very detrimental to the proprietors and to the peace of this province."[20] The French and Indian War sent the Susquehanna Company's advance party flying back to Connecticut, but they returned to Northampton County in 1760. When Governor Hamilton learned that the foreigners had reappeared on Pennsylvania territory, he ordered Lewis Gordon to visit them and "inform yourself what is doing."[21] Accompanied by the Northampton sheriff and two magistrates, Gordon set off on the dangerous mission. He suggested that the party travel incognito, "dressed as farmers in search of land . . . by which we might more easily introduce ourselves [to the New England men], learn all that was necessary and then . . . tell them our real errand and take our leave."[22] Whether or not Gordon and his companions carried out this ruse, the party got close enough to their quarry to inform the governor that the intruders had laid out townships, built houses and mills, cleared land, and planted crops.[23]

Fearful that the presence of the New Englanders would irritate the In-

. . . .

dians and escalate into full-scale war against all settlers in Pennsylvania's backcountry, Governor Hamilton proposed to burn the houses of the intruders and force them out of the province.[24] Proprietor Thomas Penn, however, preferred to eject the Connecticut people by legal means. He directed Governor Hamilton to warn the settlers off with a proclamation. Gordon delivered the writ, but as there was no way to enforce it the intruders held onto their land. Moreover, many Northampton inhabitants sympathized with the Connecticut people.[25] The seemingly unstoppable march of trespassers from Connecticut so frustrated Governor Hamilton that, in a moment of pique, he ordered the dismissal of the Northampton sheriff and swore to go to the frontier himself.[26] In the midst of this hullabaloo, Richard Peters contacted Gordon: "Much is expected from your care and zeal to rid the country of these troublesome people who will else throw everything into confusion as well as draw upon us the resentment of the Indians."[27] But the troublesome people had come to stay, and the proprietaries pressed Gordon into service as their point man in the running battle with the intruders from Connecticut. Richard Peters retired in 1762, but before he left office he awarded Gordon a lucrative lease to operate the ferry at Easton.

In 1764 George Taylor, an ironmaster, won the first of six consecutive elections as Northampton's representative in the Assembly. Taylor and Gordon were close friends. (The legislator's son studied law with Gordon and married his daughter.) George Taylor kept Gordon abreast of the debate and turmoil in Philadelphia spawned by Parliament's plan to tax all paper used for legal documents, customs declarations, political appointments, and many other applications. Some courts closed because lawyers and magistrates refused to pay the tax; however, this was not the case in Northampton County.

On December 12, 1765, five weeks after the effective date of the Stamp Act, readers of the *Pennsylvania Gazette* learned that "[Northampton] magistrates are determined to proceed in the execution of their offices without any regard to the Stamp Act." Even though Northampton's quarter sessions court did not open as scheduled in December 1765, angry inhabitants spurred the magistrates to act. "The magistrates of this county," the justices proclaimed, "taking into consideration the repeated complaints of the inhabitants, for want of a due distribution of justice, by shutting up the courts of law, have resolved, from the extreme necessity of the case, to open the courts, and proceed to business, as usual. By their order all the law offices are opened accordingly." To publicize their resolve the magistrates advised the *Gazette* that "on Tuesday, March 18, 1766, at a court held in Northampton

County, in this province, the business of the Common Pleas was gone on with without any regard to the Stamp Act."[28] There are no names attached to the letters in the *Gazette*. Even so, Gordon's name would not have been one of them, even though his participation would have been required to carry on the business of the court. Gordon had acquiesced, albeit silently, to the will of the inhabitants. In so doing, he knowingly violated his oath of office. It would not be the last time Gordon compromised his loyalty to the crown.

In 1768, the proprietaries purchased from Indians some 10 million acres that stretched across North Central Pennsylvania from the New York border to the Ohio River. This acquisition provided them with an opportunity to settle the territory with Pennsylvanians and thereby slow or even halt the advance of the New England men. In Northampton, where more than half of the population was twenty-one years of age or younger, settlers were eager to acquire land for themselves and their offspring.[29] But corruption plagued the land office. Officials had terminated a regulation enacted a few years earlier to check speculation. As a result large tracts of land ended up with speculators and jobbers who intended to subdivide the land and sell or rent small parcels to Northampton's inhabitants. The chicanery in the land office so angered Lewis Gordon that he spoke out on behalf of the residents of the county. "Had proper measures been pursued [in the land office] by the gentlemen entrusted," Gordon wrote to a senior proprietary official, "a prior settlement by our own people was very practicable and the New England men might have been entirely frustrated. But what avails it to be sensible of the mismanagement," he continued, "when [proprietary appointees] do not know how to rectify the problem?"[30] Gordon knew exactly how the problem might be solved, but his cry went for naught. Thus, double-dealing high-level proprietary officials not only bungled Pennsylvania's opportunity to thwart the Susquehanna Company but also earned the lasting enmity of many persons in Northampton.

Backlash from land office practices was predictable and swift. "At least half the county are friends to the [New Englanders]," Governor John Penn advised his uncle in 1770. The governor went on to complain that "the [Northampton] sheriff could not get four men out of the county to go with him [on a posse] though he offered them pay."[31] A year later Gordon advised a provincial official, "You cannot depend upon raising sufficient force in these parts to disperse [the New Englanders] as the bulk of the county is averse to it, and even exclaim against it."[32] From London, Thomas Penn, the governor's ailing and cantankerous uncle, fired a salvo. "Arrest those who re-

. . . .

fuse to serve on the posse," he told his nephew. As for Gordon, "if you do not find him zealous and careful in serving our interest, we shall certainly give you orders to displace him and appoint another in his room."[33] No issue created greater dissatisfaction among Northampton's inhabitants than the near-impossibility of acquiring land at what they deemed to be a fair price. Twenty years after the county had been organized, Pennsylvania's self-serving government had worn thin in Northampton.[34]

In March 1774, Parliament ordered the Port of Boston closed until the city paid for damage caused by the Tea Party. Bostonians protested that this act was yet another threat to America's liberties.[35] They vowed to resist and pleaded with other colonies to support them. In Philadelphia more than 200 prominent citizens pledged to stand by the New Englanders. They petitioned Governor John Penn to call an emergency session of the Assembly, and endorsed a congress of delegates from thirteen colonies to mediate disputes with Great Britain. Furthermore, the city men elected a committee to carry out their resolves.

When Governor Penn refused to summon the Assembly, this committee took the issues directly to the people at a mass meeting in the State House Yard. A crowd of some 4,000 cheered the actions of the committee and voted to resist British imperial policies.[36] But how would backcountry inhabitants respond to these issues? The Philadelphia Committee wrote to George Taylor and urged him to rally the people of Northampton and discuss the issues presented at the State House Yard.[37]

Because of the close relationship between Taylor and Gordon, Northampton's first mass protest meeting took place in the courthouse, rather than in the Easton town square or in a nearby field. Taylor addressed a crowd of some 200 persons. He outlined the sequence of events that had led to the meeting.[38] The popular former assemblyman declared that Parliament had trampled American rights and that an intercolonial congress would be the best way to settle American grievances. When Taylor called for a vote, the crowd, acting as self-appointed surrogates for absent neighbors, voted unanimously to take up the "common cause of American freedom."[39] They also nominated Taylor and Gordon and four other men to form a committee to link Northampton with committees in ten other counties and the capital city.[40] Northampton inhabitants also contributed more than £50 for the relief of their oppressed brethren in Boston.[41]

To help fan the resistance movement, Taylor ordered the proceedings of the meeting published in the English and German newspapers.[42] This bold

. . . .

stroke won cheers from the crowd who wanted Pennsylvania—the world, for that matter—to know that they too had drawn a line on British imperial policies. Ironically, it was Parliament, not the proprietaries, whose bungling brought men to their feet in the Easton courthouse where, on June 21, 1774, Northampton's inhabitants raised the stakes—and began to raise the Republic.

From New England to the Carolinas, from the seacoast to the frontier—in a multitude of places like Northampton County—the common cause of freedom inspired Americans to protest British policies and call for an intercolonial congress. Months of intense political debate culminated in the First Continental Congress, which convened at Carpenters' Hall in Philadelphia on September 5, 1774. To underscore the gravity of the crisis between the United Colonies and Parliament, Congress suspended trade with Great Britain and requested every city, town, and county in the United Colonies to elect a committee of observation and inspection to enforce the boycott. In a few months, hundreds of committees with more than 7,000 members operated in the colonies.[43] These committees imposed a new kind of law and order in colonial America. They accepted the promulgations of Congress as the supreme law of the land. They functioned as judge and jury. They encouraged informants and admitted hearsay evidence. They singled out persons who disagreed with the new politics and punished them with public humiliation, fines, and, in extreme cases, tar and feathers. In brief, these committees supplanted local government and served as grass-roots interlocutors for independence.[44]

On December 21, 1774, inhabitants from every corner of Northampton headed for the courthouse to elect a County Committee. The first group chosen to serve on the Committee included ten magistrates, three taverners, two innkeepers, and fourteen prosperous farmers—at least one delegate from each of the county's twenty-five townships and Easton. There were no strangers on the Committee. A mix of first and second generations, most of the men had lived in the region upwards of twenty years. Committee membership reflected the county's ethnic diversity. Persons with German roots comprised about 80 percent of Northampton's population and had settled in most of the county's twenty-five townships, but they predominated in the nine townships west of the Lehigh River and in three others. Accordingly, Germans held about half of the twenty-nine committee seats with the remainder distributed among persons of English, Scottish, Scots-Irish, Dutch, French, Swiss, and Spanish ancestry.[45]

. . . .

The Northampton Committee set to work on the day after their election.[46] The Committee of Correspondence, appointed six months earlier and chaired by Lewis Gordon, formally resigned and "received the public thanks of the county for their faithful service." The new Committee then appointed Lewis Gordon chairman and chose as secretary a man named Robert Traill, a young Scotsman who clerked for the county commissioners and studied law in Lewis Gordon's office. The Committee stipulated that at each succeeding general election inhabitants would have an opportunity to choose new committeemen. Most important, the delegates appointed Lewis Gordon, George Taylor, two Germans, a Dutchman, and an English Moravian to serve on a seven-man executive committee and authorized them to act on behalf of the full committee. So intent were the committeemen on carrying out their responsibility that nineteen of them plowed through fresh snow and ice to attend a second meeting on January 9, 1775.[47] Of the ten members who did not appear, seven lived north of Blue Mountain. At this session the Committee accepted an invitation from the Philadelphia Committee to send a delegation to an upcoming provincial convention, the announced purpose of which was to promote the nonconsumption of imported goods. The Committee directed its executive committee to represent Northampton at the conference. Gordon, however, intent on keeping a low profile, excused himself, just as he had excused himself from a convention of counties some six months earlier.

One hundred and five committeemen, representing Pennsylvania's eleven counties and the city of Philadelphia, assembled in late January 1775. Cynics joked about the convention. A gentleman of Philadelphia observed that the transactions of the convention would "consist of pious resolves to kill no wethers, and to encourage the industrious farmer to make his own coat.... This and a little inflammatory matter to keep sedition alive, now expiring, will take up their whole time."[48] In fact, delegates resolved to achieve self-sufficiency in the production of woolens, salt, nails, paper, glass, gunpowder, steel, and other items previously imported from Great Britain. The delegates also took steps that moved Pennsylvania closer to armed rebellion against the crown. First, the counties agreed that should the British force them to submit to the acts of Parliament, they would assist one another and "defend the rights and liberties of America." Second, the delegates authorized the Philadelphia Committee to act on behalf of all county committees.[49] George Taylor, for one, was not in a pious mood when he left Philadelphia. He had already decided to resign from the Northampton

Committee and give full attention to converting production at Durham Iron Company from kettles, clock weights, and pig iron to cannon and shot.

In the third week of April 1775, Gordon received a letter from the Philadelphia Committee. The committee warned that armed conflict with British troops might be unavoidable and recommended that military associations be formed in every Northampton township, "not to commence war, but for just defense."[50] The communication stunned Gordon. Had not radicals vowed to use every legal means in their power to protest British policies in North America? Gordon pocketed the letter. But a week later news of the Battle of Lexington and Concord reached Easton. Shortly afterward a member of the Philadelphia Committee named Robert Towers confronted Gordon in his office and demanded an answer to the Committee's letter.[51] While the Philadelphia tanner cooled his heels, Gordon summoned the executive committee to meet on Saturday, May 6, at Mrs. Nungessor's tavern, which was catercorner from the courthouse.[52] Secretary Robert Traill observed that "the matter recommended in the letter [from the Philadelphia Committee] . . . made a deep impression on the [Northampton Committee]." Gordon doubtless underscored the inherent danger in taking military action against the crown; nonetheless, the Committee issued a call to arms in Northampton County. Each member of the full Committee received a letter that instructed him to organize military associations in his township, elect officers, and provide each man with a good firelock, one pound of powder, four pounds of lead, a sufficient quantity of flints, and a cartridge box. The letter also called upon committeemen to meet at Easton on May 22 and to report how well their township had complied with the Committee's orders. Towers got what he came for and left Easton the next day. In truth, however, the Committee knew in advance that due to a lack of arms not more than fifty men in the entire county could turn out as they had recommended.

Committeemen rushed to enlist their neighbors in the militia. Outraged by the massacre of eight men on the Lexington green, most of Northampton's committeemen traveled to the county courthouse for the crucial meeting at the end of May. When all townships had reported, Robert Traill announced that more than 2,300 men had joined the militia. The defiant yeoman also issued a declaration:

> It being evident that the British are fully determined and bent upon the total extinction and utter destruction of American liberty, to avoid such slavery we resolve:

. . . .

1. That this Committee will execute all such measures as the Continental Congress shall in their wisdom adopt for the preservation of American liberty.
2. That all freemen should join the militia, provide themselves with arms and ammunition, and drill as often as possible to learn the military art.
3. That all shopkeepers be forbidden to sell or dispose of any arms or ammunition without the consent of one of the members of this Committee.

For readers of the *Pennsylvania Evening Post* and the *Philadelphische Staatsbote*, the message from Easton was unequivocal: The Northampton Committee had taken control of the county, and the inhabitants meant to fight to preserve America's liberty.[53]

In June 1775, Congress requested the Northampton Committee to recruit and equip a company of riflemen to join General Washington in the defense of Boston. At a meeting on June 20, the Committee directed each township "to send two expert riflemen with their rifles" to join the company. Itching to join the fray, Northampton's young men pocketed a £3 bonus and filled the company's ranks. In mid-July 1775, with the Committee looking on, eighty-one officers and men of the Northampton Company mustered in Easton's town square, elected officers, and marched off to Cambridge, Massachusetts, where they joined eight other companies from Pennsylvania's backcountry to form the Pennsylvania Rifle Battalion.[54] Lewis Gordon informed Congress that Northampton's riflemen would do credit to the county. They were "expert [marksmen] and of good figure," he boasted, "many of them being not less than five feet ten inches tall."[55]

Interestingly, Robert Traill did not record the names of those in attendance at the meetings on May 22 and June 20, the only such omissions in fifty-eight entries. Did Robert Traill, law clerk and consummate notetaker, simply forget to list the names that routinely appear at the beginning of every entry in the minutes of the Committee? Probably not. Alarmed by the Committee's decision to publish its resolves in the newspapers, Lewis Gordon doubtless directed Traill to omit the names from the minutes lest British authorities later identify committeemen—himself, in particular—as traitors.

As Pennsylvania prepared for war, the Provincial Committee of Safety turned to county committees for help in building the colony's military might. In Northampton, Lewis Gordon fielded most of the orders from the twenty-five-member committee and its nineteen subcommittees presided over by Benjamin Franklin.[56] Gordon, for example, directed a search for provincial arms loaned to the county during the French and Indian War. He sent two men to Philadelphia to learn how to make potassium nitrate, an essential chemical in gunpowder. He reimbursed officers for weapons purchased for their battalions. He appointed men to dispense powder and lead "not exceeding two rounds per man" to test the marksmanship of new recruits for the Pennsylvania Regiment in the Continental Army. On another day, Gordon supervised the collection of fifty-seven rifles made by local artisans and dispatched the weapons to the armory in the State House Yard.[57] Gordon also relayed to the colonels of Northampton's militia the on-again-off-again mobilization orders from officials in the capital city who feared the British Army would cross the Delaware at any hour. Week after week, the chairman of the Northampton Committee raced to fulfill each request from Philadelphia.[58]

The chairmanship of the County Committee had become a heavy burden on Gordon. He was not alone in praying that America and Great Britain would resolve their differences through negotiation. On the other hand, Gordon, in his role as chairman of the County Committee, reassured the Provincial Committee of Safety that we "will [uphold] every intention of yours tending to support and preserve our sacred rights as Americans and Freemen."[59] Gordon, in fact, attempted to carry out a dangerous balancing act. Beginning a decade earlier with the crisis over the Stamp Act, Gordon began to position himself so that no matter how statesmen resolved the conflict between America and Great Britain he would be counted with the winning side. But when the Committee met on May 30, 1776, to decide whether or not to support the radicals' call for independence, Gordon sent word that he was "indisposed." This excuse satisfied some committeemen, but others questioned Gordon's loyalty to the cause. Still, Gordon managed to squelch those who called for his resignation. After a lapse of one meeting, he resumed his post as Committee chairman.

In June 1776, radicals overthrew Pennsylvania's colonial government and elected delegates to meet in convention and draw up a new constitution. Until a new government could be formed, it fell to local committees and militia to maintain law and order. The Northampton Committee seized the initiative and informed inhabitants that the Committee would "keep the peace and call offenders to justice in the name of the State of Pennsylvania until it shall be otherwise ordered by the Convention or any other superior authority; for the preservation of Men's Lives, Liberties, and Reputations."[60] From June 1776 to May 1777, the Northampton Committee convened nearly once each week to mete out justice. During this chaotic period, the Committee weighed orders from the Convention, the Council of Safety,[61] Congress, local militia officers, and the commander-in-chief of the Continental Army and acted on information disseminated in circular letters, political broadsides, newspapers, and rumors passed on by persons traveling through the county. Hearsay, innuendo, and long memories accepted as evidence tainted the committee's judgment. Absent due process, defendants had no choice but to submit themselves to the mercy of this people's court chaired by Lewis Gordon.[62]

The work of this court is illustrated in its handling of charges brought against a family named Stackhouse, who, it had been rumored, were "inimical to the cause of freedom." The Committee ordered Stackhouse and his two sons to surrender their weapons. When they refused, armed militia arrested the three men and brought them before the Committee. Robert Stackhouse Jr. informed his inquisitors that he had three rifles, that the rifles were loaded, and that he would fire them at anyone who tried to take them out of his hands. The Committee jailed Robert on the spot.[63]

Nor did the Committee shy from hearing a complaint against Andrew Ledlie, the town's doctor, and Nell Hunt, the doctor's housekeeper. Responding to four men and one woman who had taken it upon themselves to act as a morals squad, the Committee confirmed what everyone in the county knew: that "Nell Hunt . . . is a common scold and a common disturber of the peace of the town of Easton; and has been so for several years last past; and that she is aided and abated in her disorderly proceedings by Doctor Andrew Ledlie who has kept her for a housekeeper and whore for many years."[64] The Committee took no action in this case, but Dr. Ledlie refused to drop the matter. Angered by the attack on his character, he petitioned the Constitutional Convention and complained of "great ill-usage by some of the inhabitants of that town [Easton] on account . . . of his attachment to the cause of liberty."[65] True patriots, the Convention opined, deserved the full protection of the state. Therefore, they directed the magistrate in Easton to "afford the petitioner all the redress and security which the nature of this case requires."[66] Dr. Ledlie went off to serve as surgeon for the Twelfth Regiment. Gossip about the doctor's relationship with Nell Hunt dried up, only to find new life in 1789, when Ledlie shot and

wounded the Northampton sheriff. The cause of this altercation is unknown; however, the sheriff happened to be the son of one of Ledlie's accusers in the Nell Hunt affair, a fact that no doubt worked to the sheriff's
disadvantage in that split second when the doctor decided to draw his pistol
and squeeze the trigger.[67]

On the eve of independence in Northampton, the treatment of persons
who disagreed with the radicals signaled the start of an era when suspicion
and persecution of one's neighbors became a blood sport. Many men
thumped their chests and proclaimed themselves patriots simply to get even
with longtime enemies and to fill their pockets. As chairman of the Committee, Lewis Gordon presided over the county's mock court, but the break-
down of traditional standards of law and order doubtless tormented him.

From July through September 1776, delegates to the Constitutional
Convention labored to frame a new charter. Meanwhile, thousands of Penn-
sylvanian's took up arms.[68] In August, the ferry at Easton transported more
than 1,500 militiamen across the Delaware to help General Washington repel the British invasion of New York.[69] The rumble of cannon fire quickened
the pace of this small army of volunteers, which included 300 Northampton
men who fell in with "flying colors, drums and fifes." Within days, however,
deserters returned to Northampton with word of the American army's defeat at New York.[70] Nearly half of the Northampton men who had marched
off in August were reported dead, wounded, captured, or missing. The battalion colonel—a former sheriff and assemblyman—was wounded and
taken prisoner. The company captain, whose father sat in the Constitutional
Convention, suffered serious injuries.[71] The captain's son, a drummer boy,
never returned. The flow of soldiers across the Delaware reversed. Militiamen had lost their weapons and ammunition, their blankets and banners,
and their pride.

Capitalizing on his victory at New York, British General Sir William
Howe turned his troops toward Philadelphia. Pandemonium gripped Pennsylvania. The state's political factions, which had battled over the formation
of a new government, declared a truce in order to defend the commonwealth. General Howe exploited the panic and offered to pardon any person
who laid down his arms and took an oath of loyalty within sixty days. Lewis
Gordon welcomed the amnesty. The conduct of the County Committee had
so offended his sense of equity and justice that he had become ill both in
body and spirit. Moreover, given the violence that infested Northampton,
Gordon rightly feared that Pennsylvania's militia-backed Revolutionary

government would wield its power to silence those who disagreed with its policies.[72]

Within days of Howe's proclamation, Gordon informed the Committee "that he would no longer attend." The Committee ordered the man who, for two years, had chaired all but one of the Committee's meetings to appear "to answer such matters as shall be objected against you." Citing his "low and weak" condition, Gordon refused, but he invited the Committee to visit him at his home, an offer the Committee declined. The standoff continued for six months until state officials placed the traitor under house arrest.[73]

Pennsylvania's Revolutionary government replaced nine of eleven colonial prothonotaries, but of these only Gordon was arrested, probably at the insistence of the Northampton Committee whom he had betrayed. Placed under house arrest, Gordon was free to travel a few miles from his home, but his detention accelerated the deterioration of his mental and physical condition. Nonetheless, Robert Levers, the county's new prothonotary, shadowed Gordon to his grave. The two men first met thirty years earlier when they both clerked for Richard Peters. In Gordon's view, Levers bore the marks of a sharper who lacked intellectual depth and the capacity to reason. On the other hand, Levers perceived the future lawyer as a representative of a class that, no matter his own achievements, would forever lie beyond his reach.

Levers, zealous defender of the common cause, had a personal motive to challenge the loyalty of Gordon and members of his family. For nearly a year Levers pestered Gordon to swear allegiance to Pennsylvania—a condition of citizenship prescribed by the legislature in June 1777—but Gordon rebuffed him. Finally, in May 1778, Gordon summoned Levers to his deathbed, raised his right hand, and swore allegiance to the state. It was a sour victory for Levers, since he could guess that Lewis Gordon had subscribed to the oath not because he had experienced a change of heart toward Pennsylvania's government but because he wanted to ensure that his substantial estate would not be confiscated by the state under the provisions of an act passed April 1, 1778. Gordon beat the deadline for complying with this law by ten days.[74] In advising Council that his long-running battle with Gordon had come to an end, Levers said only that "a few days ago, Lewis Gordon took the Test according to law."[75] A more charitable Robert Levers might have added that the longtime county prothonotary and chairman of the Northampton Committee had died soon thereafter.

. . . .

3

. . . .

ELIAS LONG

In Mount Bethel Township, clan-like ties bound together a Scots-Irish enclave hemmed in by Blue Mountain on the north and by the Delaware River on the east. But when the Revolution swept through this community, the solidarity of some 150 families splintered. As happened in other Northampton townships, the radical element in Mount Bethel branded every man a friend or enemy of the cause. Most persons in this township sided with the radicals. But some, like Elias Long, rejected the firebrands. Moreover, the dissenters made no attempt to conceal their contempt for Pennsylvania's Revolutionary government. Six months after the Declaration, Long's outspokenness led him into deep water.

In the first week of December 1776, Long and a few of his friends traveled to Easton for provisions.[1] On the journey home the men talked politics. Emboldened, perhaps, by General Sir William Howe's recent victory at New York and his subsequent march through New Jersey, Long cursed Congress, the Constitutional Convention, and the County Committee, and proclaimed loudly that they were all a "parcel of damned rascals and were selling the peoples liberties." Long had his say, and that should have been that. However, Anthony Moore and John Connelly had come up the trail behind Long and overheard his diatribe against the Revolution. When Moore, who had recently been elected to represent Mount Bethel on the County Committee, returned to Easton a few days later for a meeting of the Committee, he lodged a complaint against Long. John Connelly tagged along with Moore and confirmed the latter's allegation. As a result, the Committee ordered the Mount Bethel constable to summon Elias Long to appear for a hearing on December 13. The Committee also summoned the Marr brothers who, according to Moore, had been on the trail and had also heard Long curse leaders of the Revolution.

Long ignored the summons, so the Committee ordered Captain John Mack and a squad of Mount Bethel militiamen to bring the miscreant to Easton. After a brief trial the Committee found Long guilty as charged and sent him to the county jail for an indefinite period. After spending Christmas in prison, however, Long notified the tribunal that he was "heartily sorry for his past conduct and prayed to be released." The Committee ordered Long to post a bond of £40 for "his good behavior towards the inhabitants of the American States and especially towards the Continental Congress, the Committee of this county, or any other authority of the said states for the space of one year."[2] Long promised to behave better in the future, but he returned to Mount Bethel a marked man.

Elias Long had scarcely reached home when General George Washington crossed the Delaware River and rebuffed Howe's first attempt to capture Philadelphia. But in August 1777, Howe landed his army at Head of Elk, Maryland, marched north, and, a month later, occupied Pennsylvania's capital city. The British victory lifted the spirits of the disaffected throughout the commonwealth. Ever fearful of men like Elias Long, the Pennsylvania Assembly not only stiffened the penalty for those who refused to take the state's loyalty oath but also passed a new piece of legislation: "An Act for the Attainder of Divers Traitors if They Render Not Themselves by a Certain Day, and for Vesting Their Estates in This Commonwealth, and for More Effectually Discovering the Same and for Ascertaining and Satisfying the Lawful Debts and Claims Thereupon."[3] This law provided that any inhabitant who willingly and voluntarily served the King of Great Britain either by land or by sea as a civil or military officer, soldier, or seaman, would be attainted of high treason, and that all of his money, goods, and real estate would be forfeited to the state. Between 1778 and 1781, Pennsylvania's government proclaimed 500 persons under this act. Of this number, 36, including Elias Long, resided in Northampton.[4]

Long abandoned his wife and children and took flight in the spring of 1778. His whereabouts for the next six years are unknown. He may have joined a force of Indians and Tories who operated in northern Pennsylvania, or signed on with General Howe's troops in Philadelphia, or fled to New York City. Mount Bethel's Samuel Rea, one of six men appointed by the Assembly as agents for forfeited estates in Northampton County, swung into action as soon as he learned of Long's defection. Under the law Rea seized "the goods and chattels of Elias Long, supposed to be gone to the enemies of the United State of America."[5] Rea then contracted with Robert and

. . . .

James Richart, also of Mount Bethel, to inventory and appraise Long's property. The appraisers' tally revealed that Elias Long, his wife, and five children had made do with two chairs, two tables, two beds and bedding, a chest with lock and key, a frying pan and trammel fireplace chain and hook, an iron pot, a churn, a pail, a wheat mill and sieve, a bake tray, a reel [device used in baking bread in an oven] and barrel [earthenware jar probably used to hold yeast cake, or starter], an ax, a frame saw, hay and rye in a barrack [barn], four bee hives with bees, four cows, a horse, and a mare. The Richart brothers valued the estate at £175, of which the livestock and feed accounted for £145, and the bee hives £8. On August 20, 1778, Samuel Rea reported to the Supreme Executive Council that Robert and James Richart had sworn that the inventory was a "just apprizement according to the best of their skill and knowledge." Rea also warned that "there is so much just claims upon the estate as the whole will amount to."[6] In other words, after creditors had been paid and the Richarts, the sheriff, and Rea had received their fees, the sale of Long's property would generate no money for the state.

Agents for forfeited estates sometimes permitted wives of defectors to "borrow" personal property from their husband's estate, and they covered the transaction as a debit against receipts from the auction.[7] Rea, it would appear, did not come to Mrs. Long's rescue. In fact, there is no evidence that Rea ever auctioned Long's estate. To save trouble all around, the state's agent probably dispensed with formalities and distributed Long's goods to creditors, first-come first-served. Mrs. Long could only pray that family and friends would make room for her and her children.

In November 1782, one year after General Charles Cornwallis surrendered at Yorktown, American negotiators signed a provisional peace treaty at Paris. When copies of this document reached Northampton County in spring 1783, citizens were outraged over one of its provisions and immediately formed a countywide committee. The committee, chaired by a "virtuous, honest Whig" named Henry Geiger, petitioned Northampton's representatives in the Pennsylvania Assembly to urge Congress to modify Article V of the treaty.[8] As written, Article V urged that men like Elias Long be enabled to return home "in that spirit of conciliation which, on the return of the blessings of peace, should universally prevail." But after five years of battling Indians, Tories, and British troops, many Northampton inhabitants refused to embrace reconciliation with their former enemies. The committee made clear why they opposed a treaty that would permit traitors to return to the county:

. . . .

The scene of blood has been too lately closed, the wounds of many are still bleeding, the graves of our murdered friends and relatives are yet recent, their virtues strongly impressed in our minds, and their accumulated agonies too deeply resented for us to draw the veil of oblivion over the crimes of those who caused our sufferings. . . . The committee most earnestly entreats and enjoins you to procure a law to be passed to prevent the return into this state of such persons as during the War, have joined, aided, or assisted either the British or Indian Enemies.[9]

Congress, however, ratified the Treaty of Paris in January 1784, and Elias Long returned home. Long doubtless received a warm welcome from his family, but others in Mount Bethel treated the defector like a pariah. Consequently, upon the death of his parents in 1788, Long moved his wife and ten children over Blue Mountain. Other relatives soon joined Elias in Northampton's Lower Smithfield Township. By 1794, Elias Sr., Elias Jr., John Sr., John Jr., and Jacob Long had made a fresh start. With 200 acres, four horses, four cows, and a drove of grandchildren, Elias Long Sr. ruled the clan.[10] Nearly thirty years earlier Long had cursed Congress, the Constitutional Convention, and the County Committee. Just as virtuous and honest Whigs refused to reconcile with men who had betrayed their country, Long doubtless remained unrepentant to the end.

4

. . . .

ℋENRY GEIGER

In 1749, Henry Geiger emigrated from Germany to Pennsylvania.[1] There he joined his brother, who had settled near Philadelphia.[2] Around 1753, the Geigers moved to Northampton County and took up land in Heidelberg Township. With the outbreak of the French and Indian War (1753–63), Henry Geiger, a former soldier, joined the Pennsylvania Regiment as an ensign, or second lieutenant.[3] Geiger first manned a line of forts and blockhouses on the Northampton frontier that had been positioned and constructed under the supervision of Benjamin Franklin.[4]

Geiger performed well in the field. When senior officers at a key fort mutinied, Geiger filled the breach. "The fort is now commanded by Ensign Geiger, a sober prudent person," his superior said. He might have added that the ensign had benefited from some education.[5] For example, when supplies ran short at his fort, Geiger himself wrote to regional commander Colonel Timothy Horsefield to request immediate relief.[6] Geiger's dispatch was written in German; however, he inserted English words and spelled them as they would have sounded to him. First, he addressed the letter to "master Hassfilt [Horsefield]." Second, he repeatedly used "prowigen," a phonetic variant of provision, rather than the German "vorrat," doubtless to ensure that Horsefield, an Englishman, would not misunderstand the key word in the message. Phonic equivalents provided the means by which most eighteenth-century Pennsylvania Germans acquired a working English vocabulary.[7] Geiger boldly wove fractured English words into convoluted sentences and committed them to paper because of his fierce determination to communicate with senior persons in Pennsylvania's military and civil chains of command. As a result, twenty-three of Geiger's letters have been preserved because they reposed in official files. Moreover, Geiger's hand is so unique and clear, his letters, like those of Robert Levers, leap from a pile of archival documents or a roll of microfilm.[8]

In 1757, the army promoted Geiger to lieutenant and sent him west of the Susquehanna River, where he served under Colonel Henry Bouquet, a Swiss soldier of fortune recruited by the British army.[9] During a two-year stint in Bouquet's battalion Geiger improved upon his command of English and also acquired political savvy. Upon his discharge from the army Geiger followed the example of fellow officers and sought additional compensation for his military service. To initiate his application Geiger wrote to Colonel Bouquet:

> Most Hounorable Colonel: This with my Most Kind Complements I take this Opertunity to write to your honour wishing your hounors Good health I am very Sorry that I had not The happiness of seeing your honour before you Left Pittsburgh, I then being on Guard So as I Could not Give My Complements to your honour: I have heard by Some Gentlemen that I was in your honours favor which I am Very Much Obligated to your honour and I Shall with all Willingness Do your honour all the Good Service that I Can do Wishing the Lord will Grant your honour Good health and Good Succes that you may Finnissh this old year in health And may the New year Crown you with all happiness I begg one favour of your honour that you will be so kind as to Recommend me to his Honour the New Governour. I know that Several Officers have All Ready Gone Down for to Recommend themselves to his Honour the Governour. God bless your Honour and I Recommend My Self to your honours favor.[10]

In this letter Geiger displays a style that he perfected over the years: compliment a lot, invoke God's blessings repeatedly, make a request (twice, if need be), then bow with humility.

When the first letter to Colonel Bouquet failed to get results, Geiger wrote to him again. Geiger now turned on the charm in "French" and addressed Colonel Bouquet as *Tres Nobele et Most Hounorabele Colonele.* "I cannot forget you honour because the Gread favor that you have always get for me," Geiger began. Then, spread over many lines, Geiger invoked God's protection for his benefactor: "I pray always the Lord our God will be Your Guid Likewiss that he whass with Jesuce and Will prserven you honour from all Dangers And axidante . . . and I Recommend Me always in your

. . . .

honour favor."[11] And lest the colonel have difficulty putting a face on the writer of this letter, Geiger signed his name and added, "Lead Lieutenant." Colonel Bouquet did indeed remember the lead lieutenant who had served at Forts Bedford, Juniata, and Ligonier. In 1761, Geiger became a naturalized citizen of Pennsylvania, after which the governor appointed him a justice of the peace.[12] Thus fifteen years after Geiger set foot in Philadelphia, he took the bench in Northampton as one of twelve magistrates who served as Justices of the Lord, the King.

In 1763, the final year of the French and Indian War, Indians attacked settlers on Pennsylvania's frontier. And once again, Indians, hostile or not, became prey for some frontier troops. When soldiers stationed at Lehigh Gap killed three Indians who had been converted to Christianity by Moravians, the senior magistrate in Bethlehem ordered Justice Geiger to investigate the incident. Geiger rounded up witnesses, deposed them, and reported his findings. The three Christian Indians, Geiger declared, had been murdered. Geiger discovered that Captain Jacob Wetterholt, his onetime commander and Heidelberg neighbor, and two of his men had shot an adult male, a woman, and a boy. Geiger also informed his superior that his "neighbours been very despeass upon this actions for killing the Indian in their Neighbourhoot. . . . [Now] they muse sofere . . . the Neighboours says that they believe the officer killd the Indians for to have their goods and Not for to Destroy the Enemies and I believe mesleves." Geiger added sourly, "When the officer and soldier being in liqour then They have corge to do meschief and killy the Indian woman and boy."[13]

The settlers' fears were justified. A band of warriors tracked Captain Wetterholt to an inn and killed him. The raiders then swept through Allen and Whitehall Townships and killed twenty-three men, women, and children.[14] Geiger and his neighbors complained to authorities about the lack of protection from hostile Indians, as well as the undisciplined behavior of provincial soldiers and their officers. The colonel responsible for the Northampton frontier acknowledged that some officers may have been at fault, but he also dismissed Geiger as an agitator. "I expect to have some trouble from Justice Geiger in these parts," he reported, "as he hath already begun to give himself some airs."[15] The colonel doubtless resented the fact that Geiger had put forth his own ideas on how best to defend the frontier, and on how soldiers should conduct themselves.

Geiger's belief that the provincial government had failed to defend the frontier against Indians led him to choose a side in a bitter political dispute.

. . . .

In 1764, Pennsylvania's anti-proprietary faction floated a petition to replace the provincial government with officials responsible directly to the crown.[16] Sponsors of the petition pledged that the king would provide protection for inhabitants on the frontier. This promise appealed to Geiger and his neighbors. Geiger embraced the architect of the petition, Benjamin Franklin, as a former comrade in arms during the French and Indian War.[17] Justice Geiger crisscrossed the frontier as an advocate for Franklin's petition, a partisan activity that caught the attention of at least one Northampton official who owed his position to the old guard. "The petition for an alteration in the government meets with considerable success," prothonotary Lewis Gordon reported to the provincial secretary, "particularly on the frontiers, [where inhabitants] are made to believe they will then be better protected. In promoting this," said Gordon, "I am told Henry Geiger, one of our magistrates, exerts himself with uncommon diligence and has procured many hands to it, which I believe to be true, having had it from good authority."[18]

Geiger, it turned out, had aligned himself with the losing side on this issue. Despite his electioneering, Northampton voters went to the polls and gave the proprietary party a solid victory, thanks, in part, to intervention by spiritual leaders, who feared that under the king they would lose religious freedom.[19] Although the new Assembly adopted the petition for a royal government in Pennsylvania, a complex series of political maneuvers doomed the plan and wounded those who had proposed it. Geiger himself paid dearly for opposing the establishment. When the council secretary asked Gordon to clarify Geiger's status as a magistrate, Gordon replied that "[Geiger] has no special commission. It is a matter of little consequence whether he is put in the new commission or no."[20] Since Gordon recommended men for the General Commission for the Peace in Northampton, his remark signaled that Geiger's appointment would not be renewed. News of this sort traveled fast. In 1765, the name "Henry Geiger, Esq." appears on the Northampton tax list. When it became known that the Council did not reappoint Geiger, some person backtracked and crossed out the "Esq." Who took the trouble to set this record straight? A conscientious clerk? One of Geiger's enemies? For some person, or persons, the opportunity to take Geiger down a peg proved irresistible.

Ousted from the magistracy, a sanction rarely invoked by the colonial establishment, Geiger doubtless reminded his friends and neighbors that he had served four years on the frontier to protect them, only to be removed from office by rascals in Philadelphia. Geiger may have been so piqued over

. . . .

his dismissal that he decided to stop paying taxes. Beginning in 1770, his name no longer appears on Northampton County tax lists.[21] How did one of Northampton's most visible and vocal citizens manage to avoid the assessor and the tax collector over a period of twenty years? One surmise is that Geiger, a bachelor, sold his land and moved in with his brother and his family.

Between 1769 and 1774, "Justice" Geiger, an honorific title for life, chopped his share of wood. During this period, however, he maintained an active voice in local politics that, along with his military experience, led to his selection in 1775 as colonel of Northampton's Second Battalion. The Second Battalion included upwards of 1,000 men, most of them Germans, drawn from ten townships, which embraced some 400 square miles south of Blue Mountain and west of the Lehigh River (present Lehigh County). In the winter of 1775–76, Colonel Geiger rode circuit to sermonize his troops. The sixty-year-old soldier championed independence. He held up Tories, Moravians, and other nonresisters as enemies of the people, and lectured his men on what it meant to be a soldier. In short, Geiger had prepared his battalion for the day in May 1776 when Philadelphia radicals suddenly reached out to the back counties and asked them to help overthrow the colonial government. Nine hundred militiamen from the Second Battalion voted unanimously to support independence "at all hazards, be the consequences what they may."[22]

Following his victory over General George Washington at New York, General Sir William Howe marched south through New Jersey toward Philadelphia. Pennsylvania's government called for men to fill regiments destined to serve with the Continental Army. Driven by a desire "to serve his country," Colonel Geiger traveled to Philadelphia. There he personally submitted a petition to remind the Council of Safety that he had been a lieutenant in the last war and begged them to appoint him a captain in one of the new regiments.[23] Despite an acute shortage of experienced officers, the Council rejected Geiger's petition. Perhaps the Council rebuffed the colonel because he had reached the age of sixty. If so, they misjudged their man. Geiger's physical condition astounded men half his age. A few years later one of his fellow militia officers remarked that "Geiger, who is upwards of sixty years of age, together with all the other officers and men have encountered these high and many hills and mountains with the greatest satisfaction and discipline imaginable, and they appear to be eager to engage with the tyrannical enemy."[24]

. . . .

Geiger's failure to secure a regimental commission injured his pride. He returned to Heidelberg, nursed hurt feelings, then picked up his pen and gave the Council a piece of his mind. Tories infested the ranks of Northampton's militia, Geiger bellowed: "I have See me Selves how they behave themselve on their Duty in the Camp." The colonel then railed against a government that lacked the will to collect the fines and taxes levied on those who refused to bear arms.[25] "I believe it is in your power," he said, "to Give a Strick order to all the Commissioner in this province to Lay the Said Tax . . . then you may Depend upon that then the militia will be Ready to do their Duty." Geiger also excoriated printers for bias in reporting the news. "This macke the people in the Contrie So Confuse that if the Enemies Should Come near [Philadelphia] it Should Be very Troubelsom to Get the [militia] in Readiness for to march against the Enemies. Therefore I hop your worship will be Cearful to Give Strick order to Such Printers to not Let in their paper anything That is Contrary our freedom."[26] Nonetheless, Geiger assured the Council that he would "be alvays Ready for the Defence of this Contrie and Liberty . . . and I pray the Lord almight God that he will preserve your worship and Wholl Country from all axitans and from our Enemies."[27] But the Council had more urgent business, so Geiger took matters into his own hands.

Colonel Geiger kept watch on suspicious persons in his region. Some inhabitants, who announced that they would refuse to fight for independence, feared that Geiger would arrest them and seize their property. As a result, eighty of them signed a mutual defense pact.[28] Each member of the pact bound himself to the other with a pledge of £50; that is, if a member of the pact failed to come to the aid of a fellow member, he agreed to pay the pact £50. About this time, the Council authorized General Washington to direct militia colonels "to seize . . . all persons [in Northampton County] who are known or suspected to be Enemies of the United States."[29] Geiger knew exactly where such persons could be found. Before daybreak on December 21, 1776, the colonel and forty "true militiamen" raided a house where the suspected Tories had gathered. "They run off," Geiger explained to the Council, "except three men we took prisoner and an other We took out his own house in the same night . . . they Bound themselves each one to the other for the full Sum of £50 to go against us . . . send Me you adviss what I shall with this bad tories."[30] In fact Geiger captured and jailed seven men while a confederate captured and jailed six more.[31] The Council directed Geiger to incarcerate the men in Reading, Pennsylvia, site of the closest jail.

. . . .

Upon his return to Heidelberg, Geiger found a letter from General Washington that ordered him to muster his battalion and march to Philadelphia as soon as possible.[32] The colonel rounded up more than 600 officers and men of the Second Battalion and led them to the capital city in the first week of January 1777. At Philadelphia, Geiger encountered a rudderless ship of state. With so many members engaged in the war, the Pennsylvania Assembly had been unable to form a new government. Geiger and his men desperately needed food, kettles, blankets, and weapons. More importantly, Geiger found no superior officer to give him further orders. Geiger's men milled about the city for a week, then the colonel led them back to Northampton, a distance of more than fifty miles. Before he left town, however, Geiger visited the paymaster and collected £89 for expenses incurred in apprehending and jailing suspected Tories, and £75 to purchase blankets for his men.[33]

No sooner had Geiger returned home than the Council ordered him to march his battalion to Morristown, New Jersey, where General Washington had gone into winter quarters. "No doubt you will make all possible dispatch to reach the camp," the Council said, "where such brave men as yours are much wanted."[34] The Council also wrote to Washington and advised, "From the known integrity of the honest old German it is hoped he will be of much service to your excellency."[35] Puffed with pride, Geiger mobilized his battalion and marched sixty miles to Morristown in the dead of winter. At Washington's headquarters word of Geiger's patriotic exploits preceded him. "Geiger and his men," the Council had said, "have been very active suppressing Tories, and the principle support of the cause in that part of the county."[36]

While Geiger and his men made camp at Morristown, the Northampton Committee marched Geiger's captives from Reading to Easton, a distance of some forty miles, to stand trial. After an intense two-day interrogation—"The State of Pennsylvania vs. William Thomas and others for certain Treasonable practices committed by them against the said State, as well in signing certain papers to the prejudice of the American Cause"— the men were released after posting bail as high as £800, and promising future good behavior.[37] The Committee's decision to release the Tories stunned Geiger, "they being Toris yet as before and not true for the contrie."[38] Within weeks, however, Geiger suffered an even more devastating blow when he lost his post as commander of the Second Battalion.

Under the provisions of the Militia Act of 1777, each battalion elected

. . . .

its own officers. When Geiger discovered that only three votes separated him from the victor, he requested the Board of War to review the election. The colonel did not mince words. The three new senior officers of the Second Battalion were not fit for duty, he said. One of them had been cashiered for leaving his post at the Battle of New York in 1776. Two others had deserted when the battalion had been ordered to Philadelphia. Geiger also claimed that most men in the Second Battalion would not put themselves under the command of the newly elected officers. "Therefore," he said, "I will lay the mattre to your Worships Consideration."[39] But the Board of War declined to interfere in a local militia election and tabled Geiger's petition. The colonel tried a different tack. Geiger informed the board that the very same Tories whom he had thrown in jail last winter, and who were now free on bail, had elected the new officers. "One of the said Dangerous Persons or Tories as we Cal Them has spook very hil against the Honourable the Congress and against other Gentlemen and Officers," he said, "[and] they whas all against me [in the election]."[40] The board ignored Geiger's petition.

The irony that scalawags and Tories had defeated him in an open battalion election was not lost on the colonel. Democracy, he doubtless hollered, should not work that way. Although Geiger blamed "dangerous Tories" for his defeat, it is likely that a civilian appointee named John Wetzel, who commanded all militia in the county, engineered Geiger's removal as commander of the Second Battalion. There is no evidence for this assertion, but the newly elected senior officers of the battalion happened to be Wetzel's cronies.[41] Meantime, the war engulfed Philadelphia and then moved to the frontier. But of what use was a colonel without a command?

In 1779, Geiger ran for elective office. One of eleven candidates for five seats in the House of Representatives, the colonel did not fare well. Out of 259 votes cast in his district, which comprised the same townships represented in the Second Battalion, Geiger won only forty-seven. He added twelve more votes from the neighboring district, but received none at all from Easton and the district north of Blue Mountain. Overall, Geiger garnered only 59 votes out of 630 cast in the entire county.[42] It is likely that Geiger's reputation as a zealous soldier who marched by the book alarmed those voters who publicly espoused the cause of freedom but who, in private, embraced the middle ground. After the election the county commissioners appointed Geiger one of six tax collectors, an onerous job that provided little solace to the "Lat Colonel."

Five months after his defeat at the polls, Geiger's career took an unex-

. . . .

pected turn. At the triennial election of militia officers required by law, the men in Geiger's former battalion chose him as their commanding officer. Geiger now turned his attention to Indians and Tories who had ravaged the frontier and who, in one attack, had come within six miles of his house. When word reached Easton that a militia patrol had been ambushed, Geiger and some of his men volunteered to bury the dead. After a forty-five mile march north of Blue Mountain they reached the scene of the action at a place named Nescopec, and found "ten soldiers dead, scalped, stripped naked, and in a most cruel and barbarous manner tomahawked, their throats cut, etc., etc." Other members of the company had been taken away as prisoners.[43]

Panic spread across Northampton County. The county lieutenant assigned Geiger and more than 100 men to patrol a twenty-five mile stretch of frontier north of Blue Mountain. But the proposed deployment of the militia did not satisfy Geiger. In spring 1781, he expressed his concern to President Joseph Reed, and even enclosed a hand-drawn map to help make his point. Geiger pointed out that it had been the practice to station two to four men at each house, but this created gaps of two or three miles in the line of defense. "By that reason the frontier being open whereby the Indians may go through the Whole Countrie Without any enderniss [hinderance] and kill the poor inhabitants."[44] Alarmed by relentless attacks on the frontier, President Reed advised Geiger that he had appointed a new county lieutenant [Robert Levers], "and we hope you will not in future have the same reason to complain of the stationing of the militia."[45] Within weeks, Geiger informed Reed that the new lieutenant repeated the mistakes of his predecessors. "The proper way to defend the frontier is to hunt the enemy and not wait for him to come to you," he told Reed. "In the last war I whas officers but we Whas obliged to go Every Day upon a scout out sids the inhabitant longs the frontiers And so it should be yet and the frontier would be beter scurt [secured]."[46] To carry the fight to the enemy may have been a successful tactic when executed by trained soldiers, but the bloody toll of the Nescopec ambush reminded militiamen what might happen to them should they venture on patrol. As a result, Tories and Indians continued to burn the Northampton frontier without serious opposition from the local militia.[47]

The Treaty of Paris (1783), which marked the official end of the War of the Revolution, gave amnesty to some Tories. When copies of the preliminary Articles of Peace reached Northampton, Geiger organized and chaired a countywide committee to protest the treaty. The committee petitioned

. . . .

Northampton's assemblymen and asked them to procure a law that would "prevent the return into this state of such persons as, during the war, have joined, aided or assisted either the British or Indian enemies." The committee pointed out, "It is not to be wondered at if the feelings of the virtuous, honest Whigs were wounded at the sight of such wretches."[48] Wounded, perhaps, but also secretly discomfited. Some Whigs may have experienced pangs of contrition when they came face to face with a man whose land they had acquired at auction, whose pots and kettles hung in their kitchen, and whose beehives overflowed with honey in their meadow. The Treaty of Paris became law, but Geiger found it impossible to make peace with men who had not remained "true to their country."

In 1784, the Assembly enacted a law requiring that Justices of the Peace be elected annually. Geiger ran for office. In an election that failed to generate much interest in Heidelberg—fewer than 25 percent of the eligible voters turned out—Geiger received 31 votes, the runner-up garnered 24. The Council generally awarded the commission to the person who won the highest number of votes, but in this election they chose the runner-up.[49] In a community where meanness seemed to thrive and memories sharpened over time, a former adversary of Geiger's, whose brother sat on the Council, may have deprived him of the commission.[50] The runner-up, however, decided that he did not want the job, whereupon the Council ordered another election to be held the following year.

Geiger ran again in 1785, and received the largest number of votes, but fewer than a dozen persons cast ballots. Nonetheless, Geiger believed he had won the magistracy. Having won and lost the post once before, he wrote to Benjamin Franklin, the newly elected president of the Supreme Executive Council. Geiger began this letter with an effusive outpouring of blessings and congratulations. He then reminded Franklin that the writer was "an old friend and acquaintance from the [French and Indian War] as one of the officers when we build Fort Allen." [51]Geiger never mentioned his own election victory, nor did he petition Franklin for a favor. Geiger probably wished to ensure that when it came time to commission the next magistrate in Heidelberg Township, Franklin would recognize the soldier's name. In fact, the Northampton prothonotary certified Geiger's victory, but the Council threw it out on grounds that it was "unformal," and ordered yet another election.[52] (President Franklin was absent on the day the Council rendered this decision.)

Justice Geiger did not run for office a third time. But he complained

. . . .

long and loud to his neighbors about the rascals in Philadelphia who, once again, had deprived him of his right to serve as a justice of the peace. Unbeknownst to him, however, Geiger still had a powerful connection in Philadelphia. In 1788, Pennsylvania's president personally attempted to resolve the complaint of a petitioner in Northampton County. The president's mentor, Benjamin Franklin, suggested that the younger man might find it useful in settling the matter if he consulted Franklin's old friend, Justice Henry Geiger.[53]

5

. . . .

$\mathcal{M}$ICHAEL OHL

The Ohl family settled in Heidelberg Township about 1740. By 1774, Michael Ohl, the eldest son, had become a naturalized citizen and established himself as one of the community's prominent citizens. In addition to working a farm of more than 400 acres, Ohl, with the help of his wife and some of their ten children, also operated an inn. At the Heidelberg Church, members of the Reformed congregation regarded Ohl, like his father before him, as a guardian of the faith. When the Continental Congress requested every county in colonial America to elect a committee to police a boycott of British goods, Heidelberg inhabitants chose forty-five-year-old Michael Ohl to be their representative.[1]

With twenty-nine members present the Committee held its first meeting in Easton on December 21, 1774. This extralegal committee—like many others that sprang up in the North American colonies—sidestepped Pennsylvania's colonial government and took control of the internal affairs of Northampton County. When news of the April 19, 1775, Battle of Lexington and Concord reached Northampton, the Committee ordered inhabitants to prepare to defend themselves. Committeemen hurried to enlist their neighbors in the militia. In less than two weeks Ohl trudged over Heidelberg's fifty square miles and signed up 100 men. The recruits elected Ohl captain of the township company.[2] Later, when Congress requested Northampton to recruit and equip a company of riflemen to join General Washington at Boston, the Committee requested each township to furnish two men.

Heidelberg's Peter Frantz and John Miller yearned to claim a £3 bonus and join the fray, but they had no equipment.[3] Michael Ohl stepped forward and advanced £18—more than twice his annual tax bill—to outfit the men with rifles, powder horns, knapsacks, and other necessities.[4] However, when it appeared that the conflict between the North American colonies and Great Britain might escalate to all-out rebellion and war, Ohl's neighbors refused to share the expense of fielding the two Heidelberg men then entrenched on Ploughed Hill, overlooking Boston harbor. Ohl also discovered that some committeemen used meetings as a forum to attack Moravians. Unlike Ohl, who admired the work of the Brethren, some of his colleagues on the Committee regarded Moravians as papists and scorned them because they sought to convert Indians to Christianity and refused to bear arms. Moreover, Ohl heard rumors that these same men hoped to drive Moravians out of the county and seize their land. Disillusioned by the attitude of neighbors and fellow committeemen, Ohl resigned from the militia and the Committee.

In the last week of May 1776, some 1,300 Northampton militiamen pledged to support a new government in Pennsylvania in which every man would have a voice. Michael Ohl tried his voice and discovered that he had none. The County Committee, which had pledged to preserve law and order in Northampton until radicals could form a new state government, ordered Ohl to appear before them and answer allegations brought against him by Captain Michael Probst. Probst claimed that Ohl had publicly accused him of taking an illegal bonus of twenty shillings for every man who signed on with his company. Colonel Henry Geiger, Probst's commanding officer, took the stand and swore that he too had heard Michael Ohl "speak and utter words to that import." Following a brief caucus, the Committee reprimanded Ohl "for his low design in spreading false reports" that might damage the reputation of the militia and others in the county, and they cautioned him to avoid inflammatory speeches in the future.[5]

No sooner had Ohl returned home than the constable served him with a second summons from the Committee. At this trial a militia officer from Weisenberg Township informed the Committee that in January 1776 he and a friend encountered Michael Ohl at an Allentown inn. The officer told Ohl that he had gone to Easton to get an official muster book for his militia company, but none was available. Ohl volunteered that he had such a book and "anybody might have it that would, for he was sure that nobody would sign it." In addition, Ohl said "he would shit in such a book." The summons also charged Ohl with speaking disrespectfully about Congress and the Pennsylvania Assembly; however, the militia officer from Weisenberg Township admitted, "He did not actually hear the defendant utter such words." Colonel Geiger and two other witnesses testified that Ohl's remarks

· · · · · · · ·

had restrained many from joining the militia, caused great confusion in the region, and, in general, were "prejudicial to the general service of defending the rights of America."

The Committee found Ohl guilty as charged and ordered him to sign a recantation to be published in the English and German newspapers, to pay all costs, and to withdraw a countersuit (for slander?) brought by Ohl against his accuser.[6] When the details of the trial and sentencing of the church leader and former militia captain and committeeman from Heidelberg Township became known, Northampton's moderate faction sagged. "I, Michael Ohl," begins the confession printed in the *Pennsylvania Gazette*, "now being sensible of my folly and guilt, do ask pardon of my offended citizens, promising in future to conduct myself so as to regain their good will and approbation."[7] Folly, perhaps, but guilt? Guilty of what? Under whose laws? In what court? Offended citizens? By what name? His apology notwithstanding, Ohl had been branded a dangerous person. For him, as well as others in Northampton County who disagreed with the radicals, the worst was yet to come.

In December 1776, the British army marched south through New Jersey toward Philadelphia. With the enemy drawing closer, Pennsylvania's Council of Safety authorized General George Washington to call out the state's militia and "to seize and treat as enemies . . . every person in the said counties who are known or suspected to be enemies to the United States."[8] Henry Geiger, zealous colonel of Northampton's Second Battalion, had fingered such persons and now took it upon himself to arrest them. On December 21, 1776, Geiger and forty militiamen raided Ohl's house where suspected Tories had gathered. Geiger's prisoners included Michael Ohl, "whom we took out his own house that night."[9] That Ohl was his neighbor mattered not at all to Geiger. Moreover, both men said their prayers in the Heidelberg Union Church, albeit at different times: Geiger communed with the Lutheran congregation, Ohl with the Reformed.

Ohl and his fellow captives spent Christmas under guard in Geiger's barn. The following day Geiger, under orders, marched his captives to Reading and locked them in the jail. In mid-January 1777, guards collected the Tories and marched them to Easton to stand trial before the Northampton Committee. After reviewing the charges, the Committee freed the men on bail, on condition that they pay court costs and promise "future good behavior towards the State of Pennsylvania and the other united Colonies during the present dispute between the said Colonies and Great Britain."[10] After

. . . .

serving nearly two months in jail, Michael Ohl posted bail of £400 and became a "free" man.

When the Assembly passed a law that required every man to swear allegiance to the state, Michael Ohl was one of the first to appear before a magistrate and take the oath.[11] But this act of fidelity won him no reprieve from the prying eyes of suspicious neighbors. In January 1778, informants notified two Heidelberg magistrates that Ohl "had entertained two strange men in his home at night and was not true to the state." The justices examined Ohl, found him guilty as charged, and committed him to jail without bail.[12]

The trail of a patriot turned dangerous person ends here. But Ohl and others who had been victimized by Northampton's zealous radicals doubtless spurred the Republican Party's rise to power in the county. As a result, in 1787 Northampton broke ranks with most back counties and voted to ratify the Federal Constitution.[13]

. . . .

6

John Wetzel and John Ettwein

The founder of the Renewed Moravian Church, Count Nicholas Ludwig von Zinzendorf, named and dedicated the town of Bethlehem, Pennsylvania, on Christmas Eve 1741. The Brethren had established an outpost there to propagate the gospel and evangelize the heathen.[1] Zinzendorf's preaching so moved John Wetzel's father that he "surrendered to the Grace of the Lamb," and asked to be admitted to the Bethlehem Brotherhood. John's mother, "who accompanied her husband in his search for the Savior, also heard the call, and from that time on she walked an even road."[2]

Following his parents' spiritual rebirth, John Wetzel, the oldest of eight children, was brought up in the Moravian Church and baptized in it.[3] John, however, rebelled against the strict regimen dictated by his parents and the church. To improve his son's conduct, John's father sent him to a Moravian boarding school "for boys who had learned bad habits and whom it was not desirable to have with those in other institutions. It was a kind of reformatory" where authorities put John to work as a groom in the stable.[4] But the recalcitrant youth continued to reject the church and its ways. When he came of age, John Wetzel left home bearing a fierce grudge against Moravians.

Upon the death of his father, Wetzel returned to the homestead near the village of Emmaus, married, and began to raise a family. In 1763, township inhabitants elected him constable. In addition to collecting taxes in his jurisdiction, Wetzel provided a link in a countywide network of constables who served court papers, helped the sheriff maintain law and order, and functioned as a conduit for news and rumors. Constable Wetzel also earned a bit of hard cash, which improved his lot as a subsistence farmer. In this, his first elective office, Wetzel discovered that he possessed a flair for politics. Thereafter, the ambitious native of Macungie Township, whom some Moravians had pegged as an "unworthy backslider," forged a career that enabled him to become the most powerful man in the county.[5]

In 1765, Wetzel won election as one of six county assessors. Two years later he topped all candidates for one of the three seats that turned over annually in the three-man office of commissioner, the county's highest elective office. Then, in March 1774, the governor appointed Wetzel one of twenty-six justices of the peace in Northampton County. Although Wetzel could neither read nor write English, he had worked his way into the county judiciary system.[6] "A surly, dogged man" he may have seemed to the Brethren, but Wetzel's stubbornness and determination enabled him to move up in the world.[7]

A few months after he was named a justice of the peace, Wetzel rode to Easton to attend quarter sessions courts. There he attended an impromptu meeting chaired by George Taylor, a former Northampton assemblyman. Taylor appealed to his audience to support a plan put forth by Philadelphia radicals to resist British imperialism. In part, the radicals urged that a congress of delegates from the thirteen North American colonies be convened to mediate America's grievances with Great Britain. When Taylor called for a vote, Wetzel added his voice to the unanimous chorus of ayes. The crowd of some 200 also named a committee of correspondence comprised of Taylor, prothonotary Lewis Gordon, two German leaders, and two Moravians, one of whom represented the county in the Assembly. Because the Brethren had a long history of close ties with political leaders in England and Pennsylvania, their participation in a protest against the government aroused Wetzel's suspicion. Might not the Brethren's affirmative vote conceal their intention to spy for the British?

It is interesting that the religious sect responsible for Wetzel's disquietude comprised less than 1 percent of the population in Revolutionary Pennsylvania, or some 2,300 men, women, and children. Of that number, half lived in Northampton, where they accounted for about 7 percent of the population, some 500 lived in Bethlehem, and the remainder were scattered in so-called country congregations at Emmaus, Gnadenhuetten, Nazareth, and Bethel.

The First Continental Congress declared an embargo on trade with Great Britain to press its demand that Parliament negotiate American grievances. To enforce the boycott Congress urged every city, town, and county to elect a committee of observation and inspection. Inhabitants of Macungie Township chose John Wetzel to represent them on the Northamp-

. . . .

ton Committee, whose twenty-nine members met for the first time on December 21, 1774. When news of the Battle of Lexington and Concord reached Northampton at the end of April 1775, the Committee mobilized every able man in the county. However, Moravians refused to bear arms because of their religious beliefs, and they ignored the order.[8] At first the Committee appeared to overlook the Brethren's failure to comply with its directive, but a committeeman took the floor and attacked the Bethlehemites. Although the secretary did not identify the speaker, the rhetoric points to John Wetzel.

Wetzel reminded his compatriots that in the French and Indian War Moravians refused to bear arms to defend their county. Now, he said, the Brethren refuse to defend their country.[9] Wetzel won his point. The Committee unanimously proclaimed that any person who failed to take up arms before June 20, 1775, would be considered "an enemy to the country and all dealing and commerce with him forbidden."[10] When this ultimatum reached Bethlehem, Reverend John Ettwein, chief administrator and spokesman for the Moravian Church at Bethlehem, went on the attack. "I am not fearsome," Ettwein had once told a friend who advised him to moderate his temper, "but I don't like to let myself be made a pussycat."[11] Nor did he. Who was this man who dared to disobey orders from the Northampton Committee?

John Ettwein was born in 1721 in Wurttemberg, Germany. The precocious son of a poor shoemaker, Ettwein "grew up a rather headstrong, emotional boy. Accounts of the Savior's suffering stirred him deeply, as did the history of the early persecutions of the Christian Church; indeed he cherished a secret ambition to become a martyr himself."[12] At age eighteen Ettwein decided to cast his lot with the United Brethren and took up residence at the center of Moravian activities near Frankfort, Germany. There he attracted the attention of Count Zinzendorf, who chose Ettwein as his personal assistant. In the next seven years, Ettwein and his wife conducted church-sponsored schools for children throughout Germany. In 1750, the Brethren sent the Ettweins to London, where they continued their work as educators and where John acquired a perfect command of English. In 1754, church authorities dispatched the young couple to America. After a few years in Bethlehem they moved to the Moravian settlement at Wachovia, North Carolina, before returning to Bethlehem in 1766. Ettwein then guided the church through a difficult reorganization. In so doing he earned a reputation as an open, honest administrator who frequently carried these virtues to the extreme of bluntness.[13]

. . . .

Confronted with the edict from the Northampton Committee, Ettwein sought advice from Benjamin Franklin, one of many influential men who looked with favor on the work of the Brethren. Franklin suggested that if the church did not restrain members who wanted to bear arms, "it would operate in the minds of the [Committee] very greatly in your favor."[14] Ettwein rejected Franklin's suggestion. Instead he informed the Committee that the Brethren's refusal to bear arms was based on a fundamental principle of the Moravian Church since 1456.[15] However, the Moravian Church in Europe did not condemn war as such nor forbid its membership to bear arms. On the contrary, the church taught that in any given case each individual must determine the right or wrong of such action according to the prompting of his own conscience. But in a 1749 Act of Parliament that formally recognized the Moravian Church in the American colonies and all dominions, Zinzendorf's deputies persuaded British legislators to exempt Moravians from bearing arms and taking oaths. The law provided that Brethren could pay money and make affirmations in lieu of these two obligations. Moravians sought the same exemptions in Pennsylvania because they wanted to make common cause with Quakers, Mennonites, and other peace churches, thereby keeping the door open for Moravian missionaries to proselytize among these sects. Therefore, in the interest of unity, authorities in Bethlehem obliged church members to put aside the right of conscience on the matter of bearing arms and taking oaths.[16] And if Brethren required additional moral suasion on this matter, they had only to look to John Ettwein, who held that "resorting to arms ordinarily was equivalent to murder."[17]

Franklin requested Congress to nudge the Pennsylvania Assembly to pass a resolution that urged militiamen to "bear a tender and brotherly regard" toward Moravians, Quakers, Mennonites, and other peace churches, and recommended that nonresisters "cheerfully assist" militiamen whose families suffer because of time spent in public service.[18] The Northampton Committee circulated the resolution, but in that frontier county the time for brotherly love had passed.[19]

As the June 20 deadline approached, negotiations between Ettwein and the Committee had reached an impasse. Both parties, however, suddenly faced a new challenge: Congress requested every county in Pennsylvania to form a company of riflemen to join General George Washington at Boston. The Northampton Committee promptly directed every township "to send two expert riflemen with their rifles" to Easton. Anticipating that the Brethren would refuse to obey the order, the Committee informed them

. . . .

that "unless Bethlehem would furnish 2. men within 3. days, the Committee would proscribe the Bethlehemites in the newspapers as enemies of the country."[20]Ettwein shot back that Bethlehem would furnish no men and that it was not their affair but the township's.[21] However, Ettwein offered to share the cost of equipping the rifle company, a gesture that earned a reprieve for the Moravians and temporarily silenced John Wetzel.

With 750 native sons in the line at Boston, the reality of the undeclared war with Great Britain struck Pennsylvania. On July 1, 1775, the Pennsylvania Assembly appointed a committee of safety and directed it to manage the military build-up of the province.[22] The Assembly also issued quotas to each county for the manufacture of rifles, bayonets, cartridge boxes, and knapsacks, and urged all inhabitants to contribute men and money for the "freedom, welfare and safety of their country."[23] In a matter of months, the Assembly and Congress poured more than £1,500 into Northampton for war matériel.[24]

The Committee of Safety also drew up rules and regulations for Pennsylvania's militia. Militiamen, however, rejected the plan because Quakers, Mennonites, Moravians, and members of other peace churches had been exempted from military service. The Committee of Safety reported the discord to the Assembly. "The [militia] conceive," the committee said, "that where the liberty of all is at stake, every man should assist in its support, and where the cause is common, and the benefits derived from an opposition are universal, it is not consonant to justice or equity that the burthens [of war] should be partial."[25] This argument divided families, towns, townships, and Pennsylvania, province and state.

The rhetoric of war and independence and who should serve in the militia intensified in the winter of 1775. Some inhabitants chose sides. Many, however, chose silence. They comprised a small army of fence sitters who shifted their position like weathervanes. For or against, patriot or Tory, who could tell? John Wetzel argued that the ranks of dissenters and the undecided concealed traitors to the cause. Congress fueled the unrest by alerting each colony "to arrest and secure every person whose going at large may endanger the safety of the colony, or the liberties of America."[26] Wetzel and other zealous patriots pointed at nonresisters like Moravians, Quakers, and Mennonites. They also fingered suspected Tories and harassed neighbors who had unwittingly spoken out of turn. Freedom, it turned out, was not a common cause in Northampton, or in Pennsylvania.

In Philadelphia, militiamen organized a Committee of Privates to provide a voice for the common soldier.[27] In fact, leaders of this committee hoped to organize 30,000 militiamen into a political faction that would champion the cause of freedom.[28] The campaign to politicize the militia gathered momentum in January 1776. In a letter circulated among back county leaders, the committee said they wished "to know the sense of the militia in general on any part of the [rules and regulations] which may need amendment, so that any future application to the Assembly may express the desires of [all militia in the province]."[29]

John Wetzel, who by virtue of his magistracy now styled himself a colonel, seized the opportunity to assist the committee. The colonel traveled from house to house in Salisbury and Whitehall Townships and urged members of Northampton's Second Battalion to sign a petition addressed to the Assembly. This petition begged the Assembly to make the public defense less burdensome for individuals. At the same time, similar petitions were submitted to the Assembly by battalions in other counties. The petitioners argued that Quakers, Moravians, Mennonites, and other nonresisters who did not join the militia had no expense for arms and accoutrements, yet they were fined only the trifling sum of fifty shillings per year. As a result, the petitioners said, many other inhabitants "neglect to join the militia by which means the public cause suffers."[30] John Ettwein had a different opinion. Wetzel, he charged, had incited the petitioners against Moravians and other nonresisters because they claimed exemption from military service on religious grounds.[31] Angered by Ettwein's criticism, Justice Wetzel attempted to persuade militiamen that they should not bear the burden of fighting a war while some persons in their midst invoked God's word to avoid it.[32]

Despite numerous petitions, the Pennsylvania Assembly refused to accommodate militia demands to increase fines on nonresisters, or to alter its stance against independence. Radicals of all stripes agreed that the composition of the Assembly must be changed. With an infusion of new members, most of them from the back counties, radicals believed that the balance of power in the Assembly would shift in their favor. In a series of adroit maneuvers, radicals forced the Assembly to increase the number of elected representatives. This strategy backfired. In a by-election on May 1, 1776, radicals failed by a narrow margin to win control of the Assembly. In Northampton, voters elected one radical and one moderate assemblyman.

Throughout the month of May, radical leaders, assisted by a few congressmen, worked to overthrow Pennsylvania's provincial government. But

. . . .

to form a new government whose congressional delegation would vote for independence, the radicals needed support from the back counties. Radicals as well as moderates showered rural counties with propaganda. In Northampton the Committee met on May 30, 1776, considered the alternatives, and voted to overthrow the colonial government. The Committee also chose a delegation of six men, of which John Wetzel was one, to represent Northampton at a Provincial Conference of County Committees that had been charged with laying out a plan for creating a new government. "The Committee," huffed Ettwein, "poor ignorant people, . . . sent deputies [like Wetzel] to Philadelphia."[33]

In the third week of June 1776, ninety-seven delegates, nearly half of them militia officers, worked day and night to complete their task. The feverish activity at Carpenters' Hall transformed strangers into confederates. In an address to the people of Pennsylvania, the president of the conference said, in part: "We beg that you would endeavor to remove the prejudices of the weak and ignorant, respecting the proposed changes in our government, and assure them that it is absolutely necessary to secure property, liberty, and the sacred rights of conscience to every individual in the province."[34] Two days later the president closed the conference with an address to men determined to raise a new nation. In brief, he declared to conference delegates and provincial militia: "You are not about to contend against the power of Great Britain in order to displace one set of villains to make room for another. . . . You are about to contend for permanent freedom . . . immortalize your names . . . [establish] a lasting foundation for the liberties of one-quarter of the globe . . . remember the name of Pennsylvania."[35] Colonel Wetzel doubtless prided himself on helping to suppress "all authority under the crown of Great Britain."[36] On the other hand, he cared not one whit about an individual's sacred right of conscience. He vowed to remove the prejudices of weak and ignorant Moravians by driving them out of Northampton County. For John Ettwein, however, the pledge by the conference president to protect the sacred rights of conscience of all citizens cast a ray of hope. (Ironically, in the matter of bearing arms and taking oaths, the Moravian Church in America had earlier denied these rights to its membership.) Ettwein met with church leaders at Bethlehem. They discussed conditions in Northampton and decided on a course of action: "To remain quiet and to await the help of the Lord has been our endeavor. . . . We shall, therefore, observe it strictly as regards the [constitutional] convention and its election [of delegates]. We do not see how a Brother can have anything

. . . .

to do with it or be active in the overthrow of the government under which we have enjoyed so many benefits."[37] As the Brethren soon discovered, no such benefits would be forthcoming from Pennsylvania's Revolutionary governments.

In June 1776, radicals closed the provincial courts until a new government could be formed. As a result, the Northampton Committee became the sole arbiter of justice in the county. Under orders of the Committee, squads of militiamen rounded up suspected Tories and tossed them into jail to await trial. Meeting weekly, more often when necessary, this tribunal adjudicated crimes of bribery, slander, and theft, arbitrated personal quarrels, directed the recruitment of soldiers for the Continental Army, and dispensed money for needy families of militiamen.

Not even John Wetzel escaped the Committee's scrutiny. When he returned from the convention in Philadelphia, the Committee summoned Wetzel to answer charges that seven months earlier a disgruntled member of the militia had sold his gun to him for thirty shillings.[38] Wetzel probably intended to resell the gun at a profit, whereas he should have turned it over to men in Macungie chosen at a special election to collect guns for the militia. The Committee found Wetzel guilty as charged, and ordered him to hand over the gun to the collectors "and pay some costs."[39]

Wetzel's mishandling of the gun was a minor infraction, but it marked the second time in a month that he had stood before the Committee. Earlier, one of Macungie's elected gun collectors informed the Committee that Wetzel had received expense money from both the township and Congress for recruiting riflemen for the Northampton company that joined General Washington's army in the summer of 1775. A Moravian, whose sister-in-law was Wetzel's eldest, and perhaps the closest, of his four sisters, substantiated this charge. Nonetheless, the Committee found in Wetzel's favor and ordered the gun collector to publicly beg the colonel's pardon and, in the presence of the accuser's militia company, to acknowledge that his words were "false and groundless."[40]

The Declaration of Independence was read in Easton on July 8, 1776, a day set earlier by the Provincial Convention for the election of delegates to the Constitutional Convention.[41] To win control of the convention, radical leaders had directed county committees to prepare ballots in advance with a slate of militia officers only. This tactic worked in Northampton, where the people elected an eight-man delegation that consisted of two officers from each of the county's four militia battalions. Because he was not a militia officer, Wetzel did not qualify as a candidate; however, his seniority on the Committee doubtless gave him a say in nominating candidates.[42]

When the Constitutional Convention convened at the State House in Philadelphia on July 15, the delegates undertook not only to draw a new charter, but also to seize control of the legislative and executive branches of government. Delegates issued a series of ordinances to secure law and order in the state. As one of numerous emergency measures, the convention appointed Wetzel and nine others to serve as interim justices in Northampton. More importantly, the convention issued two ordinances that targeted disaffected persons and secret enemies of the state. The first ordinance ordered battalion officers to disarm any person who refused to join the militia. The second decreed that all residents must pay allegiance to the State of Pennsylvania or face trial and possible forfeiture of their property.

While the Constitutional Convention was in progress, Moravians followed Ettwein's advice and remained silent. Nonetheless, when Ettwein learned that the new constitution merely required members of the Assembly to swear their belief "in one God the Creator and Governor of the Universe," he condemned the convention in an unsigned article that appeared in the *Pennsylvania Post*, and in the German newspapers:

> If the Christian States in Europe hear Pennsylvanians have made a new constitution that . . . mentions not a word of the bible, Christ, or Christian religion, much less Protestantism, a Presbyterian Meeting House, a Roman Catholic Church, an Episcopal Church, a Mosque, Synagogue, or Heathen Temple, [all of which] have now in Pennsylvania equal privileges—if blasphemers of Christ and the Holy Ghost or the ever blessed Trinity, despisers of Revelation and the Holy Bible, may be legislators, judges, councillors, and presidents or governors in Pennsylvania, Wo unto the city, Wo unto the land![43]

To mollify Ettwein and countless others who opposed the original draft of the oath, the convention added to the declaration: "I believe in one God the creator and governor of the universe *and rewarder of the good and punisher of the wicked. And I do acknowledge the scriptures of the old and new testament to be given by Divine inspiration*" (emphasis in original).

Ettwein's outburst gave Wetzel and other patriots one more reason to crack down on Moravians. Northampton militia stopped and searched a

Moravian wagonload of flour headed for Bethlehem in the mistaken belief that it carried weapons destined for the British.[44] Militia colonels twice rode into Bethlehem and confiscated firearms.[45] Six armed militiamen descended on the Moravian community at Emmaus where they seized an elder named Andreas Giering and hauled him off to Allentown. The militiamen accused Giering of being a Tory, "arraigned" him, then freed him after he paid "costs" to a jury-rigged "court of inquiry."[46] It made little difference to some inhabitants that Moravians had made available communal living quarters at Bethlehem and Emmaus to care for wounded soldiers. While collecting supplies to treat the sick, Giering was "roughly treated and beaten" by a stranger who reportedly mistook the Moravian elder for a Tory.[47]

The convention issued an ordinance that imposed a fine of £1 a month and a special property tax on men who refused to bear arms. The ordinance also authorized county commissioners to collect the money and disburse it to the families of poor militiamen.[48] Ettwein appealed to the Northampton commissioners to delay collection of the fine until after the election of the new Assembly, which, he believed, would "very likely revise" the Convention ordinance.[49] The minister also argued that Moravians had been held up as enemies to the land, disarmed, excluded from the election of the Convention, prohibited from holding civil or judicial offices, and denied work in favor of militiamen. "All this," he concluded, "could be looked upon as punishment enough." Why, Ettwein inquired, did Revolutionaries punish Brethren whose only desire was "to be granted freedom to be friends of all men?" Like many other persons in Pennsylvania, Ettwein could not bring himself to accept the collapse of Pennsylvania's colonial government and the ascension of the rabble.[50]

Under Ettwein's leadership "the Brethren unanimously resolved not to pay the fine willingly, but to wait until it was taken from them."[51] The Moravians did not wait long. A county commissioner with a company of armed militiamen soon appeared in Bethlehem and compelled the Brethren to pay up.[52] At Gnadenhuetten, an isolated Moravian country congregation, militiamen seized a yoke of oxen and blacksmith tools to extract payment of the fine.[53] Thus, Northampton authorities made it clear that they would prosecute persons whose religious beliefs placed them at odds with the law.

On Tuesday, November 5, 1776, Pennsylvanians elected the first government under the new constitution. In addition to casting ballots for county officials, Northampton voters chose six men to represent them in the Assembly. Elected annually, assemblymen could serve no more than four

. . . .

years in seven. Moreover, sitting assemblymen could hold no other public office, except in the militia.[54] In a contest rigged to clinch the election of militiamen, battalion officers who had represented Northampton at the Constitutional Convention won five seats. Wetzel carried the sixth seat. Clearly, the colonel had built support for a kind of maverick candidacy: militia rank and file voted for him, even though he was not one of them. And why did Wetzel choose not to rise within the militia? Listening to his own muse, he probably placed himself a cut above the sort of man who forked dung.

The First Assembly of the Commonwealth of Pennsylvania convened for a few days even as General George Washington's outnumbered army attempted to stem Lord General William Howe's advance on Philadelphia. The Assembly quickly announced that it would "enact a militia law . . . and take such measures that would put the defense of this state on a just and equitable footing, so as to encourage those worthy [militiamen], who, freely and virtuously, step forth in the defense of their country."[55] But so great was the immediate need for soldiers that General Thomas Mifflin visited several counties and offered ten dollars to every man who "joined [the army] before December 20, seven dollars to those who came forward before December 25, and five dollars to all who enlisted after that time and before December 30" on condition of serving for six weeks."[56] Wetzel and two other Northampton assemblymen accompanied Mifflin on this recruitment drive. Wetzel's colleagues included a storekeeper named James Ralston, one of three assemblymen charged with bringing in the militia bill, and Jacob Arndt, a veteran of the French and Indian War, who had the ear of state authorities at the highest level.[57] The militia bill doubtless became the principle topic of discussion between the general and his traveling companions.

With so many assemblymen at war it was impossible to raise and hold a quorum in the Assembly.[58] However, following Washington's victory at the Battle of Trenton, Pennsylvania's Revolutionary government began to take hold. Assemblymen tackled business that ranged from setting their daily rate of pay to debating the militia bill. It is interesting that the Northampton delegation divided evenly on the pay issue. Whether the naysayers demanded a higher or lower per diem, or none at all, is unknown. But thirty shillings a day seemed right to Wetzel, and he voted for the bill.

Despite the chaos attendant on organizing a new government in wartime—a process that included the election of Philadelphia merchant Thomas Wharton Jr. as president—the militia bill worked through the Assembly. Finally, on March 17, 1777, after six weeks of debate, the Assembly passed the Militia Act.[59] By institutionalizing the militia, the radical-dominated Assembly had created a paramilitary political faction that also functioned as an internal police force. This faction became known as the Constitutionalist Party, so named because its members defended the state constitution of 1776, while members of the emerging opposition party were identified as Republicans.

The Militia Act required that "one reputable freeholder" in each county be nominated to serve as lieutenant with authority over all militia.[60] John Wetzel's fellow assemblymen named him Lieutenant of Northampton County, a three-year appointment that paid him fifteen shillings for every working day. Wetzel, who reported directly to President Wharton in his capacity as Captain General and Commander-in-Chief of the Commonwealth, had achieved a position that enabled him to control large sums of money, to dispense patronage, and to exercise dictatorial power over local civil and judicial officers. No county official in Pennsylvania before or since has been vested with so much power.

Authors of the Militia Act had created a detailed operations manual for the state's militia with 8,000 words in thirty-two subsections. Following the letter of the law, Wetzel recast Northampton's battalions of farmer-soldiers. Aided by five sublieutenants and the constable in each of the county's twenty-five townships, Wetzel first compiled a "true and exact list" of every man between the ages of eighteen and fifty-three capable of bearing arms. The lieutenant then divided the county's manpower into six battalions with about 600 men each, and subdivided each battalion into eight companies.[61] Battalion and company elections elevated 750 men to the status of field or line officer. This military bureaucracy sustained the undeclared state of marital law that had existed in Northampton County for nearly a year.[62]

The Militia Act compelled nearly all men to serve in the militia, but the law also gave every man the choice "either to serve in person or to find a sufficient substitute."[63] In theory it was a simple idea: men unwilling to serve paid those who did. In a state where thousands refused to bear arms on religious grounds, payment for substitutes ensured that each individual would contribute to the defense of freedom. But the law opened the door for villainy:

> If any person shall neglect or refuse to serve or find [a] sufficient substitute in his place within three days after [being called into actual service],

. . . .

the lieutenant is hereby *required* to provide, hire or procure on reasonable terms a substitute for such person . . . and to charge such sum together with reasonable expenses for procuring the same, to such delinquent, to be recovered by distress and sale of his goods and chattels, lands and tenements by warrant under the hands and seals of any two justices of the peace of the county where such person resides.

The Militia Act may have seemed "just and equitable" to assemblymen who voted for it, but for Lieutenant Wetzel and his cronies this law provided an opportunity to take advantage of Moravians and other Northampton citizens who, for one reason or another, refused to bear arms.[64] Ettwein complained that the Militia Act "gave opportunity for much corruption." He pointed out that Lieutenant Wetzel and his five sublieutenants said to prospective substitutes: "This is your opportunity to make money; I need a man for company X and company Y; ask as much as you please; the Moravians have to pay it."[65] Ettwein also protested that "the lieutenants have laid exorbitant, immoderate fines. They have taken the tools of honest tradesmen and thereby distressed not only them but the country. They did not consider justice and equity in getting substitutes, but exacted ten times the sum of an equivalent of personal service." Ettwein computed that the rate at which fines and fees were collected from the Brethren would have enabled the state to hire 10,000 troops a year at £60 per man.[66] But when Moravians complained that they could not pay the fines, magistrates informed them: "You must pay or be put in prison until the money is forthcoming."[67] Nonetheless, Ettwein rose above the tumult and urged the Brethren to stand fast. "Paying for a substitute in the militia," he reminded them, "was merely hiring a murderer instead of being one."[68]

Ettwein also accused Wetzel of encouraging renegade militiamen to carry out forays against helpless Moravians. Militiamen rode into the isolated Moravian settlement at Gnadenhuetten, seized 20,000 board feet of lumber, and hauled it to Allentown as "war tribute." Militiamen later returned to Gnadenhuetten, seized two Moravians, and attempted to force them to serve two months in the militia. When the men refused, the militiamen held them for ransom. Unable to pay £100, the prisoners were forced to cut fifty cords of wood each—a combined stack four feet wide, four feet high, and 800 feet long—for the militia's use. After months of this kind of treatment, the greater part of the Moravian community at Gnadenhuetten took the oath of fealty.[69]

. . . .

But when Wetzel and two magistrates ordered some fifty Brethren at Bethlehem to attend drill, pay a fine, or go to jail, Ettwein went on the attack. "We will not presume to reason with you gentlemen," he said, "but we must say that the present mode of [executing the militia law] is highly oppressive and quite intolerable." Ettwein requested Wetzel to defer the execution of the judgments until the matter could be appealed to a higher authority. "We doubt not," Ettwein concluded, "but you yourselves would give us a testimonial in that a strict execution of the militia law must inevitably rob us of our property and liberty and be the utter ruin of the Brethrens' settlements."[70] Wetzel and his cronies howled. Fines for nonperformance of militia duty would, indeed, bleed the Brethren white and hasten the day when Wetzel and his cohorts would lay claim to their land.[71] Operating with no personal supervision—express riders carried circular letters back and forth between the president and county lieutenants—Wetzel manipulated laws to suit his own purposes, and no local official, including the sheriff, dared challenge him.[72]

The Militia Act compelled men to bear arms. The Test Act, which became law on June 13, 1777, required all males over the age of eighteen to appear before a magistrate and swear allegiance to the State of Pennsylvania.[73] Persons who refused the oath were held "incapable of holding any office or place of trust in this state, serving on juries, suing for any debts, electing or being elected, buying, selling or transferring any lands, tenements or hereditaments, and shall be disarmed by the lieutenant."[74] Although legislators had given the county lieutenant only a minor role in the enforcement of this law, Lieutenant Wetzel used the Test Act to strengthen his hand, as was evident in his dealings with a man named George Kriebel, a member of a religious sect founded by Caspar Schwenkfeld (whose followers were known as Schwenkfelders).

One Saturday afternoon in July 1777, a militia captain fined young Abraham Kriebel for having failed to turn out on exercise day. George Kriebel, Abraham's father, asserted that his son had just turned seventeen, not eighteen as the officer had claimed, and he refused to pay the fine.[75] Justice Frederick Limbach, one of John Wetzel's cronies, issued a summons for the delinquent. A constable arrested Abraham and ordered the elder Kriebel to accompany his son to the magistrate's office, where Lieutenant Wetzel also waited. Under questioning by Limbach, Abraham said he did not attend drill because he was only seventeen. When Limbach asked for evidence, George Kriebel said that he would prove it in writing. The trap had been sprung. Waving a copy of the Test Act, Limbach cried out: "We can't take your evidence until you take the Test." George Kriebel stated that he could not take the Test at that time. "And why not," asked Wetzel?

KRIEBEL: "I promised allegiance to George III when I naturalized and I am afraid I might be guilty of perjury before God, and in my conscience, and moreover, it is very uncertain upon which side the victory will fall out."

WETZEL: "So do you declare yourself for George III of Great Britain?"

KRIEBEL: "No sir."

WETZEL: "Then you won't take the test."

KRIEBEL: "No sir, not at present."

Wetzel then ordered the magistrate to send Kriebel to jail. "And you shall not come out," the lieutenant thundered, "even if you pay me £1,000 cash upon the nail." Limbach lowered his voice. "Well, George," the magistrate said to his neighbor, "you see I can't help it—you better take the Test and stay at home." Kriebel reiterated his refusal to take an oath, but said that he would consult his friends. Wetzel screamed at Kriebel, "I will do my utmost to have all those that will not take this test drove out of the country—leaving their estates behind." When Kriebel inquired about where such people might go, Wetzel bellowed: "They may go unto Lord Howe, or wherever they please, but shall never come back again amongst us."[76]

In his deposition Kriebel said that Wetzel "spoke in a very haughty manner but to relate all that [the lieutenant] had said would be too troublesome." (Would that Kriebel had not found it so!) George Kriebel concluded his declaration with a summation of his position. "I promised Mr. Wetzel and Mr. Limbach that I would be true to the state in paying any lawful taxes or other charges," he said, "and in carting or any thing they should want, except in bearing arms, which was against my conscience, but all the rest . . . I were willing to do it." But Kriebel's appeal fell on deaf ears. Justice Limbach fined Abraham Kriebel £1.12.6 and dispatched the boy's father to the Easton jail.[77] The mittimus stated that George Kriebel refused the oath and that he had "made declaration for King George of Great Britain."[78] In a cunning maneuver, truth had been bent to fit a crime.

A short while later, a Mennonite by the name of Henry Funk fell victim to a citizen's arrest. Upon hearing the evidence, Limbach charged Funk with being a spy and failing to take the oath and sent him to the Easton jail.[79] Together, Kriebel and Funk petitioned Pennsylvania's Supreme Executive Council for a special hearing. The application cited Justice Limbach's conduct as "a daring violation of the principles of the constitution, of the known law, and of his sworn duty."[80] The Council advised Limbach that the petitioners' case should be reconsidered, and that if he had difficulty taking such action, he should consult with two other justices. Moreover, if, after such consultation, Justice Limbach still found reason not to release the prisoners, then all parties must appear for a hearing in Philadelphia. "But there is reason to hope," the Council concluded, "that this will not be found necessary."[81] Simply put, the Council warned Limbach and Wetzel not to take the law into their own hands. Limbach freed the prisoners, but both he and Wetzel shrugged off the admonition from the six-month-old government.

Wetzel's vendetta against nonresisters doubtless interfered with his duties as county lieutenant. Under the authority granted him by the Militia Act, Lieutenant Wetzel should have prepared county militia to march, if need be, to defend their country. But when President Wharton ordered Northampton's militia to hurry south and help the Continental Army stop General Howe's attack on Philadelphia, only about 400 men, or 25 percent of those called out, reported for duty.[82] Furthermore, had the state not sent Wetzel £4,500 for arms, supplies, and substitutes, even fewer men would have turned out.[83] Despite patriotic slogans and fines, most Northampton militiamen, like their comrades in other counties, refused to leave their families. As a result, the British army overpowered General Washington's men and, on September 26, 1777, paraded through the streets of Philadelphia.

In the end, the most zealous patriots—militia rank and file and their political leaders—who had sworn to defend the state and its constitution, sidestepped responsibility for defeat at the hands of the British. Intimidation, rather than a hot fight, was the patriots' drift. From militia privates to assemblymen, radicals blamed the American defeat on Tories and disaffected men, many of whom refused to bear arms and swear allegiance because of their religious beliefs. Crack down on these people, said the patriots, and rewrite existing statutes, pass new statutes, stiffen the penalty for noncompliance with state laws. But no amount of finger-pointing and denial could conceal the fact that the British occupation of Philadelphia had dealt a political blow to the Constitutionalists.

While General Washington's army regrouped at Valley Forge, Pennsyl-

. . . .

vania's radical-dominated Second Assembly enacted a law aimed at Tories, and another that required all male citizens over eighteen to swear allegiance to the state no later than June 1, 1778. Persons who failed to comply with these laws faced loss of citizenship, confiscation and sale of personal property and land, and banishment from the commonwealth.[84] But even before copies of these new statutes reached Northampton, Wetzel had stepped up his campaign against nonresisters. A squad of ten armed militiamen swept through Emmaus and the nearby countryside and arrested twelve Moravians and seven others and tossed them into the Allentown jail.[85] Ettwein describes what followed:

> On the [following day], Wetzel sat with some militia officers as a court of inquiry and had the prisoners brought before him. They were asked whether they had paid substitute money? Some had paid. Others said they had not yet been able to make an appeal [as permitted by law]! Still others said they would pay as soon as it would be legally required of them. Thereafter each was asked in turn whether he would take the Test? One replied: Not now. Another: No! Others said: I want to consider about it further.[86]

Wetzel sent all nineteen men to the Easton jail and ordered them held without bail. Roped at the neck and tethered to a guard, the prisoners stumbled through Bethlehem "like sheep [led] by a pack of wolves."[87] Based on the "proceedings of the court and other proper information," reads the mittimus, the men were found "guilty of several transgressions against the interests and liberties of the state."[88] There were no accusers, no witnesses, and no sworn statements at this trial. In fact, one of the magistrates fetched to sign the mittimus refused to do so because he knew nothing about the case. At Wetzel's bidding, however, the sheriff informed the magistrate that it was his duty to sign the document.

So menacing was the militia's presence in Northampton that when the imprisoned men sought a hearing, local magistrates refused to review their complaint. Moravian leaders appealed to the Supreme Court, which ordered a panel of Northampton magistrates to hold a special hearing and review the matter. But Wetzel did not appear to press charges, so the panel dismissed accusations against the nineteen men and released them from jail without conditions. Wetzel doubtless absented himself because he did not want to press charges in a proceeding shadowed by the Supreme Court. But two

. . . .

days after the Brethren had returned to their homes in Emmaus, Wetzel struck again and summoned them to appear in Allentown.

Wetzel not only renewed his demand that the Brethren pay substitute money, but he also informed them that he now had a person who would swear that they were disaffected against the state. Andreas Giering, one of those summoned, countered that "he could prove that the [Brethren] were friends of the country." At this "Wetzel flew into a rage. He rushed up and down in the room and stamped with his feet, and threatened to beat and shoot Giering."[89] In the end the "court of inquiry" granted the Brethren a week to pay fines of £53 each; nonetheless, Wetzel continued to harass Giering. At Wetzel's request, magistrate Robert Levers issued a warrant for Giering's arrest on grounds that he "had been unfriendly toward independence."[90] The Moravian surrendered to the constable, who delivered him to the Easton jail to await trial at quarter sessions court on June 18, 1778. At his arraignment Giering again refused to take the Test, whereupon one of the judges ruled that if he did not swear within thirty days, his estate would be sold. Giering pleaded with the Supreme Court to review his case, but this body rejected his appeal. After seven weeks in jail, he paid a fine, swore allegiance to the state, and returned to Emmaus.[91]

The Militia Act and the Test Act shook the Church of the United Brethren. A few Brethren had no scruples against bearing arms or taking the Test. Most, however, followed Ettwein's lead and said: "We will not yield though we should rot in jail!"[92] To gain relief from Wetzel's predatory attacks on church members, Moravian leaders petitioned Congress and the Pennsylvania Assembly. Ettwein, who drafted and delivered the memorials, discovered that many members of both bodies sympathized with the Brethren. But the skilled diplomat also found no congressman or assemblyman who would step forward and challenge the enforcement of either the Militia Act or the Test Act, the twin cornerstones of public policy under Pennsylvania's Revolutionary government. However, some radical assemblymen recognized that Wetzel's behavior might become a political liability to Constitutionalists and prevailed on the president to restrain his lieutenant in Northampton County.

As President Wharton was ill, Vice President George Bryan informed Wetzel that Moravians and Schwenkfelders were not to be feared. Therefore, Bryan said, "it is the wish of government not to distress them by any unequal fines . . . or by calling them to take the oath at all." Also, "we wish it to be understood that Council and the Assembly desires to avoid any noise

. . . .

from the people mentioned above."[93] Bryan also requested Robert Levers "to interpose himself in a prudent way [to stop] the tumultuous and riotous treatment" of Moravians and Schwenkfelders in Northampton.[94] Levers opposed Wetzel's tactics, but he believed the Brethren should comply with the laws of the state. "The Honorable Assembly is the Eye of the Law," Levers informed Ettwein, adding, "We ought in good conscience to pay obedience thereto, for '*the Powers that be are ordained of God*'" (emphasis in original).[95] Wetzel immediately leapt to his own defense. He informed Bryan that despite complaints to the Assembly by Moravians and Schwenkfelders, he had merely been enforcing the laws of the commonwealth. "The bad behavior of the Tories in this county," he said, "and those in particular who have been some time ago committed to the Easton jail, merit no leniency, notwithstanding I have treated them . . . in such a manner as no part of my conduct shall or may be looked upon as rigorous, or my actions ever deserve the name of persecution." Moreover, Wetzel concluded, "I will promote peace and harmony, and suppress anything that would give our Council or Assembly distress or trouble."[96] Wetzel's mea culpa may have put some persons at ease, but even as he crossed his heart the lieutenant continued to plot against the disaffected.

The Council soon received three petitions from seventy-five officers of Northampton's First, Second, and Fourth Battalions. In nearly identical memorials, the commanders demanded that Moravians be denied the privilege of petitioning any legislative body in the commonwealth until they swore allegiance to the state. In a striking demonstration of raw political power, Wetzel had rallied his troops and used them to warn the government to stand fast.[97] Furthermore, even as the petitions arrived in Philadelphia, Wetzel and Limbach conspired to bring to trial a group of Mennonites who refused to bear arms and swear oaths because of their religious beliefs. Since Vice President Bryan did not include Mennonites in his letter, had Wetzel merely taken advantage of a loophole? Or was the lieutenant testing the resolve of state authorities? But even as the Council contemplated how it might shorten the reins on the lieutenant in Northampton County, the war in Pennsylvania moved from Philadelphia, which had been abandoned by the British, to the Pennsylvania frontier.

On July 3, 1778, at a site just sixty-five miles northwest of Easton, the enemy massacred more than 200 soldiers. When Wetzel learned that a force of about 750 Indians and Tories was marching toward settlements on the Delaware, he panicked. Wetzel informed Bryan that he had "ordered out

. . . .

half of the battalions of the county, but by all accounts it is not a sufficient number to withstand the [enemy]." Wetzel also urged Bryan to hasten to Northampton, or as Wetzel's scribe put it, "we humbly beg your interposition on the premises."[98] In Philadelphia, the guerilla war unleashed on helpless settlers by Tories and Indians brought action. The Board of War sent arms and ammunition to Northampton. Congress ordered units of the Continental Army and Count Casimir Pulaski's Legion to help turn back the invaders. But in Northampton, militiamen south of Blue Mountain refused to be drawn into battle. It was not their fight, they said. To drill, shoot mark, and drink whiskey was one thing, but they had no intention of serving as human targets. Thus, Wetzel found himself in the precarious position of levying fines on ordinary militiamen who refused to muster or pay for substitutes. Tensions eased when the enemy, worn out by a long campaign, began to pull back. The emergency past, Wetzel and his cronies immediately resumed their drive to bankrupt Moravians and seize their land. This scheme to get even and to get rich also generated an immediate residual benefit for the county lieutenant. By holding up the Brethren as a common enemy, Wetzel blurred factional disputes within battalions, and in doing so he dampened the rivalry between battalion commanders, which might have led one or all of them to challenge his authority.

On September 7, 1778, a constable accompanied by two armed militiamen confronted Ettwein at an inn near Bethlehem. The constable informed the minister that he had a warrant, signed by Justice Frederick Limbach, summoning all men in Bethlehem and three nearby Moravian settlements who had not taken the oath of allegiance to appear before magistrates at an Allentown tavern one week hence. "You must give me the names of all male inhabitants of Bethlehem," the constable told Ettwein. "If not," he said, nodding in the direction of the militiamen, "I'll take them by force." Ettwein, who had charmed visiting dignitaries from near and far, invited the constable and the guards to have dinner with him. Afterwards, the constable agreed to let his host execute the warrant. In return, Ettwein gave the constable a receipt for the warrant, which certified that the constable had done his duty.[99]

No sooner had the constable departed than one of Northampton's assemblymen arrived in Bethlehem. He informed Ettwein that the Mennonite affair had caused an uproar in the Assembly, and that both moderates and radicals, including the speaker, had vowed to amend the Test Act.[100] When Ettwein showed his visitor the warrant issued by Limbach, the legislator im-

. . . .

mediately informed Justice Limbach "that a supplement to the Test Law, for the ease and relief of all quiet minded persons in this state" was being discussed in the Assembly. He indicated that the amendment might come to a vote in a matter of days and urged Limbach to suspend any prosecution until the proceedings of the Assembly were known.[101] At Ettwein's request, Northampton's representative on the Supreme Executive Council also advised Limbach to "suspend the rigorous execution of the Test Act" until the Assembly had finished its business.[102] Despite these appeals, Limbach refused to rescind the warrant. Ettwein hurried to Philadelphia.

On September 10, the day Ettwein arrived in the capital city, the Assembly took up the Test Act, but radicals fended off attempts by moderates to modify the statute and merely closed a few loopholes in the original legislation. Thus, although some members of the state's Second Assembly had begun to agitate for modifications in the Test Act, radicals refused to allow the issue to come to the floor. Working against time—the Assembly adjourned the following day—Ettwein distributed copies of Limbach's warrant to legislators sympathetic to the Moravians.

Hoping to avoid a calamity like the one that had befallen the Mennonites in Northampton, an uneasy Assembly appointed a committee to study the warrant and then consult with Ettwein.[103] While awaiting the committee's response, Ettwein conferred with Speaker John Bayard, who expressed hope that the Moravians would be able to escape prosecution until the next Assembly, when he believed the Test Act would be amended. "We have made a sharp weapon," the Speaker acknowledged, "and mad men have got it into their hands, and we must try and get it from them again."[104]

The committee appointed to review Limbach's warrant wanted to know how Wetzel and Limbach could be prevented from prosecuting Moravians until the next Assembly. Council lawyers studied the matter and carved a loophole in the statute. The Test Act, they advised the Council, could not be applied to the Moravians because the law contained no provision for administering the oath to a mass of persons at the same time and place; therefore, the warrant issued by Justice Limbach was illegal.[105] The lawyers also believed that the court would set aside Limbach's warrant. The special committee appointed to assist Ettwein hoped the delay would give the Moravian leader time to lay his case before the next Assembly. In the meantime, they said, if Wetzel and Limbach attempted to enforce the warrant, Ettwein should report them to the Council at once.

Wetzel had been informed of Ettwein's mission to Philadelphia.

Nonetheless, when the Moravian leader returned to Bethlehem, Wetzel ordered him to appear in Allentown on September 15, at 10 A.M., or "be fetched by a guard." Against the advice of colleagues, Ettwein decided to obey the informal summons. Justice Limbach conducted the interrogation. "I have a witness," he told Ettwein, "who swears that you have prayed for the King." Ettwein replied that he prayed every Sunday for all kings, princes, and lords, and for all our enemies, but he denied that the name of King George of Great Britain had been spoken in the Brethrens' church since the Declaration of Independence.[106] Limbach attempted to trap Ettwein into admissions punishable by law, but he failed to shake the Moravian leader. Finally, Limbach suggested a compromise: he would visit Bethlehem and take the oath from those men who would do so voluntarily. Confident that no Bethlehemites would step forward, Ettwein agreed and took his leave. Wetzel, who had eavesdropped on the examination from an adjoining room, asked Limbach what he had done with Ettwein. "Nothing can be done with him," Limbach replied. "He has too many good friends in the Congress and the Assembly."[107] Meanwhile, Ettwein worked on the petition to be presented to the upcoming Assembly.

In the election of 1778 moderates won more than half of the seats in the Third Assembly. This number fell short of the two-thirds majority required to pass legislation, but it gave moderates leverage, and they made good use of it. In return for legislation that would relax penalties set forth in the Test Act, moderates agreed to endorse radical candidates for president and vice president. The amendment to the Test Act—passed on December 5, 1778—prohibited all persons who refused to take the oath of allegiance from "being elected to or holding any place of trust" under Pennsylvania government and from serving on juries; but all other penalties, incapacities, and disabilities imposed by any former act of Assembly would cease.[108] The compromise satisfied Ettwein. "The Brethren neither desired to hold office nor to be elected thereto," he said, "and to be freed of jury duty represents a real benefaction for us."[109]

The Brethren lived under these restrictions until 1786, when the Assembly agreed that "since the independence of America is established and a general peace concluded, it is judged expedient and reasonable to afford to those persons who are now willing and desirous another opportunity of testifying their allegiance and fidelity and thereby adding to the security of the commonwealth."[110] A few months later, Ettwein, who had once dreamed of becoming a martyr, stepped forward and swore allegiance to Pennsylvania.[111]

. . . .

But Ettwein's change of heart came too late. By 1785, confiscatory fines had bankrupted the Moravian Church. A precipitous decline in the number of new male converts crippled existing church programs and prevented the development of new ones. Income from congregational industries failed to support the aged and provide pensions for retired ministers and church workers. In fact, the church was no longer able to stand alone as a distinctive religious community. Ettwein, who in 1784 had been consecrated a bishop even though he had never studied theology, had been slow to realize that a new day had dawned in America. He lamented, "Our youth takes pleasure in the world and its follies and no longer prizes simplicity and the imitation of Christ." Nonetheless, Ettwein continued to work tirelessly to help Moravians transform the church from an exclusive brotherhood to one "set within the fully rounded life of human society." By 1795, Ettwein had preached the gospel in every one of the fifteen states except Delaware and Kentucky.[112] Bishop John Ettwein died in 1802.[113]

The amendment to the Test Act passed in December 1778 put an end to Wetzel's scheme to drive the Brethren out of Northampton. Rebellious militia colonels also challenged Wetzel's authority. Several battalions claimed that "Mr. Wetzel" had lined his pockets at the expense of militia rank and file and called for his ouster. Both the Assembly and the Council investigated this allegation, but Wetzel survived the attack on his integrity and retained his job as county lieutenant until March 1780, the full term to which he had been appointed.[114] Given their slim majority in the Assembly, radicals had no intention of roiling the water in a fight over one of their own appointees. Wetzel may have been happy to leave office, but questions about his performance dogged him. In 1783 the controller general examined Wetzel's accounts for the years 1777 to 1779 and found that a considerable balance was still due the state.[115] Then, in 1785, a former militia colonel sued Wetzel to recover money he had advanced in 1778 for substitutes in his battalion. Wetzel, in turn, petitioned the Assembly for relief.[116] How the Assembly resolved these issues is unknown. But it appears that Wetzel managed to wriggle free of financial liability incurred during his term as county lieutenant.

In 1784, Wetzel reflected on his record of public service and declared himself a candidate for Assembly. But Wetzel, like John Ettwein, failed to recognize that a new day had dawned. Although more than 1,000 Northampton inhabitants turned out for this election, Wetzel garnered only sixty-three votes. Worse, in his home district, which included Macungie

Township, he received just three votes.[117] Wetzel had made many enemies who prevented him from resuming his political career. But time is a great healer. Wetzel outlived nearly all of his contemporaries and slowly acquired the patina of a hero of the Revolution. In 1812, the legendary patriot chaired a committee that, along with other concerned citizens, successfully petitioned the Assembly to partition Northampton and create a new county called Lehigh, so named for the river that ran along its eastern boundary, with Allentown as the seat.[118] Wetzel must have savored this political victory. For more than fifty years inhabitants of this region, which included Macungie Township, had been trying to convince the legislators that they should have their own county and courthouse. Notice of John Wetzel's death at age eighty-six appeared in Lehigh County's first newspaper, *The Unabhaengiger Republikaner* (The Independent Republican). In this paper's inaugural edition, the editor wrote: "I shall oppose all men who, under the mask of Federalism, promote the interests of the king of England."[119] Wetzel, himself, might have written that line.

. . . .

7

. . . .

ℰLIZABETH KURTZ

In a series of treaties concluded between 1682 and 1768, Native Americans sold about two-thirds of their land in present Pennsylvania to William Penn and his heirs. Although the Penns sold or leased most of this land to friends and immigrants, they reserved for themselves seventy-eight tracts, or manors, totaling about 550,000 acres. One such tract in Northampton County, the Manor of Fermor, embraced some 20,000 acres north and west of Easton. William Parsons, a former surveyor-general of the province who, in 1752, had been appointed prothonotary of Northampton County, believed the Fermor tract should be settled as soon as possible. Parsons feared that if this land remained vacant, it would form a barrier between Easton and the western part of the county and thereby place Bethlehem in a position to become Northampton's principal center of trade. Governor Thomas Penn and Richard Peters, secretary of the land office, shared Parsons's concern and authorized him to open the manor for sale.

Parsons discovered that some land in this tract had been occupied by squatters. Instead of running off these interlopers, Parsons surveyed their claims, and thus enabled them to make proper applications and purchase the land. In carrying out this business Parsons and his crew surveyed a parcel staked out by Christopher and Elizabeth Kurtz. But when Parsons showed the Kurtzes his survey of their claim, Mrs. Kurtz protested that they had been shorted. Parsons admitted that he may have erred in his calculations and promised to return another day and check his marks. The Kurtzes were satisfied that justice would be done. However, the advent of the French and Indian War prevented Parsons from fulfilling his promise. He served as a senior officer on the frontier before dying of natural causes in 1757.[1]

Nearly a decade after Parsons's death a new secretary of the land office discovered that overlapping boundary lines invalidated a number of surveys in Fermor Manor. To resolve this mess the secretary ordered the provincial deputy surveyor to resurvey "the whole [Fermor] manor tract and lay it out in pieces so as to accommodate the settlers as equal as might be."[2] It fell to prothonotary Lewis Gordon to inform some settlers, including Christopher and Elizabeth Kurtz, that they must give up land exceeding the acreage allotted to them under the new surveys. Gordon, however, informed the Kurtzes that they could keep the sequestered land by paying him £15. Mrs. Kurtz smelled treachery and chased Gordon off her property.

Gordon sent a constable to read the law to Mrs. Kurtz, but she "assaulted, beat, and abused" the official. A magistrate ordered Mrs. Kurtz to appear in court and answer charges of hindering this constable in the execution of his office, "and in the meantime to be on her good behavior." Moreover, the magistrate required Mrs. Kurtz's husband and son to post a bond of £20 each to guarantee her appearance in court.[3] As family friend Colonel Henry Geiger later described the incident, "poor Hophel Coutz hat no money to pay [Gordon] so that small tract of land was took from him."[4] Mrs. Kurtz, however, remained convinced that villainous persons in Northampton had conspired to steal her land, and she intended to get it back.

When Governor John Penn visited Bethlehem in April 1769, the Kurtzes presented their plight to him. Governor Penn took great pains to acquaint himself with the Kurtz's claim and offered them a sympathetic ear.[5] As a result, in 1772 the Kurtzes brought action in the Northampton Court of Common Pleas to recover the land taken from them, which had since been sold to three men. But when the Kurtzes could not prove that they had any legal right to the land, the justices dismissed the action and it never came to issue. Nonetheless, Mrs. Kurtz continued to badger the court. She became "so turbulent and troublesome that the justices were obliged to commit her to prison during the court in order to preserve decency and decorum and to proceed on business."[6] However, this spirited woman refused to accept defeat, and she continued to marshal support for her cause. When Richard Penn visited Bethlehem in 1774, she secured an audience with the former governor, who, like his cousin, also professed interest in the Kurtzes' problem.[7]

The turmoil that engulfed Pennsylvania in 1776 slowed the Kurtzes' pursuit of justice, but it did not stop them. In the early months of the War of the Revolution, retreating American soldiers spilled into Northampton. Elizabeth Kurtz opened her home and garden to them—for a price. In October 1776, Congress paid her $64 for feeding militia, providing supplies to the army, and caring for the sick and wounded. And in April 1777 she received an additional $89 for boarding and nursing six men who belonged to General Charles Lee's guard.[8] Then, in the middle of the turmoil following the British capture and occupation of Philadelphia, the Kurtzes petitioned the Assembly, which had fled to Lancaster, for redress of their grievance. What led these two to launch their petition at this perilous moment? Perhaps they were emboldened by a section of the state constitution that promised, "All officers of government are trustees and servants [of the people], and at all times accountable to them."[9] Motivation aside, on March 1, 1778, a memorial from "Chistopher Kurtz and his wife, Elizabeth, setting forth that they had been unlawfully deprived of a considerable quantity of land and praying relief," was read in the Assembly. The speaker sent the memorial to the committee on grievances—where it was tabled.[10] Elizabeth and Christopher Kurtz soldiered on.

In the fall of 1780, the Kurtzes secured the assistance of Speaker of the Assembly Frederick A. Muhlenberg to help them bring an "action of trespass and ejectment against [the three men] who possessed some of the land [the Kurtzes] claimed." The court appointed a distinguished attorney to conduct the suit for them.[11] How did the Kurtzes gain the assistance of Speaker Muhlenberg? They probably turned for help to their neighbor, Jacob Arndt, Northampton's elected representative on the Supreme Executive Council. In 1770, Arndt and his wife had entertained the Speaker's father, Reverend Henry M. Muhlenberg, when the leader of the Lutheran Church in Pennsylvania came to Easton to preach and administer sacraments of the church. A friendship blossomed between Arndt, a man who believed that "God in Christ directed all his steps toward the salvation of his soul," and Reverend Muhlenberg.[12] Not surprisingly, when Arndt brought the Kurtzes' plight to the attention of Speaker Muhlenberg, he walked through an open door and found an attentive ear.

In 1781, at the June term of the Northampton court, "the Kurtz matter [by consent of parties] was referred to six reputable freeholders. . . . The case was ordered on trial, the jury sworn, and the dispute stated. But as many difficulties were raised which a view of the premises would have prevented, [the trial] was dropped" and it was agreed that the six freeholders would act as referees. In September 1781, the referees made their report, and a judgment against the Kurtzes was entered in the docket.[13]

Nonetheless, Elizabeth Kurtz continued to press her claim for land she believed had been wrongfully taken from her. Soon after returns were posted for the 1782 elections, she wrote to William Moore, the state's new president. Mrs. Kurtz complained to the president about the manner in which the justices at Easton had handled her claim. President Moore requested Robert Levers, the Northampton prothonotary, to clarify the matter. "For more than twenty years past [Mrs. Kurtz] has been a constant plague to the governors and assemblies of Pennsylvania and to the court at Easton," Levers responded. "Her claim is founded on some loose conversation that passed many years ago between William Parsons, Esq., and her. Everything has been done for her formerly and latterly that this court could effect, but in vain, she would not be pacified." Levers informed President Moore about Speaker Muhlenberg's intervention and the finding of the referees. "This old woman," said Levers, "knew the verdict of the court when she occasioned your Excellency the trouble to write to me on the subject. For your Excellency's satisfaction," Levers puffed, "I send a copy of the report."[14]

But Levers failed to convince Moore to put the Kurtz matter to rest. In their desire to seek every possible remedy in the pursuit of justice, President Moore and the Council tried a new tack and sought help from a venerable Northampton magistrate named Aaron Depui. "Sir," said the Council to Depui, "Mrs. Kurtz has been applying to Assembly and Council with a complaint respecting some land of which she alleges her husband had been unjustly deprived. . . . We have only to request that you would at the next meeting of the court, have the matter particularly enquired into, and if she is entitled to any redress let it be obtained, so as to free this Council from her repeated applications."[15]

Neither Depui nor the court hurried to respond to the Council's request. When a year passed with no action on her complaint, Mrs. Kurtz wrote to newly elected President John Dickinson. "The enclosed papers are submitted to your serious consideration," she said. "They will show in what manner I have lost my all, and for seventeen years have been endeavoring to regain my land but all to no purpose, owing to the villainy of some persons in Northampton County. I request . . . that the Council will be pleased to give such orders as will be of service to me. I cannot speak English, therefore Mr. Levan [from Berks County and a member of the Council] will interpret for me, in which case I can verbally lay all my complaints before you."[16] The Council did not wish to entertain Mrs. Kurtz in its chambers, so they asked Frederick Limbach, one of Northampton's German magistrates, to reason with her.

. . . .

But Mrs. Kurtz was impatient. When she received no response to her petition, she addressed a second letter to Dickinson, and traveled to Philadelphia to deliver it to the president. (No doubt the Council's letter to Limbach and Kurtz's second letter to Dickinson crossed in the mail.) "His Excellency the president and the Council will pardon me," she said, "for making one more application for a redress of my grievances. Your last letter to Esq. Depui had no effect and it does not appear that anything will be done in consequence of it. I therefore request that your Honors will be so kind as to give such order as will make my further attendance unnecessary and that my effects may be restored to me, for which I pay the taxes and have not the enjoyment thereof."[17] It was clear to the Council that "the old woman" had no intention of dropping her case any time soon.

Aaron Depui did in fact follow up on the instructions he received from the Council. But it was not until the June term of court in 1783, more than a year after the Council had requested that he query the Northampton justices on its behalf, that the Northampton court reviewed the judgment handed down against Mrs. Kurtz in September 1781. The court confirmed the decision rendered earlier: Mrs. Kurtz had no legal right to the land. Depui asked Robert Levers to pass the word to the Council.

Hoping to clarify this matter once and for all, Levers addressed President Dickinson and laid out each and every step of the confrontation between Mrs. Kurtz and the authorities, beginning with her "misunderstanding" with William Parsons. At one point in this recitation, Levers lost his temper. "This woman is married, her husband not discontented, and her children satisfied with the land they have, and own more than they can pay for besides," he bellowed. Levers offered additional details and then wrapped up what he hoped would be his last letter on the subject of Mrs. Kurtz. "With submission," Levers told the Council, "I will take the freedom to say, that this woman becomes exceeding troublesome to the court, as well as to individuals; her age and infirmities make her a true object of pity and concern and therefore she ought to be treated as she used to be, or perhaps now merits." Levers had one more blow to deliver, but it did not come from him, as he took pains to point out. "Were [Mrs. Kurtz] discountenanced at Philadelphia, we might be in hopes of getting rid of her. . . . I presume to mention this last, as it was the desire of the justices, as well as the Gentlemen of the Bar that it might be mentioned."[18]

But Mrs. Kurtz was as yet unwilling to lay down her sword. Six weeks after Levers hoped he had settled the matter, Mrs. Kurtz wrote a third letter

. . . .

to President Dickinson and told him that the letter to Limbach "has had no effect but to make me travel many miles for no purpose. He promised to meet me at a certain place in order to settle the matter, but he never came. This is playing the fool with a poor old woman [who cannot speak English]. It is well known," Mrs. Kurtz argued, "that I am not asking the property of another person. I want only what belongs to me. I most earnestly request you will give me some relief."[19]

The Council had had enough. Similar to the magistrates in Northampton County, the councillors wished Mrs. Kurtz well and prayed that she would not bother them in the future. In a few months, however, the Council received a letter from Colonel Henry Geiger, a former militia officer who had known Christopher and Elizabeth Kurtz for thirty years. "I begs leave to inform you that this woman the wife of Stophel Coutz desire of me to give you information of her demands of an small tract of land upon the dry land Then what I know of that land I know so much that before the last war by Mr. William Parsons . . . "[20] Geiger's detailed and sympathetic description of Mrs. Kurtz's travail drew no response from the Council.

Having determined that the Council would not help her, Mrs. Kurtz again took her case to the Assembly. On September 7, 1785, she submitted a petition that was assigned to a committee for further study. One week later the committee reported that they were "of the opinion that the petitioners claim is inadmissable in as much as she enjoys all the land surveyed for her use by order of commissioners appointed [in 1766] to do justice to the settlers on the [Manor of Fermor], without having paid any consideration or obtained any official right for the same: that her case was tried by jury of the proper county, who after viewing the lands were unanimously of opinion that her claim was ill-founded, therefore, that the interference of the Assembly where the judicial authority is competent is improper and the prayer of the petitioner cannot with propriety be granted."[21] This statement by a committee of the Assembly should have ended the matter, but Mrs. Kurtz continued her fight for justice.

In May 1786, Mrs. Kurtz pulled on President Benjamin Franklin's heart strings. "Your petitioner," she wrote, "*a poor old woman, infirm with age*, hath been deprived of her property . . . relying on your Excellency's well known goodness of heart, and desire to have strict justice done in all cases, handed unto the Council Chambers yesterday a petition stating her grievances to you, but unfortunately for her your Excellency happened not to be present, this being the case, she fears that attention will not be paid to [her petition]. . . . Your

. . . .

humble petitioner will ever pray for your Excellency's long life and good health and a happy reward for your good deed hereafter" (emphasis in original, probably by Franklin's secretary's hand).[22] Franklin did not respond to this letter, but, as will be seen, Mrs. Kurtz's anguished plea left its mark on him.

Within months of writing to President Franklin, Mrs. Kurtz filed another petition with the Assembly. The petition was read a second time on September 1, 1786, and sent to a committee, which later returned it to the Assembly, where it was tabled.[23] A year later Mrs. Kurtz filed a similar petition with the Assembly, but it met the same fate as the one she had submitted the previous year.[24] Undeterred by her lack of success, Mrs. Kurtz wrote to Assemblyman Thomas Mifflin. (Mifflin was President Benjamin Franklin's protégé who, in 1788, with the statesman's blessing, succeeded Franklin as President of Pennsylvania.) Although Mrs. Kurtz's letter to Mifflin has not been found, Mifflin's letter to Northampton magistrate Valentine Opp leaves no doubt that Mrs. Kurtz, with help from Benjamin Franklin, persuaded Mifflin to help her regain her land. "Mrs. Kurtz," Mifflin wrote to Opp, "has requested me to write to you and to prevail on you to call on Justice Geiger, and with him to proceed to the land claimed by her. This I wish you to do and to bring with you to the next Session of Assembly a true and just state of her claim that Justice may be done."[25] The following note appears at the bottom of Mifflin's letter to Opp: "So also desires Your Humble Servant [signed] B Franklin."

Opp and Geiger must have encouraged Mrs. Kurtz to press her claim, for on September 13, 1788, she again petitioned the Assembly. One week later the petition was read for a second time and referred to members of the Assembly from Northampton County. On October 2, 1788, this committee submitted its report and returned the petition to the Assembly, which, yet again, tabled it without further action.[26]

Questions linger. How did Elizabeth Kurtz persuade English-speaking scriveners and lawyers to work pro bono and submit thirteen letters and petitions on her behalf to the Northampton Court, the Supreme Executive Council, the Assembly, and Presidents Moore, Dickinson, Franklin, and Mifflin? Even more baffling is why, given the state of emergency, legislators and state officials repeatedly took up Mrs. Kurtz's petitions? It would have been a simple matter for high officials in Pennsylvania's Revolutionary governments to send Mrs. Kurtz and her petition packing. But they did not, which says quite a lot about some of the men elected to carry out the state constitution of 1776.

. . . .

Efforts to learn more about the young woman and her husband who took up land in the Manor of Fermor about the middle of the eighteenth century have reached a dead end. Despite assertions that she paid taxes on the disputed land, no person named Kurtz appears on applicable returns of Northampton taxpayers. Moreover, no person named Kurtz appears on the rolls for Northampton County in the first United States Census of 1790.

. . . .

8

· ·

*J*OSEPH ROMIG

On April 6, 1776, Pennsylvania's provincial Assembly enacted a law that decreed that all persons who refused to fight in defense of the United Colonies be disarmed.[1] This statute required each of nearly 300 townships in the province to choose by ballot three persons to collect weapons from persons "disaffected to the Cause of America." In Macungie Township, Northampton County, the inhabitants selected Jacob Behr, Peter Haas, and Jacob Stephen, a trio who averaged thirty years in age, to enforce the law.[2] The new officials drew up a list of disaffected persons and targeted those who might possess weapons. Some persons attempted to sell or hide their arms, but the collectors, aided by watchful neighbors, ferreted out the dodgers and reported them to the County Committee. The Committee ordered those who had attempted to violate the law to hand over their weapons, and to pay a fee to the collectors of arms and the constable "for their trouble and expense in attending the Committee."[3] Most disaffected persons in Macungie obeyed the law; however, a man named Joseph Romig defied authorities.

Joseph was one of six sons of Frederick Romig, who had settled in Macungie around 1743. Because Frederick's sons worked the land adjacent to their father's tract, the area became known as the Romig settlement. In 1764, Frederick Romig converted to the Moravian faith. Thereafter, the records of the Emmaus Moravian Congregation contain many references to members of the Romig family, which also included six daughters. Joseph's name, however, appears only in connection with the baptism of his twin children at his father's home; there is no mention of Joseph's communion, marriage, or death in church records. As his father's influence over him weakened, Joseph doubtless slipped away from the Moravian Church. Nonetheless, Northampton authorities treated Joseph like a Moravian, a sect whose members, many persons believed, were "disaffected to the Cause of America."⁴

When the gun collectors called on Joseph he told them they were no better than "common thieves and robbers" and denounced them as heathens.⁵ In addition, he advised them that they had no right to confiscate his gun. Flustered by Joseph's rebuke, the collectors retreated. But they returned a few days later and, "in a calm and discreet manner," again demanded that Joseph surrender his weapons. Joseph admitted that he had arms "but would not deliver them up," whereupon collectors Behr, Haas, and Stephen brushed Joseph aside and searched his house. The officials discovered a gun, but Joseph claimed that the weapon belonged to a lodger. Frustrated in their attempts to carry out their duty, the collectors reported the incident to the Committee.

Meantime, the Macungie militia heard that Joseph had thumbed his nose at the collectors. After a day of drill and shooting mark, topped off with a bout of drinking, twenty-five militiamen raided the homes of Frederick Romig and two of his sons and seized their guns. It being a Saturday, the whiskey patriots knew in advance that the Romig family would be attending communion services at Emmaus.⁶ But the men did not attack Joseph's house. They may have been worn out from the exertion of sacking three homes in one afternoon, or, more likely, the pack had no desire to tangle with Joseph Romig, whom they probably guessed would be at home rather than in church with the rest of his family.

When the Committee learned about Joseph Romig's behavior, they "legally summoned" him and his brother, John, to appear before them at Easton on June 6. Earlier, John had arrived on the scene to help defend his brother. Constable John Merkle and his son delivered the summons. John Romig read the court order and told the constable "that he shit upon it." Joseph snapped at Merkle and said that he and his brother "would come if they pleased; if not, they would stay home." Advised of the constable's confrontation with the Romigs, the Committee ordered "Captain Trexler of Macungie township with a sufficient party of his men to bring Joseph Romich and John Romich [sic] before the Committee to be held at Easton on June 13 at one o'clock in the afternoon to answer such matters and things as shall be objected against them." Captain Trexler delegated the task to Lieutenant Henry Wetzel. Accompanied by four guards, Wetzel visited the Romig brothers and notified them that he had orders to bring them to Easton. Then, possibly because John Romig had been married to

. . . .

Henry Wetzel's sister, the late Benigna Wetzel, the lieutenant suggested that the use of force might be avoided if Joseph and John agreed to appear voluntarily before the Committee. The brothers accepted Wetzel's offer. Later, however, they decided not to make the twenty-five mile journey to Easton on June 13. Embarrassed by defiant Moravians, the Committee ordered Lieutenant Wetzel to "bring them down by force" on Saturday, June 15.

In passing, it should be noted that when militiamen served as internal police, contemporary documents, such as the Minutes of the Northampton Committee, invariably refer to them as "guards." This appellation is probably not accidental. Guard, as in "calling out the guard," accurately describes the work of militiamen engaged in local police work, such as rounding up Tories and securing their personal property. In Northampton, it appears that militiamen served far more time as guards than in combat with the enemy.

When Captain Trexler learned of the Committee's action, he personally took command of ten men and set off to arrest the Romig brothers. When the squad arrived at Joseph's house, they saw and heard no one. Captain Trexler ordered his son, a member of the guard, to crawl closer to the house and investigate. Peter Trexler crept to a point beneath a window and peered in. Joseph, he signaled to his father, "had a gun in his hand." Peter then called out to Joseph and begged him to put down his gun and open the door. Terrified by the sight of armed men who had surrounded his house, Joseph replied, "We are in a passion and do not know what we might do." John Romig called out and said that if the militia "would not kill them" he would open the door. Peter then observed that Joseph had placed the gun behind a stove. At that instant, Captain Trexler and four men, who had quietly gained entrance to the house "by lifting up the latch of the outer door without any force," burst into the room and seized the gun and also a tomahawk. Captain Trexler discovered that the gun, a fowling piece, had been loaded with heavy shot and primed to fire. The guards took the Romigs into custody.

At their trial on June 15, the Committee found Joseph and John Romig guilty of opposing the resolves of the Assembly and of disobeying the summons of the Committee. As a result, the Committee informed the Romigs that unless they voluntarily signed a recantation drawn up by the Committee and paid all costs, their names would be published in the English and German newspapers as enemies of the country. The Romig brothers signed the recantation, which appeared in the *Pennsylvania Gazette* on July 10, 1776:

. . . .

We do voluntarily acknowledge that we were duly waited upon in an orderly, decent, and discreet manner by the persons appointed to take arms from disaffected persons, and that we did most imprudently refuse to deliver up the same, also did refuse to pay any obedience to the summons of the Committee, who were then obliged to send a party of [militiamen] to compel us to answer for our misconduct; and that we did then resist their authority by loaded firearms. Being now convinced and made sensible of our error, we do humbly ask pardon of our injured and incensed countrymen, promising to deliver up our firearms immediately to the persons appointed for that purpose; and that we will in future demean and conduct ourselves in such a manner as to recommend us to the friends of American liberty.[7]

This recantation must have terrified the newspaper's disaffected readers. But Joseph Romig's clash with local authorities failed to dampen his contempt for the Committee.

To silence protestors of every stripe, Pennsylvania's radical-dominated Assembly enacted laws that required all men to serve in the militia and to swear allegiance to the state.[8] After the British captured and occupied Philadelphia in September 1777, the Assembly declared a state of emergency and appointed a Council of Safety to govern the commonwealth. The Council passed an ordinance that authorized the seizure without a prior trial of the personal property of any person who joined the British army, or gave aid or intelligence to the enemy. To enforce the ordinance, the Council appointed commissioners in each county and authorized them to examine witnesses, break open doors, jail those who resisted authority, and call civil and military personnel to help them if needed. The Assembly later approved this ordinance, then expanded it in March 1778 with an act that provided for the confiscation of real estate as well as personal property.[9]

Joseph Romig doubtless made enemies among his neighbors in Macungie, none more dangerous than Lieutenant Henry Wetzel's brother, County Lieutenant John Wetzel. John Wetzel despised Moravians. Exercising the power of his office, Wetzel "persecuted Joseph Romig with unrelenting perseverance."[10] The hostility between Lieutenant Wetzel and Romig came to a head in the fall of 1777. Citing the ordinance issued by the Council of Safety, Wetzel accused Joseph Romig of being inimical to the war against Great Britain. The county lieutenant also leveled similar allegations against two of Joseph's brothers and four of his neighbors. Fearing for his

. . . .

life, Joseph left his family and fled north of Blue Mountain. Wetzel called out fifteen militiamen and proceeded to round up cattle and horses that belonged to Joseph and the six other alleged Tories.

John Wetzel's zeal came at a price. Of the fifteen men mustered for the four days of guard duty, eleven received £3 while the other four received a pair of shoes valued at 45 shillings in lieu of pay, plus 15 shillings in hard money. When the clerk reviewed his accounts, however, he reduced the amount of cash paid to Edward Lyons, one of the men in need of shoes, from 15 shillings to 7 shillings 6 pence with no reason stated. Expenses which contributed to the overall cost of the guard included £17.13.10 for seven quarts of whiskey, oats and hay, six bushels of forage for horses taken from the Tories, breakfast for fifteen men prepared at Colonel Wetzel's house, dinner for two at Colonel Breinig's, and four days service by Archibald Engel, the clerk, and Colonel Wetzel, who earned better than £1 a day. What is more, John Heinley received 10 shillings for hauling goods, which, along with hay, stabling, and the expense of driving cattle and horses to Allentown, together with an additional meeting attended by the clerk and Lieutenant Wetzel, pushed total expenses for the strike against Joseph Romig and the others to £69.7. Presumably, the state would bear none of these costs. The clerk made book entries that he intended to cancel out when he received £10 from Joseph Romig and each of the six other alleged Tories, who had been ordered to pay the costs of Wetzel's operation against them. Moreover, rank had its privileges. The clerk not only paid Wetzel for time served but also for providing his men with whiskey and breakfast.[11] From top to bottom, patronage permeated the militia. This practice did little to improve the military readiness of the civilian guards, but it provided grist for Pennsylvania politics.

In spring 1778, Joseph Romig returned home. Informed of Romig's presence in Macungie, Wetzel dispatched guards with orders to bring in the traitor, dead or alive. Romig resisted arrest and escaped his would-be captors, wounding one of them in the process. When last sighted, Joseph appeared to be heading for the British lines at Philadelphia. Wetzel reported this information to the Supreme Executive Council, whereupon the vice president proclaimed Joseph Romig a traitor and ordered him to give himself up and stand trial for treason. Further, the proclamation directed the sheriff of Northampton County to read the proclamation at Easton, "*if it could be done with safety*" (italics added), and post it in ten public places throughout the county.[12] The guard shot by Romig, a man named Lawrence

. . . .

Nihell, received £40 "in part pay of expenses and loss of time occasioned by being wounded when in the country's service."[13] Nihell made a full recovery, thanks to the ministrations of John Wetzel's family, who received payment of £16 for the wounded soldier's board and room.[14]

As set forth in the "Act for the Attainder of Divers Traitors," the Northampton sheriff seized and sold at auction Joseph Romig's personal property. Colonel Stephen Balliet, one of six county agents for confiscated estates appointed by the state, supervised the proceedings. Balliet later remitted the proceeds of the sale to the state treasurer, less expenses, which included direct costs for guards, haulers, appraisers, cattle feed, criers, travel, and advertising, as well as Balliet's 5 percent commission and a fee for the sheriff. Joseph Romig's goods sold for nearly £400; however, expenses reduced the amount received by the state to just over £300.[15] Although the law made no provision for the wives and children of traitors whose property had been seized, Balliet permitted Mrs. Joseph Romig to retain some household goods for her own use in return for posting a bond in the amount of £100. (Balliet also extended this courtesy to the wives of three other traitors.)[16] The life-sustaining items selected by Mrs. Romig included three beds and bedding, a chest, a pan, an earthen pot, two pewter dishes, four earthen dishes, four wooden plates, seven pewter spoons, two tubs, a hemp break, a lamp, a cask of vinegar, a plough and gears, a dark brown cow, and two hogs. Mrs. Romig's walnut chest, a table and benches, two iron kettles, a washing tub, a woman's saddle, a spinning wheel, a grinding stone, three books, three cows, three calves, eleven sheep, and two horses all found new homes.[17] Not long after the Romig auction, Balliet approached some of the wives he had befriended and asked them to help him locate unimproved land forfeited by their traitorous husbands. "The women," he informed the state treasurer, "could not or would not give me the least information about it. I could get no deeds, warrants, not anything relating to these lands from them. They said their husbands had taken them along with them the time they went off to the English army."[18]

After his escape from John Wetzel and his guards in 1778, Joseph Romig wandered about the counties of Berks, Bucks, and Philadelphia and eked out a living as an itinerant blacksmith.[19] Sometime in 1779, Joseph learned that Balliet intended to sell his "plantation in Macungie, which contained about 105 acres, a log house and barn, 8 acres of meadow, and 80 acres of upland cleared and under good fence."[20] Joseph sent word to Balliet that the land he had occupied for many years actually belonged to his father.

. . . .

Nonetheless, Balliet proceeded with plans to dispose of the property. He employed a surveyor to confirm the boundaries of the parcel. He also paid a little over £12 to John Wetzel, whose three-year term of office as county lieutenant had expired, to appear before a justice and swear to the facts in the matter of Joseph Romig. Finally, in May 1781, the property was sold to an outlander.[21] Forced from their home, Joseph's family moved in with his brother, John. Meantime, Frederick Romig died and left the forfeited estate to Joseph; however, the executors discovered that while Joseph's father had obtained a warrant for this land, the parcel had never been patented. Moreover, the land office denied the executors' application for a patent.

Under the terms of the Treaty of Paris, which brought the War of the Revolution to a close, Joseph Romig and other Tories received amnesty. Joseph returned home, but his former neighbors probably shunned him, because in 1788 the forty-eight-year-old Macungie native moved to Canada, from whence he returned a year later. Determined to claim his inheritance, Romig appealed to the state supreme court; however, it appears that the court rejected this motion. Joseph likely resumed his life among family members in the so-called Romig settlement. Conjecture on his standing in Macungie after 1790 is more difficult. For the rest of his life, however, people likely fingered Joseph Romig as the Moravian who not only had resisted the authority of zealous radicals but also, in the lone recorded instance of its kind during the Revolution in Northampton County, had boldly shot one of his tormentors.

9

· ·

*J*ACOB STROUD

Around 1760, Jacob Stroud, fresh from a five-year stint in the English Army, returned to his home in Lower Smithfield Township north of Blue Mountain.[1] A few years later the veteran of the Battle of Quebec opened a general store and tavern at a major trail head on the edge of the frontier. For travelers headed to and from Pennsylvania's wilderness, Stroud's place became a welcome landmark.[2] The short, thickset, teetotal storekeeper soon became the unofficial leader of the region—a sort of baron, many inhabitants would have agreed.[3] Hence, when the County Committee organized the Northampton militia in 1775, forty-year-old Jacob Stroud was named to lead the battalion mustered north of Blue Mountain.

To assess Northampton's readiness for war, the County Committee requested Stroud to verify the number of men and equipment under his command. The colonel gathered the information, but he may have misinterpreted the Committee's directive; he mistakenly delivered it to the Committee of Safety in Philadelphia. More likely, however, Stroud ignored the local chain of command so that radical leaders in Northampton and Philadelphia would understand that, north of Blue Mountain, he was in charge.[4]

On July 8, 1776, Northampton's inhabitants elected eight militia officers, Jacob Stroud among them, to represent the county at Pennsylvania's Constitutional Convention. In Philadelphia, convention delegates nominated Stroud to sit on two key committees, one of which prepared an essay on human rights while the other created a frame of government. Some historians have argued that the political theories of Locke, Harrington, Hume, Montesquieu, and Blackstone influenced the delegates who drafted Pennsylvania's Constitution of 1776.[5] It is doubtful, however, that the sermonizing of these philosophers affected Stroud, whose view of the world faded at the end of his own lane.

From the onset of the Revolution, inhabitants north of Blue Mountain lived in fear of attacks by Indians and Tories.[6] Stroud believed that, in an emergency, settlers should abandon their isolated homesteads and run for safety to his place, which stood in the shadow of Fort Penn. But talk did not lead to preparation. In July 1778, settlers perished when Indians and Tories struck the region of northern Pennsylvania framed by the Susquehanna and Delaware Rivers. Stroud informed Lieutenant Wetzel, head of the Northampton militia, that "Coshishton [Cochecton] was entierly cut off yesterday morning by a parcell of torys and Indians, massacreing all Men, woemen, and children. I beg a line from you directing me what to do, whether to retreat with the inhabitants or stand with a handful of men to be destroyed."[7] There is no evidence that Wetzel responded to Stroud's cry for help; indeed, it appears that the lieutenant took no action of any kind to aid inhabitants north of the mountain.

Giving voice to the anger of his people, Stroud informed the Council that Fort Penn would be the best line of defense for settlements along the Delaware River. Study a map, he advised the leaders in Philadelphia. "If it can be thought Best not to have the frunteer heare," he said, "I could wish the Councyl in their wisdom would point out the place." The colonel closed his letter with a parting shot at Northampton authorities. "Wee have our Eyes on you [Council]," Stroud said, "as wee have no other place to apply for Relief."[8]

In the spring of 1779, Indian and Tory war parties renewed their attacks on inhabitants of the Northampton frontier. Wetzel ordered militiamen north of Blue Mountain to engage the enemy, but those men took orders only from Colonel Stroud. Wetzel laid this problem before President Joseph Reed, who reminded Stroud that a well-regulated militia was the only proper and effectual force against the enemy. "As you therefore possess a good share of the esteem and confidence of the people, I shall hope and do recommend it to you as the best service you can perform to your bleeding country to do away as far as possible the effects of former opinion and strive by a general concurrence with the other gentlemen in the militia to give them vigor and efficacy."[9] While this letter was in the post, Reed received another message from Wetzel, who now accused Stroud of insubordination.[10] An angry president summoned Stroud to appear before the Council to answer charges of inciting the people to oppose the authority of the

. . . .

county lieutenants and of obstructing the execution of the law. Furthermore, lest the colonel disappear into the woods, Reed ordered a trusted deputy to hand-deliver the summons.[11]

On September 10, 1779, Lieutenant Wetzel, five sublieutenants, and Colonel Stroud appeared in Council chambers for a hearing. At the end of the day, the Council issued the following resolutions:

> *Resolved,* That the conduct of Colonel Stroud, in arraigning the authority of the lieutenants, and the legality of their appointments, is highly disapproved of by this board, it being their clear opinion . . . that the Assembly have a legal constitutional power to appoint lieutenants, and that they ought to be respected accordingly.

> *Resolved,* That disputes between officers appointed to promote the same service, and especially one on which the safety and security of the people so much depend, is highly prejudicial to the public welfare; that, therefore, it be recommended to the parties now before the board, to lay aside all animosities, and, in future, treat each other with kindness, and conduct the public business with harmony.

> *Resolved,* That in consideration of Colonel Stroud's good character as an officer, his activity and zeal in the public service, the board think proper to pass over on farther proceedings herein.

Reed's jawboning had no effect on the militia officers. Public business? Kindness? Harmony? Zeal? The president had no idea how the world turned in Northampton, especially in Stroud's domain north of Blue Mountain.[12]

In May 1780, Stroud won reelection as colonel of his battalion. (Stroud led this battalion from 1775 to 1793, when the Assembly repealed the Militia Act.) But the colonel and his men were unable to stop the fierce attacks on their neighbors by Indians and Tories. Desperate to halt enemy assaults on frontier inhabitants, Reed offered bounties for Indian and Tory scalps, a stopgap measure that met with little success. Stroud argued that more militiamen would turn out if they were paid for past service. At the same time, however, an assemblyman from Stroud's district charged that the colonel "had sported with public money."[13] This report helped set the stage for a serious confrontation between the colonel and the Council.

When illness forced the Northampton County lieutenant to resign,

President Reed urged Prothonotary Robert Levers to take on the additional job of county lieutenant. The new lieutenant discovered that his sublieutenants were in the process of pressing charges against Colonel Stroud. Levers, who had nursed a grudge against Stroud ever since the two store-keepers competed in the skin trade, lost no time in forwarding the brief to Reed.

1. For endeavoring to suppress the power of the [county] lieutenant and sublieutenants, thereby assuming the power by which no part of the frontier had proper security except his own house, his views being that those people who live between him and the enemy should move down and work his land on shares.

2. For inveigling the militia about his tavern for the sake of sordid gain, while fellow citizens lose their lives and properties.

3. For asserting that the townships of Delaware and Upper Smithfield were not worth defending, he must therefore conclude the lives and properties of these people cannot be equal to his.

4. For maliciously calling people Tories who were earnestly entreating some militia to be stationed at their houses, nothing could be more barbarous.

5. For cowardice and incapacity when marching his battalion to face the enemy, by his absconding into another state, and having been heard to say that a man of his importance ought to be very careful of himself.

Clearly, the sublieutenants, all of whom lived south of the mountain, had had their fill of Jacob Stroud and intended to cut him down. Reed agreed and authorized Levers to court-martial the colonel.

The trial opened on August 1, 1781. Stroud's adversaries leveled four new charges against him, including abuse of legislative authority with contemptuous language, disrespect to the Supreme Executive Council, and scandalous behavior in signing a paper unbecoming the character of an officer and a gentleman. After jury selection, the judge adjourned the court until August 20. In the interval, the judge requested Levers to seek clarification from the Council on "How far a militia officer is amenable to a court-martial for his conduct when not in actual service." To this question President Reed responded, "We do not conceive a militia officer amenable to a court-

. . . .

martial when not in actual service." At the same time, he added, "we think it proper that the court martial should make inquiry into any unofficer-like conduct and report in what particulars such officer has misbehaved, though it may not come within the Articles of War." Reed had shrewdly blocked Stroud's potential escape route.

The court reconvened as scheduled. Levers informed Reed that, "having gone through the examination of Colonel Stroud's witnesses on the north side of Blue Mountain, the court adjourned on August 22, to reconvene on September 3 in Easton." Meanwhile, Levers wanted to know whether the jury and state's witnesses would be paid. Reed responded that officers have always considered serving on a court part of their duty, "but as this demand is so novel, we will consider farther upon it and give you an opinion in the next letter."

However, the next letter never arrived. Fearing that British General Henry Clinton might attack Philadelphia to reduce the pressure on General Charles Cornwallis's army in Virginia, Congress ordered Pennsylvania to call up the militia to defend the state's capital city. Amid the turmoil that followed, the court-martial of Colonel Jacob Stroud unraveled, to wit, vanished from the record. Perhaps the jury had been persuaded that it was too great a burden for them to travel over the mountain and continue the trial in Easton. (Levers groused to one of his correspondents that some men believed crossing Blue Mountain was like crossing the Alps.)[14] Moreover, two of Stroud's allies protested to President Reed that the colonel was the victim of a vendetta. Whatever the facts in this matter, the captain of Pennsylvania's ship of state suddenly found himself beset with a multitude of problems, the least of which was Jacob Stroud.

Stroud's "acquittal" lifted the spirits of his friends north of the mountain, and it even made him new friends elsewhere in the county. In fact, Stroud's appeal among Northampton voters was so strong that they promptly elected him to the first of three terms in the Pennsylvania Assembly. The colonel's improbable victory, coming as it did just weeks after the court-martial might have poisoned public opinion against him, doubtless reminded state officials that guardians of the frontier, no matter their faults, commanded loyalty from their neighbors.[15] Indeed, in the two succeeding elections, Assemblyman Stroud won an even larger share of the votes.[16] But in November 1784, just two months after he had won laurels as a political hero, Stroud failed in his bid for reelection by a substantial margin. The story of his defeat has a contemporary ring.

. . . .

In the running battle between Republicans and Constitutionalists over the Test Act, Stroud stood firm. When a petition to modify the act landed in the Assembly early in 1784, the colonel voted to table it. Then, in September, Republicans attempted to push through a revision of the Test Act. Republicans tasted victory, but nineteen Constitutionalists, including Jacob Stroud, stomped out of the chamber and eluded efforts by the sergeant-at-arms to bring them back. This maneuver made it impossible to obtain a quorum in the Assembly and thus killed the bill. Two months later, at the annual state elections, Constitutionalists crowed about their ability to shut down the Assembly and won control of the legislative body in a landslide.

Stroud, however, did not share in his party's resurgence because some speculators in Northampton believed that he had been much too cozy with Connecticut land-grabbers. In 1753, land speculators in Connecticut discovered a flaw in Penn's charter and claimed the upper third of Pennsylvania. The operators surveyed the land, publicized their speculation, and sold lots to settlers from Connecticut. In many cases, however, Pennsylvania speculators claimed prior rights to the same land. Claims and counterclaims led to bloodshed and court battles that continued into the nineteenth century. Long before his election to the Assembly, however, Stroud had become well acquainted with the newcomers who colonized the region around Wyoming. He not only supplied the settlers with food, guns, and ammunition and forwarded their mail but also doubtless purchased land in the speculation.[17]

In 1784, the Assembly, fearful that the conflict between the Connecticut people and Pennsylvania land claimants would surge out of control, sent a delegation, of which Stroud was a member, to investigate the situation at Wyoming. There, Stroud was heard to advise the New Englanders not to deal with Pennsylvania land claimants until higher authorities had heard their case. But the New Englanders told Stroud they feared their case would never be heard in court. The assemblyman shot back: "Do you think I don't know better who helped make and repeal the laws of this state?" Stroud's position on this matter angered Northampton land speculators, who crossed party lines and stifled the colonel's bid for reelection to the Assembly.[18]

This political setback, however, did not affect Stroud's reach and popularity north of Blue Mountain. In 1787, one of Stroud's visitors gushed that the colonel "keeps a store, tavern, grist mill, saw mill, a farm with nearly three hundred acres of wheat—and the most hands I ever saw at one place."[19] A decade later, Stroud, who had accumulated some 10,000 acres,

. . . .

surveyed a parcel of land adjacent to his compound and laid out a town—his town, to be precise. "A condition of building will be a part of every contract," the colonel announced in 1799, "and therefore no person need apply for a lot unless he is determined to become an improver of the town, which will hence forward be called Stroudsburg."[20]

For more than fifty years Stroud had focused his energy not on raising the new commonwealth or the new republic, but on obsessively expanding and filling the space around him. Moreover, the colonel intended to pursue his mission for days without end. "I do not like dying," he told a minister. "I believe that God made man to live forever."[21] In this, however, Jacob Stroud miscalculated, for he passed away in 1806 at age seventy-one. It is not surprising that his cortege contained more persons "than had up to that time been brought together on any occasion on the north side of the Blue Mountain in Northampton County."[22]

10

. . . .

George Taylor

In 1736, George Taylor found employment as a clerk at an iron plantation located near Philadelphia. When one of the owners died, Taylor, age twenty-six, married his widow. Thereafter, he assumed an active role in the management of the business.[1] The young ironmaster also participated in a rebellion. Near the close of King George's war (1744–48), the Pennsylvania Assembly refused to take steps to defend Philadelphia from a possible attack by French forces.[2] Concerned that the Assembly's inaction might result in disastrous consequences for the province, Benjamin Franklin urged fellow citizens to form a volunteer militia and defend themselves. About 10,000 men, George Taylor among them, responded to Franklin's call to arms. They organized themselves into companies, elected officers, and drilled with weapons. John Penn maintained that the militia had been founded on contempt for government and that its existence would lead to anarchy and confusion. Some persons feared that Franklin might use the militia for political purposes. But at the end of the war, Franklin's army disbanded without having fired a shot or casted a vote. Nonetheless, this successful uprising for the public good doubtless made a lasting impression on Captain-elect Taylor and many of his peers.[3]

In 1752, Taylor moved aside at the iron plantation to make way for his stepson, who had come of age and inherited the business. A year later Taylor acquired a lease to operate Durham Iron Company, a business that straddled the boundary between Northampton and Bucks County, about ten miles south of Easton. When the Durham lease expired, one of the lessors, William Allen, a wealthy power broker and leader of the Proprietary Party, persuaded Taylor to run for the Northampton seat in the Assembly.[4] Buttressed by his sound reputation as a businessman, Taylor rode the coattails of Allen's party in 1764, and won the first of six consecutive terms in the Assembly. Party leaders expected much from the newcomer and placed him on sensitive committees. Taylor served on the committee of grievances, which had full authority to subpoena persons, papers, and records. He also helped draft instructions to Pennsylvania's delegates to the Stamp Act Congress, as well as a petition to Governor John Penn that castigated the government for failing to take action against those responsible for the massacre of savages on the frontier:

> Murders [in Lancaster and Cumberland County] have been long since committed, and the offenders are not yet apprehended, nor, as we have even understood, has a single warrant been issued for the purpose. Murders perpetrated at noon-day, in a populous borough [Lancaster], before a number of spectators, and yet, as 'tis said, the names of the criminals remain undiscovered. There is a manifest failure of justice somewhere. From whence can it arise?—Not from the laws—they are adequate to the offense. It must then be either from a debility, or inexcusable neglect in the executive part of government, to put those laws into execution.[5]

In addition, Taylor served on committees that introduced bills concerning roads and highways, navigation on major rivers, election procedures, custody of the insane, the formation of Bedford County, relief of the poor, bills of credit, and the construction of a courthouse in Easton.

The death of Taylor's wife in 1769 doubtless contributed to his decision not to run again for the post of assemblyman. In an open letter published in the *Pennsylvania Gazette*, he informed his constituency: "With the highest sense of gratitude, I take this method of returning you my sincere acknowledgment for the honor you have done me. . . . It is now with regret I am obliged to inform you, that the situation of my private affairs will not permit me to serve you . . . any longer. . . . I am, with my best wishes for the prosperity of Northampton County, your most obedient servant."[6] But Northampton's inhabitants brushed aside Taylor's announcement and elected him to a sixth term in the Assembly. A year later, however, Taylor, age fifty-four, declined to run. Although personal problems surely contributed to this decision, Taylor's quitting likely signaled much more. His contempt for Parliament's colonial policies grew, as did his frustration at being unable to garner political support to increase Northampton's representation in the Assembly. Ensconced in Northampton, Taylor devoted himself to the magistracy, which had been awarded to him shortly after he won his

. . . .

first term in the Assembly. He also entered into a relationship with his housekeeper, with whom he had five children.

The matter of Northampton's representation in the Assembly had been a bone of contention from the outset. The act that formed the county in 1752 authorized the inhabitants to elect one person to represent them in the Assembly, whereas the three original counties—Philadelphia, Chester, and Bucks—each sent eight representatives to the State House. Old-guard assemblymen thus ensured that political power would remain in their hands. By 1764, however, some Northampton inhabitants had begun to clamor for additional representation in the Assembly. In fact, when Taylor arrived in Philadelphia, he found that a special seven-man committee had been assigned to study the matter. This committee submitted a report to the Assembly, which tabled it.[7] The following year Northampton County and its western neighbor, Berks, joined forces to press for additional representatives. This bill too was tabled after one reading. In 1768 the two counties tried again. This time the bill came to a vote, but the Assembly rejected it.[8] Two years later Berks and Northampton submitted yet another bill that passed by a "great majority." However, an amendment to the bill provided that only county residents could stand for election. This maneuver targeted William Allen, who, although he was a resident of Philadelphia, had represented Cumberland County for fifteen years. A majority in the Assembly voted for the bill as amended and sent it to the governor for his signature. But on its way to the governor's desk, the bill mysteriously disappeared.[9] Given Allen's clout, this development probably came as no surprise to political insiders. Even so, the party leader's heavy-handedness likely added furrows to George Taylor's brow and helped seal his decision not to run for reelection.

Taylor's successor sponsored bills in 1772, 1773, and 1774 that would have provided additional representation in the Assembly for Northampton County, but legislators tabled each of them. However, the last bill filed had two lives. In mid-December 1774, the once-rejected bill suddenly reemerged in the Assembly, came to a vote, and moved on to Governor John Penn, who signed it on Christmas Eve.[10] But for the people of Northampton, the boon from the provincial Assembly and Governor Penn arrived too late. On December 21, 1774, at the request of Congress, the inhabitants of this frontier county, with George Taylor in the forefront, elected a committee of observation and inspection to police a boycott of British goods that had been decreed by Congress. This committee promptly seized responsibility for law and order in Northampton County.

. . . .

In the wake of the Boston Tea Party, Parliament cracked down on the North American Colonies. Some of Taylor's former colleagues in the Assembly proposed that delegates from the thirteen colonies convene in Philadelphia to consider measures to safeguard American liberties. Moreover, they implored each county to approve their plan. Justice Taylor quickly organized and chaired a public meeting at the Easton courthouse. Northampton, along with every other county in Pennsylvania, rallied to support radical leaders who had risen to challenge British imperial policies.[11]

News of the Battle of Lexington and Concord in April 1775 shocked Pennsylvanians. In Northampton, the Committee mobilized several thousand men who organized themselves into militia companies and elected officers. In Philadelphia, the Assembly appointed a committee of safety and directed it to prepare the province for war. George Taylor made a hurried appearance before this committee. The ironmaster had again leased Durham Iron Company, probably because he anticipated the outbreak of armed conflict with Great Britain.[12] Citing his experience in manufacturing round shot for the provincial government during the French and Indian War, Taylor informed the committee that he would produce cannonballs for £20 a ton.[13] When the committee resisted, he settled for £16 a ton. Two months later, however, Taylor complained to the committee that he would lose money on the present contract, at which point the parties settled on £18. Between August and October 1775, employment surged at Durham as the ironworks cast and delivered nearly 4,000 rounds of 18-, 24-, and 32-pound missiles— about thirty-five tons—with a contract value of more than £630.[14] Patriotism and commerce had converged.

In October 1775, George Taylor returned to the State House as one of two Northampton representatives in the Assembly.[15] At its opening caucus the Assembly added Taylor to the Committee of Safety. He later shouldered numerous assignments on committees, including one that prepared rules and regulations for the militia. On July 20, 1776, the Constitutional Convention, which had seized control of Pennsylvania's government, elected nine men, including Taylor, to serve as delegates in the Continental Congress. Thus, on August 2, 1776, Taylor became a signatory to the Declaration without having been in a position to vote for it.[16]

In the first election under the laws of the Commonwealth of Pennsylvania, Northampton voters chose George Taylor as their representative on the Supreme Executive Council. The Council, with one representative from each county, raised a quorum and convened for the first time on March 4,

. . . .

1777. Taylor attended every Council meeting for five weeks. Then, wracked by illness, he returned to his home in Durham. In May, Taylor advised the Council secretary that he had been overcome by a violent fever but promised to return as soon his health would permit.[17] However, Taylor's political career had come to an end. At Durham Iron Company Taylor discovered that in his absence the business had suffered from the "unsettled state of affairs and scarcity of hands."[18] Matters worsened when Joseph Galloway, owner of the Durham works, fled behind enemy lines. As was the law in such cases, the commissioner for forfeited estates seized the Durham property. Because of these problems with his business, Taylor neglected to register his slaves. "It is but a few days ago that I ever heard of an Act of Assembly for recording negroes [*sic*]," he wrote to prothonotary Robert Levers, "and by mere accident might have been innocently guilty of the breach of a law, before I knew there was such a law in being." Taylor apologized for his tardiness— he beat the deadline for registering slaves by one week—and paid a fee to register Tom and Sam, "both about thirty years [old]."[19]

Taylor fought to regain the Durham works from the commissioner for forfeited estates. He appealed to the Council, won a stay in the proceedings, and later, with three partners, acquired the company at public auction. But it was a pyrrhic victory. Taylor's health had failed, and he found himself in dire financial straits.[20] In February 1781, a business associate, who called on Taylor a day before his death at age sixty-five, observed that "[Taylor] was always sending [to me] for money and I had none to give him. But poor old gentleman, I believe his dunning is almost at an end."[21] When the executor finally settled Taylor's affairs in 1799, he discovered that the ironmaster's estate was insolvent.

Signers of the Declaration of Independence occupy a special place in the pantheon of American heroes. Throughout the nineteenth century relatives and town boosters went to great lengths to claim a Signer as their own. George Taylor presented a challenge to local historians because he had lived in Chester, Bucks, and Northampton Counties before dying in New Jersey. Taylor, however, was buried at Easton, which gave Northampton first rights to the former master of the Durham Iron Company. (Chester County, where Taylor resided for about seventeen years, seems not to have claimed him as a Signer.) The people of Northampton cemented their claim to Taylor by erecting a lasting memorial to him. In 1854, public-spirited citizens of Easton contributed to a fund to celebrate the opening of the Belvedere and Delaware Railroad, which linked Easton and the Lehigh Valley to Elizabeth, New Jersey. But the celebration did not deplete the funds in the treasury, so the Easton council decided to use the surplus to erect a monument to the memory of its "great and illustrious citizen." Taylor's body was removed from the yard of St. John's Lutheran Church and reinterred in the Easton Cemetery. A twenty-two-foot-high marble shaft marks the site. On the top of the shaft is carved a draped American flag with an eagle at the crest. In July 1885, George Taylor and the monument that marks his resting place inspired the following tribute from a local citizen: "[The monument] tells of noble deeds; of great worth; of renown; a patriot dead; a country's loss, a nation's grief."[22]

II

· · · · · · · · · · · · · · · · · ·

𝒫HILLIS

On March 1, 1780, the Pennsylvania Assembly passed An Act for the Abolition of Slavery.[1] Representative George Bryan, former vice president of the Supreme Executive Council, authored the bill and shepherded it through the Assembly. A friend of Bryan's referred to the new statute as "the law for freeing of Negroes hereafter born"—a prosaic description of the legislation, albeit a more accurate one.[2] This law, the first abolition legislation in the United States, "freed not a single slave; it held in lifelong bondage all children born before the law became effective; and it consigned to twenty-eight years of servitude every child born of a slave after March 1, 1780."[3] The law also required slave owners to register their property; unregistered slaves would be eligible for their freedom upon reaching maturity, regardless of their date of birth.

In Northampton County, thirty-four citizens registered fifty slaves.[4] Michael Hart, who operated a hotel and general store in Easton, kept two slaves. One of them was a young female named Phillis. In October 1780, the Hart's housekeeper, a woman named Mrs. Brills, discovered that Phillis was pregnant and informed her mistress. Mrs. Hart spoke privately with Phillis, who acknowledged her condition and, when pressed, stated that Mr. Hart was the father of the child. These are the essential points of Phillis's deposition subscribed to by Robert Levers on November 6, 1780.

Save for whispered innuendos and caustic glances aimed at Mr. Hart, Phillis's plight would have gained little notice in the Pennsylvania backcountry prior to the Revolution. In fact, 150 years later a scholarly study of eighteenth-century documents concluded that in colonial Pennsylvania slaves were well fed, were not overworked, had time of their own (which they were not too tired to enjoy), had certain days off, and were trusted and treated like members of the family.[5] Which brings us back to Michael Hart.

Mr. Hart's dalliance with his slave was no secret, although Mrs. Brills and Mrs. Hart may have been the last to learn of it.

How did Phillis come to be deposed by Robert Levers? Did Mrs. Hart arrange the meeting with the magistrate? If so, did she contemplate suing her husband for divorce? Or did Phillis herself, aided by Mrs. Brills, arrange for the deposition, having been told that a sympathetic court might grant her immediate freedom? Or did "The Pennsylvania Society for Promoting the Abolition of Slavery, for the Relief of Free Negroes Unlawfully Held in Bondage, and for Improving the Condition of the African Race" hear of Phillis's case and come to her aid? And what of the child? Did Mr. Hart send Phillis out of the state so that her child would not be born on free territory? Or did he permit her to have the child in Pennsylvania, knowing that the children of registered slaves would become servants until they were twenty-eight years of age? The fate of the child is unknown, but Phillis remained with the Hart household as a bound servant.[6]

Phillis's words are as fresh and telling now as they were on the day she appeared in Robert Levers's office. Her deposition provides the raw diction of how one master systematically raped his slave:

> The examination of Phillis, a Negro slave, the property of Michael Hart of the Town of Easton . . . shopkeeper, came before me, the subscriber, one of the Justices of the Peace in and for the County of Northampton. And first the said Negro Phillis says that about three years ago, when the said Michael Hart kept shop in Easton in the house opposite Meyer Hart's [father of Michael], and the same house that the subscriber now lives in, that he, the said Michael Hart, used to call the said Negro Phillis to light him in the stable, he used to promise her ribbons and blow out the candle and make her stay with him in the stable, and then made her lay down in the stable, he used to pull up her clothes, and put into her his xxxxx and had carnal knowledge of her body.[7] And at other times whilst the said Michael Hart lived in the same house, he would get up in the night whilst Mrs. Hart was in bed, and go down stairs as if he wanted a drink of water, and then call her, the said Phillis, from up stairs out of her bed to get water for him, and then he would lay the said Negro Phillis down on the kitchen floor and have carnal knowledge of her body in the same manner as before. And whilst the said Michael Hart lived in the same house in this manner he had carnal knowledge of her a great many times, sometimes but seldom, and sometimes very of-

. . . .

ten. That after said Michael Hart had moved out of the said house into the new house where he now lives, about two or three weeks after, he used, when Mrs. Hart was gone out, to send her [Phillis] upstairs, and then follow her, and sometimes to throw her on the bed and sometimes on the floor, and have carnal knowledge of her as before. And in the same manner frequently afterward whilst Mrs. Hart was gone abroad in Easton, as well as when she went to Philadelphia, sometimes in the daytime and sometimes in the nighttime. That she at last found herself with child, and Mrs. Brills, the housekeeper, first discovering her the said Phillis to be with child, she told it to Mrs. Hart who called said Negro Phillis, up stairs alone and asked her if she was with child. That she answered her mistress she was; that Mrs. Hart asked her who was the father, that she, the said Phillis, told her that her master was the father of the child then in her body. And the said Phillis solemnly declares that the said Michael Hart was the only person who ever had carnal knowledge of her, the said Phillis, since he the said Michael Hart first laid her down in the stable as aforesaid and knew her carnally. And that the said Michael Hart, whilst she was with child, wanted to have again carnal knowledge of her but that she absolutely refused him. And further this deponent saith not.[8]

And further we need not say.

12

MATHEW AND MARY MYLER

In the aftermath of the Battle of Lexington and Concord on April 19, 1775, some Americans began to wonder whether or not the British, like the French before them, would use Canada to stage attacks on the United Colonies. Encouraged by reports that many Canadians sought closer ties with Americans and might join the fight against Great Britain—talk of a fourteenth colony circulated—the Continental Congress dispatched an army to capture Montreal and Quebec.[1] From the start, however, this expedition floundered. In fact the army might have been forced back had it not been for a man named Moses Hazen, a native of Haverhill, Massachusetts. Hazen had distinguished himself during the French and Indian War as a lieutenant in campaigns at Crown Point, Louisburg, Acadia, and Quebec. Rewarded with a pension by the British government, the forty-year-old Hazen retired to a farm near St. Johns, Quebec. As American troops marched toward Montreal in the fall of 1775, a fort at St. Johns blocked their advance. Ill-prepared for harsh weather and a long siege, the Americans floundered until Hazen and some of his neighbors provided them with food and clothing. Thus replenished, the expedition seized the fort and moved on to capture Montreal. (Most Canadians, it turned out, did not welcome the Americans.) Meantime, Hazen, whose property the British had burned to the ground, traveled to Philadelphia. Although Congress had misjudged the tenacity of the British and the arctic-like weather in the St. Lawrence River Valley, it refused to give up on the Canadian operation. As a result, in January 1776, Congress resolved to raise a second Canadian Regiment under the command of Colonel Moses Hazen. Hazen returned to Canada and recruited about 500 men; however, after the American defeat at the Battle of Quebec on December 31, 1775, the invaders withdrew from

Canada. Hazen's men joined the retreat, and by late summer, when his regiment reached Albany, New York, all but 100 had deserted.

The Canadian misadventure had come to a close, but Congress decided to continue Hazen's regiment and authorized the colonel to raise men in "any and all of the United States." Men who agreed to serve for the duration of the war in "Congress's own," so-named because Congress bore the expense of recruiting and maintaining this regiment in the field, received a $20 bonus. In the countryside near Chambersburg, Pennsylvania, a town situated in the western part of Cumberland County, Hazen's recruiters found many eager volunteers, including Mathew Myler.[2]

In the spring of 1777, Hazen's regiment joined General George Washington's army in New Jersey. To prevent Lord General William Howe's army from advancing through New Jersey and attacking Philadelphia, Washington placed pickets along main roads and struck at Howe's flanks. On June 22, 1777, Washington's men attacked Howe's rear guard at Brunswick, New Jersey. It was in this skirmish that Mathew Myler probably suffered the wounds that landed him in a hospital at Trenton.[3] Mary Myler, who had followed her husband to camp, visited Mathew in the hospital and brought him a "silver watch made by Stroud of London, with a steel chain and a carnelian stone with a head engraved on it."[4] When Mathew asked his wife "how she had come by the watch," Mary told him that she "had bought it [from Sergeant] O'Brian of the same regiment and company and paid [him] £10 in hard cash."[5] During this visit Mary also gave Mathew a $30 bill and a $15 Virginia bill to change. Mathew did as his wife requested and gave her the proceeds of the transaction.

In August 1777, authorities transferred Myler to the Invalid Corps in Philadelphia where he performed duties consistent with his injuries. When General Howe invaded Pennsylvania early in September, Myler helped transport injured soldiers to Bethlehem, Allentown, and Easton in Northampton County, where private dwellings, churches, and a fulling mill had been transformed into hospitals.[6] Before his departure from Philadelphia, Myler sold his watch "to one Ross, a vendue crier, for £13."[7]

In Northampton, Myler and his wife lived at the fulling mill hospital in Easton, where Mary served as a nurse. While on duty at nearby Bethlehem, Myler chanced to run across a friend from Cumberland County named James Grier, a captain in the First Pennsylvania Regiment. Hazen's regiment and the First Regiment had joined forces in the action at Brunswick, where Myler had become a casualty. Captain Grier, who had been wounded

. . . .

at the Battle of Brandywine, informed Mathew that Mary Myler had stolen his "silver watch, two $30 bills, one $15 Virginia bill, and some other bills," the value of which he could not then recall.[7] The theft, Mathew reckoned, must have occurred in May or June 1777, while Hazen's regiment and the First Regiment were bivouacked in New Jersey. Mathew may also have been tormented by the possibility that his wife had obtained the bills from Grier as payment for a sexual favor and, in due course, had lifted his watch. The sergeant's accusation so upset Myler that he informed his medical officer that his wife had stolen Sergeant Grier's watch and money.[8]

Military authorities gave short shrift to Myler's letter. But Grier may have intended to pursue his grievance in the Northampton Courts, for both Mathew and Mary Myler, each in the other's presence, went before magistrate Robert Levers on January 9, 1778, and gave sworn depositions in this matter. Mathew began his testimony by recounting his stay in the Trenton hospital and Mary's visit, at which time she gave him a silver watch and money, including a $30 bill, to change. Mathew swore that Mary brought another $30 bill and an $8 bill to Philadelphia and bought "a black petticoat and a gown which now is or lately was at [the house of] Mrs. Barnet," wife of the tanner in Easton, where Mary stored her clothes. In addition to these bills, Mathew stated, "When Mary came to Philadelphia she had other small bills amounting to $120 or thereabouts." According to the deponent, his relationship with his wife took a turn for the worse just a few days prior to their appointment with Levers. Mathew stated that as he and Mary walked from Mr. Spangenberg's [tavern] to the fulling mill, Mary upbraided him for his drunkenness. Mathew retaliated by upbraiding Mary for buying curtains belonging to Mr. Shanon, even though Mathew had previously warned her that the curtains had been stolen. Mary responded angrily. "Ah, you villain," she said, "it is well you know no secrecy to upbraid me with, or else you would upbraid me with having [stolen] Captain Grier's . . . watch which I made you wear."

Mathew related that when he and his wife came to the fulling mill he sat down with her on the side of the bed. Mary was in "high temper" and he endeavored to coax her into a good humor. "She being then a little elevated with liquor," Mary told Mathew that she had once possessed two $30 bills, a $15 Virginia bill, an $8 bill, and some small bills along with Captain Grier's watch. Later that same night, Mathew continued, Mary summoned an orderly, "his name he knew not," who confined Mathew in the guardhouse. Mathew had come to the end of his deposition, but the matter of the curtains stuck in his craw. As an afterthought, Mathew requested Levers to note for the record that Mary had borrowed £6 from Mrs. Barnet to purchase the curtains from Mr. Shanon.

Mary's recollection of events differed wildly from her husband's testimony. She swore that sometime in the summer of 1777 she bought a watch from one John Clark who lived near Chambersburg in Cumberland County. She paid £10 for the watch, £5 in cash and the remainder with money received from pledging a gown. She confirmed that the watch had a steel chain and seal. She also testified that "when she bought this watch her husband was present, and that she gave it to him soon after, and that he afterward gave it to her to take care of." As for Captain Grier, Mary testified that she "did not know him, never remembered having seen him, and utterly denied ever having any of his property in her possession, or taking anything from him." She also denied ever possessing a $15 Virginia bill, or giving Mathew Myler such a bill or any of the bills mentioned by him in his examination. Levers concluded the deposition by asking both parties to sign the document. With a bold and seemingly practiced flourish, Mathew signed his name "Mat Myler." Mary made her mark.

Like thousands of persons who resided briefly in Northampton during the Revolution, the Mylers probably moved on after Levers deposed them. There is no evidence that Captain Grier or Mathew Myler brought charges against Mary Myler. Moreover, about a month after Levers had deposed the Mylers, Grier returned to active duty at Valley Forge. Promoted to major, James Grier spent the next two years in the field as commander of Company C in the Tenth Pennsylvania Regiment. Major Grier probably chalked up to experience the misfortune he had allegedly suffered at the hands of Mary Myler. And even after Mathew Myler charged his wife with being a thief, it appears that the couple continued to share the same bed. It was a bout of heavy drinking, probably a regular pastime, that led Mary and Mathew to speak out on matters which, upon sober reflection, both may have wished had been left unsaid. Doubtless this couple had previously endured cross winds of gale force intensity, but their marriage survived, at least to the point of the depositions. Could it be that Mathew and his wife requested Levers to depose them simply to clear the air? After all, Mary sat at the same table with Mathew when he had his say, and Mathew, of course, heard Mary present her version of events. Moreover, the fact that the picayune matter of the curtains nagged

. . . .

Mathew who, in turn, badgered Mary over them, suggests that this marriage had heretofore proceeded along normal spousal lines.

Save for Sergeant O'Brian, a name Mary probably invented, the identity of persons cited in the depositions has been verified in other sources, with the notable exceptions of Mathew and Mary Myler. The deposition places Mathew in Cumberland County, but the only male members of the one Myler family identified in tax and militia records of that county are Elias, Michael, Titus, and Eli. In addition, Mathew Myler's name does not appear on the roster of Hazen's regiment, the Invalid Corps, or anywhere else among the thousands of indexed names in the *Pennsylvania Archives*. Thanks to Robert Levers's passion for detail, Mary will be remembered not only as the woman who married Mat Myler but also as the woman who gave her husband a watch made by Stroud of London, complete with steel chain and a carnelian stone with a head engraved on it.

13

*I*SAAC KLINKERFUSS

In February 1776, the Count of Hanau, a small principality in the Duchy of Hesse, Germany, agreed to provide England with men who would serve as soldiers in America. The nearly 700 peasants dragooned for the foreign legion included a young man named Isaac Klinkerfuss. The green troops marched 250 miles from Hanau to Stade, on the Elbe River.[1] There they joined more than 3,000 men from the Duchy of Brunswick, under the command of General Friedrich von Riedesel, and set sail for England. In April, an army comprised of some 7,000 British and German soldiers boarded a fleet of thirty-six ships and sailed from Spithead, England, bound for Canada. Two months later the flotilla dropped anchor in the St. Lawrence River off Quebec. The army spent the winter near Montreal. Then, under the command of General John Burgoyne, the soldiers marched south to capture Albany and take control of the Hudson River Valley. But on October 16, 1777, American forces under General Thomas Gage defeated Burgoyne's army at Saratoga, New York. Both generals signed a convention providing that Burgoyne's troops would surrender their arms and be granted free passage to England on condition of not serving again in North America during the war. Some 2,300 British and 1,900 German survivors of the battle, including Isaac Klinkerfuss, marched to Boston. British troops were barracked on Prospect Hill, the German troops on Winter Hill; both elevations were situated about three miles west of Bunker Hill in present Somerville, Massachusetts.[2]

In December 1777, however, Congress ordered Burgoyne and his troops to suspend their embarkation until England ratified the convention. But the king refused to sign the document, "possibly because the British government feared that this might involve a recognition of the United States."[3] Moreover, when England declined to pay for the upkeep of its troops, Congress ordered the men to march to Charlottesville, Virginia, where food and fuel were more abundant than in Boston. The forced march of three British and three German regiments began on November 9, 1778.[4] Meanwhile, more than 700 desertions had reduced the number of Brunswickers and Hessians barracked on Winter Hill. Some deserters joined the Continental Army. Isaac Klinkerfuss wandered into Boston and found work.[5]

In May 1779, one of Klinkerfuss's employers recommended him to American General William Heath, who gave the Hessian deserter a safe conduct pass. Klinkerfuss, however, lost both his pocketbook and the pass. The soldier then moved eight miles out of Boston where he worked for a brief period. In June, Klinkerfuss headed south. Two months and 300 miles later he arrived in Mansfield, New Jersey, a village situated just south of Trenton.

Klinkerfuss had difficulty finding work in this region, so he followed the Delaware River north until he arrived at Valentine Beidleman's mill in Phillipsburg, New Jersey, a riverbank town opposite Easton. From August to October 1779, Klinkerfuss worked for Beidleman, who then sent him to work for his neighbor, a man named Abraham Haynze. Haynze hired Klinkerfuss for the best part of a year. During this period the itinerant laborer from Hanau met a girl from a neighboring farm and proposed to her. But Klinkerfuss's good fortune soon faded.

Dr. Andrew Ledlie of Easton, one of a breed of patriots whose participation in the Revolution appears to have been motivated by nothing more than a desire to feather their own nests, had inveigled the United States Board of War to appoint him District Commissioner of Prisoners. Despite the highfalutin title, this post ranked low on the scale of appointments; nonetheless, conniving and malicious incumbents could cause much mischief. Among his duties, Commissioner Ledlie kept an eye on prisoners who had been temporarily paroled in the community. As a result, when Ledlie heard that Haynze employed a former German soldier, he consulted his list of parolees and did not find Klinkerfuss's name among them. Guessing that Haynze's hired man was a deserter, Ledlie set out to bring him to justice.

As a first step, the doctor directed Haynze to let him know should Klinkerfuss decide to move on. Klinkerfuss did, in fact, plan to marry and move on, so he boldly went to Easton and asked Ledlie why he could not leave Haynze's place. Commissioner Ledlie informed the Hessian that since he had no papers, he must post security or go to jail. Klinkerfuss, of course, had no security to offer, so Ledlie immediately had him locked up in the

. . . .

Easton jail. When Haynze learned that Ledlie had seized his hired man, he and a neighbor approached the doctor and offered to give security for Klinkerfuss's release. Ledlie, however, insisted that he had to have security from three men, so Beidleman trudged to Easton and the three men posted bond in the amount of £3,000 Continental money to secure Klinkerfuss's release from jail.

After the harvest season in 1780, Klinkerfuss, now married, worked place to place. In spring 1781, Beidleman urged Ledlie to let the Hessian go not only because he had proved his worth to the community, but also because his wife was pregnant. Dr. Ledlie told Beidleman that he would free Klinkerfuss on condition that the German pay him two half-joes.[6] Klinkerfuss's friends advised him not to pay the doctor, saying that money alone would not clear him. Meanwhile, Ledlie changed his tune. Having learned that Klinkerfuss was a mason, he demanded that the German come to Easton and work for him, at which point Klinkerfuss prevailed on two of his former employers to lend him money so that he might buy his freedom from Dr. Ledlie. But the doctor now refused to accept the bribe and informed Klinkerfuss that he had to work for him if he wanted his freedom. However, the doctor promised Klinkerfuss that as soon as he finished work on his house, he would let him go. Ledlie also warned the German that if he did not begin work the next day, he would send him to jail.

Klinkerfuss spent the month of November 1781 working for Ledlie. Afterwards, Beidleman asked Ledlie when he intended to clear the Hessian. Ledlie replied that he had already written to the Commissioner General of Prisoners and requested that Klinkerfuss be cleared. But Ledlie lied to Beidleman, for he intended to wring more work out of Klinkerfuss. In fact, a few weeks before Christmas, 1781, the doctor visited Klinkerfuss's father-in-law and left word that he wanted Klinkerfuss to quarry 300 or 400 loads of stone for him. Klinkerfuss informed Ledlie that he would not work without pay. An angry doctor directed Beidleman to come to Easton and pick up his bond, as he intended to put Klinkerfuss in jail. The Hessian's friends rallied to his defense and advised him to lay his case before Justice Robert Levers. Thus, on March 7, 1782, the jailer brought Klinkerfuss to Levers's office, where Levers, who simultaneously served Northampton County as prothonotary and county lieutenant, examined him.

Later, when Levers raised the Klinkerfuss matter with Ledlie, the doctor told him to mind his own business. Instead, Levers moved to strengthen his case against the commissioner by asking Beidleman and Haynze to come

. . . .

to Easton and, in Ledlie's presence, give depositions on the Klinkerfuss affair. Both men agreed and the parties met with Levers on March 25, 1782. The testimony given by Beidleman and Haynze corroborated Klinkerfuss's deposition in every detail. At one point, Levers interrupted and suggested to Beidleman that Ledlie might have said only that, in return for money, "he would *try* to get Klinkerfuss discharged" (emphasis added). Beidleman shook his head. "The words were," he said, "that if Klinkerfuss gave Ledlie two half-joes he would discharge him." Levers then asked Beidleman whether Ledlie had informed him that Klinkerfuss was indebted to the doctor when he asked for the two half-joes. Beidleman declared that he had never heard anything of the sort. In response to the same question, Haynze recalled that Ledlie had told him that Klinkerfuss was indebted to him, but did not mention any particular sum or for what. Ledlie left Levers's office in a rage. The next day he wrote to his nemesis:

> If you have thought it proper to take down the depositions of Beidleman and Haynze in the Isaac Klinkerfuss affair, I hope you will likewise send my account of the matter which shall be in as few words as possible. Prior to my mentioning anything about money to either Beidleman and Haynze, except to receive their bond for Klinkerfuss's release from jail, Klinkerfuss became indebted to me for the sum of six pounds specie for curing him of a second infection of the venereal disease, which is my lowest price, and was the sum mentioned by me to them. It was not my business to make them acquainted with [the venereal disease] until I was obliged to by this unjust attack upon my character, as it would hurt my business by exposing private disorders of my patients. As to my promising Klinkerfuss an exemption from exchange [for an American prisoner], the words in my letter to the War Office concerning it were: that five or six of the Hessians who were married here were desirous of staying if consistent with the [secretary's] instructions and the good of the country.

Ledlie had one more blow to deliver. "I told this to both Beidleman and Haynze," he informed Levers, "but they being Germans, it seems they have not attended to or understood [me]. I shall waive saying anything about their political principles at present."[7]

A few days after Levers had taken depositions from Beidleman and Haynze, Mrs. Klinkerfuss called on him. In response to her request that he

. . . .

help secure the release of her husband from the Easton jail, Levers promised to write a line to General Benjamin Lincoln, Secretary of the Board of War. "Whilst other prisoners have their liberty," Levers advised Lincoln, the imprisonment of Isaac Klinkerfuss "appears to be the result of anger and resentment, rather than a just punishment for demerits." Levers then set forth Klinkerfuss's history from the Battle of Saratoga in 1777, to February, 1782, when Ledlie confined the Hessian in the Easton jail. On that occasion, said Levers, the Commissioner was so angry "that he beat Klinkerfuss in a very cruel manner, making, as it is said, a hole in his head with a stick Ledlie wears." Levers urged that justice be done:

> Mrs. Klinkerfuss tells me that her husband is, in a few days, to be sent to off to Reading [Pennsylvania]. She tells me that he has ever used her with tenderness and affection, and has an infant sucking at her breast. Klinkerfuss bears a general good character among the neighbors at Phillipsburg, and can bring undoubted good security for his appearance at all times. In behalf of this poor woman and child, I therefore use the freedom to solicit in her behalf that if it may be judged consistent with the public weal, her husband, Isaac Klinkerfuss, may be permitted to remain with her and be discharged from his confinement in the Easton jail upon giving such security as may be required.[8]

Levers sealed his letter to General Lincoln and delivered it to Mrs. Klinkerfuss, who, together with Beidleman and Haynze, planned to go to Philadelphia and personally deliver it to the general. But Ledlie caught wind of Levers's tactic, and immediately wrote to the Board of War. "Not only has Levers injured me in my office as Deputy Commissioner of Prisoners," Ledlie advised the Board, "but even my private character. . . . Notwithstanding the opposition, I shall exert myself and use means to procure as many prisoners as I can, and send them to Reading as soon as possible."[9]

Some elected officials viewed the Klinkerfuss affair as nothing more than the latest confrontation in a longstanding feud between Ledlie and Levers. Animosity between the two bureaucrats doubtless helped blow the issue out of proportion, but other elected officials cited the Klinkerfuss affair as a prime example of how an agency of Congress—in this case, the Board of War—encroached on the laws of a sovereign state. Levers, for example, in his role as county lieutenant, had warned Ledlie that prisoners should not be jailed without an order from a local magistrate. In fact, when word of the

Klinkerfuss incident reached President William Moore, he asked Levers to clarify the matter. "I hope," Levers responded, "it will not appear to your Excellency and General Lincoln that I have not done, or attempted to do anything, but what an honest man, and a man of feelings will be ever constrained to."

> So far from enforcing an order for the confinement of the Hessian prisoners of war, I have pitied them in their state of vassalage in which some of them are constrained to remain in this town, and have only complained that a Hessian prisoner has been cruelly abused and unjustly confined by Doctor Ledlie. . . . When Klinkerfuss's wife came to me, I knew my speaking to Doctor Ledlie would be of no avail, so I advised her to prevail on Mr. Beidleman and Mr. Haynze to go with her to Philadelphia and that I would write a few lines [to General Lincoln] if it could be of any use.

Levers concluded his letter to President Moore with a summary of the Klinkerfuss matter that diplomatically left intact the reputation of every participant, including his own. "I am ever cheerfully ready to give every assistance according to my abilities to the officers in every department," said Levers, "and as Doctor Ledlie is an acknowledged District Commissioner of Prisoners . . . I shall in a particular manner from the injunction of Council, as well as from my inclination to perform the trust reposed in me, endeavor to render every necessary service."[10] Trapped by his own loquacious rhetoric, Levers artfully buried the hatchet, and the parties moved on. As for the intrusion of the "Federal" government in the affairs of sovereign states, that issue would be argued on a larger stage a few years hence.

In his letter to President Moore, Levers included copies of his examination of Isaac Klinkerfuss, the depositions of Valentine Beidleman and Abraham Haynze, as well as his unopened letter to General Lincoln, which had been returned to him by the Hessian's wife. Ledlie, it seems, had beaten Levers to the punch. A few days before Mrs. Klinkerfuss was to have departed for Philadelphia, Ledlie freed her husband. Upon his release from the Easton jail, Klinkerfuss returned to his wife and child. In his later years, it is said that he became an influential citizen of Sussex County, New Jersey.[11]

. . . .

14

. . . .

*H*ENRY LEGEL

In June 1778, the British abandoned Philadelphia and marched back to New York. Pennsylvanians cheered, but state authorities warned that Tories and Indians might now attack the backcountry. In Northampton, the militia and other officials ignored reports that war parties had begun to infiltrate the region north of Blue Mountain. Moreover, Prothonotary Robert Levers chose this moment to pick a fight with an army officer over the disposition of items found on the body of a dead soldier. This was a trivial matter; however, to defend his principles and his territory, Levers made an issue of it. The resulting fracas had local watchers on their toes.

The quarrel began when passers-by pulled a dead man from the Lehigh River at Easton. Since the sheriff had passed away a week earlier, a spectator sent for Robert Levers. The dead man wore a uniform, which tagged him as a soldier in Count Casimir Pulaski's Legion. Levers searched the soldier's pockets and found two $7 Continental bills, two fourpenny lottery tickets, a tobacco box, a receipt for an overdue loan, and an old prayer book. Upon examining these items, Levers identified the dead soldier as Henry Legel, and directed a constable to deliver the man's money and personal effects to his office for safekeeping.[1]

Count Pulaski was one of several European military men who offered their services to the United States during the Revolution.[2] As the Continental Army had no experienced cavalry officer, Congress authorized Pulaski to "organize and raise a corps of 68 horse and 200 foot."[3] Pulaski's second-in-command, a former Prussian officer of Hussars named Colonel Michael de Kowatz, decided to marshal the corps outside Bethlehem because he hoped to acquire saddles, gloves, and other accoutrements from Moravian artisans. The Brethren, however, could not provide the equipment owing to a lack of materials and the placement of a hospital in their town.

Nonetheless, Count Pulaski and Colonel de Kowatz maintained cordial relations with the Moravians and, on more than one occasion, earned the Brethren's gratitude by posting guards at the residence of female Moravians when it appeared that unruly troops might threaten them.[4] Nonetheless, some inhabitants complained about the conduct of the general's troops. The people "expect protection and not violence and oppression from troops raised and supported at their own expense," the Board of War informed Pulaski. Some irregularities happen among all troops, the Board said, but from the charges leveled against the Legion "we conclude their conduct to be more reprehensible."[5]

The death of one of Pulaski's men stirred the rumor mill in Northampton. Levers, a man who observed the letter of the law, raised his guard when Colonel de Kowatz called on him and demanded Legel's money on grounds that the money retrieved from the dead soldier's pockets "belonged to the states." Levers advised de Kowatz that "he did not think himself indemnified to release the money" until the charges for an inquiry had been paid. Levers also informed de Kowatz that he had decided to "consult and receive the directions of the court in this matter." Levers subsequently asked the court to request Colonel de Kowatz to appear before them so that the incident might be settled. Moreover, he warned the court that de Kowatz would make it appear that the money was not the property of the dead soldier. That Colonel de Kowatz should be treated with suspicion and hostility came naturally to Levers, for he believed that rather than turn to outsiders for help, especially European-blooded aristocrats, Pennsylvanians should rise and fight for the cause of freedom.

The bailiff advised de Kowatz that the court wished him to make an appearance at quarter sessions court, but the colonel protested that he had a prior engagement in Bethlehem on the third Tuesday of June and therefore could not be present. Subsequently, Colonel de Kowatz honored the court's request that he meet Justice John Arndt at widow Nungessor's tavern in Easton and discuss the matter. Justice Arndt reported to the court that "Kowatz was indifferent" about the fact that Levers had taken the money, but that de Kowatz judged he had a right to the money because the deceased man was his soldier. The colonel also said he would balance his accounts by debiting the impounded funds in Levers's name.

When the court convened it took into consideration Levers's application, Colonel de Kowatz's response to Justice Arndt, and the fact that it would cost money to summon and qualify a jury, to view the body, and to

. . . .

hold an inquest. As a result, the court "directed and ordered" Levers to pay the charges of holding an inquest and the cost of drawing the deceased out of the water from the monies remaining in his hands, and that the "remainder of the money be restored to Colonel de Kowatz" along with Legel's personal effects.

After Levers paid the coroner five shillings for hauling the corpse, one pound for examining the body, seven shillings six pence for the coffin, and three shillings for digging the grave, he had exhausted Legel's money.[6] Meanwhile, word reached Easton that the enemy had massacred several hundred soldiers northwest of town. In full cry, Levers warned the Council that Easton might be next, and he begged for help.[7] Given these circumstances it is unlikely that Colonel de Kowatz stopped at the courthouse to retrieve Henry Legel's lottery tickets, the tobacco box, the receipt for an overdue loan, and the old prayer book.

15

· · · · · · · · · · · · · · · · · · · ·

*E*VE YODER AND *E*STHER BACHMAN

After the British captured Philadelphia in September 1777, Pennsylvania's Revolutionary government instituted draconian measures to wring loyalty from the state's inhabitants. The Act for the Attainder of Divers Traitors punished persons who assisted or joined the army of the King of Great Britain.[1] The Act for the Further Security of the Government amended the Test Act, which required all men to swear allegiance to the state.[2] These laws prescribed that persons who violated them forfeit all personal and real property to the commonwealth.[3] The Attainder Act explicitly set forth the method of the law. The amendment to the Test Act, however, granted magistrates discretion in dealing with persons who refused to take the oath. In Northampton, discretionary judgment gave rise to prosecutorial malfeasance. Here, in this frontier county, the cunning interpretation of a law that purported to safeguard the "welfare and happiness of the good people of the commonwealth" enabled appointed officials to victimize countless persons, among them, as will be seen, two Mennonite women, Eve Yoder and Esther Bachman.

In the spring of 1778, the actions of Northampton's Lieutenant John Wetzel and Justice Frederick Limbach gave Vice President George Bryan a headache. The state needed zealous patriots who supported the cause of freedom. Wetzel and Limbach, however, used their appointed positions to line their own pockets at the expense of Moravians, who, because they refused to bear arms and swear allegiance to the state, were forced to pay excessive fines. In fact, the turmoil in Northampton so concerned some assemblymen and congressmen that they prompted the vice president to reprimand Wetzel. "Moravians and Schwenkfelders are not to be feared, either as to numbers or malice," Bryan advised Wetzel. "Therefore, it is the wish of the government not to distress them by any unequal fines, or by calling them to take the oath at all."⁴ Wetzel immediately responded to his superior. "Sir," he said, "I can with pleasure assure you that I . . . will ever endeavor to suppress anything that would tend to give our Council or Assembly disturbances or trouble."⁵ Lieutenant Wetzel lied. The commander of Northampton's militia had already plotted with Limbach to dangle the Test before Mennonites. Were these two men so obtuse that they missed the fact that Bryan's injunction, by extension, included Mennonites? Not at all. Wetzel and Limbach simply chose to ignore the vice president. They probably foresaw that the commotion generated by the death of the state's president, along with the upcoming British evacuation of Philadelphia, would shield their activities from official scrutiny. Therefore, the conspirators proceeded against the Mennonites shortly after June 1, 1778, the deadline established by the Assembly in the amendment to the Test Act for swearing allegiance to the Commonwealth of Pennsylvania.

In the first week of June, constable Yost Walp traveled through Upper Saucon Township and summoned eleven Mennonite men to appear at quarter sessions court in Easton.⁶ On June 17, the bailiff herded the Mennonites into the dock of the courthouse. Justice Limbach ordered the men to swear allegiance to the state. The Mennonites, however, refused the proffer because they had religious scruples against swearing oaths, whereupon Limbach ordered them to forfeit their personal property and leave the state within thirty days.

Drafters of the amendment to the Test Act failed to specify who should dispose of forfeited property, an omission that Wetzel and Limbach had intended to turn to their advantage. But Colonel Stephen Balliet, citing authority granted to him by the Assembly, stepped in ahead of Wetzel and Limbach and seized the Mennonites' estates. A month earlier, the twenty-three-year-old colonel, who had led a battalion of Northampton militia in the Battles of Brandywine and Germantown, won an appointment under the Attainder Act as one of Northampton's agents for confiscated estates.⁷ Balliet chose two men, Joseph Kooken and Simon Snyder, who had served under him at Brandywine to inventory and appraise the Mennonite properties.⁸ Balliet also ordered Captain John Stahl, one of his company commanders, to muster men from Northampton's Second Battalion, seize the Mennonites' goods, and guard Kooken and Snyder while they performed their task. Thirteen members of Sixth Company, Second Battalion, volunteered for the special duty. Because most of these men, and their families before them, had toiled alongside the convicted Mennonites for decades, what

. . . .

motivated them to help carry out this mission? Patriotism? Curiosity? Per diem pay? As ordered, Captain Stahl and his company marched first to John Geisinger's place. The sight of first-name neighbors bearing down on his house with rifles, pikes, and clubs at the ready stunned the Mennonite and reduced his wife and children to tears.

Kooken and Snyder spent a full day searching John Geisinger's house and farm. In addition to horses, cattle, wagons, saddles, farm equipment, stoves, beds, chests, kitchen utensils, books, and grain, they inventoried and assigned a value to empty bags, cloth remnants, and a sack of feathers. Kooken and Snyder estimated the value of this estate at £937. John Geisinger posted a bond to retain his household goods until the auction; however, drovers seized his cattle and penned them in a field adjoining John Bahr's mill. In the next three days, Kooken and Snyder inventoried the personal property of the remaining Mennonites, which had a total estimated value of nearly £5,000.

Shamed by their assignment, or so it would seem, the men in Stahl's company drifted away. At the close of the first day, four noncommissioned officers went home. On the second day, five additional men deserted, followed by four more on day three. Only Captain Stahl remained to guard Kooken and Snyder during their final day of work. At the conclusion of this tour of duty, Stahl submitted a bill for his guard detail. Eight years after the fact, in 1786, Stahl's payroll reached the desk of the state controller general, who audited the bill and authorized payment to each man for time served at the rate of 1 shilling 4 pence a day for privates, double that for noncommissioned officers, and 3 shillings 18 pence for Captain Stahl, a grand total of £1.17.8.[9]

The inventory and appraised value of the estates confirmed what most people in Northampton had suspected: the Mennonites in Upper Saucon ranked among the wealthiest persons in the county. Across Northampton, and in nearby parts of Bucks and Berks Counties, the upcoming auctions kindled gossip and dreams.[10] Meantime, news reached Philadelphia that Balliet had used his authority as an agent for confiscated estates to seize the Mennonites' property. Because the Test Act provided no procedural rules on this matter, the Council stepped in and declared that the county sheriff should seize the estates of persons who refused to take the Test. (The Assembly appointed all agents for forfeited estates; sheriffs served at the pleasure of the Council. In this matter the Council doubtless wanted to flex its authority.) Northampton, however, had just buried its sheriff. Therefore, the

. . . .

Council moved quickly and replaced the deceased official with Colonel John Siegfried, Balliet's comrade-in-arms at the Battles of Brandywine and Germantown.[11]

To ensure that all parties understood its executive order, Council notified the Northampton agents that the sheriff would have sole responsibility for seizing the estates of persons convicted under the Test Act.[12] The Council also wrote to Sheriff John Siegfried and reminded him that it was his duty to seize the estates of persons who refused to take the Test. Most important, this letter to their new sheriff reveals that the councillors doubtless disagreed on how to interpret and apply the penalty phase of the Test law. "It may, perhaps, be proper," the Council hedged, "to let the heirs of those persons know, that the grain, grass, etc., growing on the ground, are part of the *real estate*, and therefore not forfeited." But the discussion in Council did not stop there. "It will not be necessary," the Council cautioned Siegfried, "to remove the personal estate immediately after taking inventory when the possessors will give security for their delivery on demand; much less will it be proper to sell immediately." Continuing their retreat from strict enforcement of their understanding of the Test Act, the councillors added: "In some cases, applications may be made to Council for lenity, and the possibility of this ought not to be foreclosed."[13]

Siegfried, whose parents and grandparents were Mennonites, decided that he would rather fight the British than be county sheriff.[14] But Councilman Jacob Arndt, who had posted bond for the colonel, urged Siegfried to take the office for three months until the fall elections, a compromise the sheriff-designate accepted.[15] Siegfried's interest in his new post grew when friends pointed out to him that the Mennonite auction might bring as much as £10,000, and that he would receive a percentage of gross receipts for services rendered. Siegfried also learned that he would have authority to disburse part of the proceeds from the sales for advertisements, auctioneers, haulers, horses, guards, clerks, provisions, and whiskey. But on July 3, 1778, as Siegfried prepared to carry out his duty, Indians massacred several hundred soldiers at Wyoming, a settlement on the Susquehanna River near present Wilkes-Barre, about sixty-five miles northwest of Easton. As a result, preparations for the state-ordered auctions came to a halt.

Justice Limbach's sentencing of the Mennonites disturbed many Northampton inhabitants, among them, Doctor Felix Lynn. Taking a cue from the Council's letter to Siegfried, Dr. Lynn urged the Mennonites to appeal their case, and volunteered to draft a petition. The Mennonites ac-

. . . .

cepted Lynn's proposal and signed the petition.[16] At the bottom of the petition Lynn added a statement that praised the character of the Mennonites and pleaded their case. Lynn signed this endorsement, as did eleven neighbors of the accused men, including schoolmaster Nicholas Kooken, whose brother had served in Captain Stahl's guard.[17] Midway through the petition, Lynn cut to the heart of the appeal. "We humbly conceive the process against us," he wrote, "has not been according to the spirit of the law, or the intention of the legislature with regard to the peaceable industrious part of the people, which error is imputed to [Limbach] not clearly understanding the full meaning of the first and third clauses of the Test Act [as amended April 1, 1778]."

Doctor Lynn planted two questions in the minds of the Council. Had Limbach sentenced the Mennonites without having read the law? (Given the lapse of time between the publication and distribution of statutes in Revolutionary Pennsylvania, this was not an idle question.)[18] And even if Limbach had read the law, did he intentionally bypass intermediate steps in the sentencing, one of which provided for a three-month stay of execution for defendants who refused to take the Test? Doctor Lynn's strategy, however, went for naught. News of the massacre at Wyoming and the Mennonites' petition arrived in Philadelphia about the same time. Council focused on the crisis at hand, and the petition got lost in the shuffle.[19]

Jacob Bachman, son of George Bachman, then sent a second petition to the Council on behalf of his mother, Esther, and several small children, "who are likely to be much distressed except your honors will be pleased to grant some redress." This petition too closes with a statement by friends of the accused: "We the subscribers being neighbors to the above petitioner do recommend the above case as truly worth your consideration, and any favor showed will be gratefully acknowledged." In addition to Doctor Lynn and two members of the Kooken family, John, Casper, and Jacob Rumfeld—three members of the guard mustered from Sixth Company who had deserted after short service—signed this plea. Even more astonishing, the plea for mercy bore the signature of Captain John Stahl, the very same commander who had stuck to the task of dispossessing the Mennonites to the bitter end. Jacob Bachman's petition reached the Council on July 7, where it was tabled for possible consideration at a later time.[20] In mid August, Jacob sent a third petition to the Assembly. He protested that he had leased from his father a plantation, together with the stock thereon, which had since been seized by the agents for confiscated property, and so he prayed the Assembly would order them to be returned. After one reading, the Assembly tabled the petition.[21]

Near the end of July, Siegfried notified Northampton's inhabitants that the personal property of the convicted Mennonites would be sold on August 24 and 29, and on September 1, 2, and 3. In all, these auctions probably attracted upwards of 2,000 spectators. Three hundred and fifty persons, most of them men, made one or more successful bids. The auction of some 3,000 items, which included nearly 50 horses, 130 cattle, 130 sheep, and 45 hogs, created a frenzy. Lieutenant John Wetzel bought a cow, a calf, a bull, and a horse. Justice Limbach, who earned £79 for serving as clerk at the auctions, picked up a hand screw and a half-bushel of grain. Constable Yost Walp found a dresser to his liking. Jacob Stahl (father of Captain Stahl?) paid a staggering £590 for "a whole team." A blacksmith named Anthony Kleckner traveled twenty miles to acquire a set of blacksmith tools for his son and a chest for his new daughter-in-law.[22] Siegfried found a bargain at nearly every auction. His purchases included a sheep, three hogs, a piece of uppers leather, iron rods, a chair, two stools, two bedsteads, yarn, two books, and a Bible, for a total expenditure of £33. So hot was the action that even the two men who had signed petitions on behalf of the Mennonites fell under its spell. Captain Stahl carried off two porringers.[23] Schoolmaster Nicholas Kooken acquired four cow chains, a harrow, two sickles, and a dresser. Assemblyman Peter Burkhalter also turned out for one auction, probably not only to observe the proceedings first hand but also to mingle with his constituents, who returned him to office six times in eleven years, including four consecutive terms, the limit allowed by law. Buyers snapped up almost every item, except for Casper Yoder's pigeon net. This net probably went the way of John Geisinger's whiskey, three kegs of which had been inventoried but failed to reach the sale.

And how did the crowd react when Jacob, Henry, and Ann Bachman spent some £170 to buy back pieces of the family property? Or when John Geisinger's wife called out and paid £140 to hold onto a wagon, horse, mare, and colt, and offered another £5 to retrieve an iron kettle? A few folks doubtless cackled at the spectacle of Mennonites bidding on property that formerly belonged to them. Others must have frowned and furtively sought out kindred souls. But the reaction of most persons in the crowd would have eluded the sharpest observer, for many in Northampton had learned to conceal their leanings on any matter linked to Pennsylvania's Revolutionary government behind stony stares and silence. In the end, the auctions grossed

. . . .

£6,289, a little more than the appraised value of £5,886, but far lower than some numbers that had been tossed about.[24] In the end too the auctions stranded eleven Mennonite families in empty houses that had been stripped of every object that could be removed and sold, from spools of thread to heirlooms that had been carried across the Atlantic.

The forfeiture and sale of their personal property impoverished the Mennonites, but banishment would have destroyed these families. With fresh determination, Eve Yoder and Esther Bachman requested that the Assembly mitigate the severity of the court's decision and permit their husbands to remain with them. The two women employed a scrivener and bravely opened their hearts to him.[25] Their husbands had been peaceable and quiet, they said. They had never meddled in state affairs. They had paid taxes and fines, furnished teams for the Continental army and, in some cases, had served as drivers, work for which they had yet to be paid. The sheriff sold all of their property for a sum of £40,000. Not a morsel of bread had been left for the children. Moreover, they had no means to keep their children warm, especially at nights when they had to lie on the floor without beds. Some of the men's wives were pregnant and would soon give birth. Finally, the women appealed to assemblymen to have some regard for the "scriptures of truth: 'What God hath joined together, let not men put asunder,' and that our husbands may be permitted to continue to dwell with us, and that our children may not be taken from us."[26]

This petition arrived at the State House on September 10, one day before the scheduled adjournment of Pennsylvania's Second General Assembly. A petition that arrived in the closing hours of a session would almost certainly have been tabled and handed to the next Assembly. But the homely supplication of Eve Yoder and Esther Bachman shook the radical-dominated Assembly, which immediately sent the petition to the Council and recommended that it launch an inquiry into the matter. The Assembly also told the Council that if the facts set forth in the petition were found to be true, they should "grant such relief to the [Mennonites] . . . as they may think proper by a draft on the state treasurer."[27] The Assembly, however, said nothing about the fate of the men. On the crucial issue of banishment, the Assembly doubtless employed private channels to reverse Limbach's order. Confronted by the bitter fruit of their legislation, the radicals gave ground. But benevolence in this case did not signal a change in their ideology. With annual elections at hand, radicals simply hoped to counter adverse public reaction to the barbaric treatment of Mennonites

. . . .

and Moravians in Northampton County by Lieutenant John Wetzel and Justice Frederick Limbach. The radicals' cynical maneuver notwithstanding, moderates won more than half of the seats in the Third Assembly. Although they did not win the two-thirds majority required to pass legislation, moderates gained leverage that enabled them to negotiate with leaders of the state's Third Assembly and obtain a relaxation in the penalties set forth in the Test Act.

Vice President George Bryan believed it would only add to the difficulties of the Mennonites to have them stand before the Council and support the allegations in their petition. Therefore, he requested Doctor Felix Lynn and Northampton Assemblymen John Ralston and Peter Rhoads to investigate the matter on the spot, "that on your report and advice an order may be sent to the state treasurer to the sheriff of your county to relieve their present difficulties."[28] This committee completed their work in two weeks, and reported that the Mennonites had grain enough to support their families for one year, since the last harvest was left to them for their own use. They acknowledged, however, that the families may have been in want for a few days because the seizure occurred just before harvest. Abraham Geisinger's wife, they said, was about to deliver a child, but she had no bed. Henry Zell was robbed of all his cash shortly before his personal goods were seized, and he was, at times, somewhat delirious. Finally, the trio reported that, as nearly as they could determine, the sum arising from the sale of the estates amounted to only about £9,000.[29] Bryan had his report, but final resolution of this matter stalled.

Meanwhile, Philip Boehm, paymaster for the Northampton militia, asked Bryan to order Siegfried to hand over £3,000 of the proceeds from the auctions, "as the militia have become very clamorous for want of their pay." Bryan obliged. Siegfried also debited the proceeds to pay charges related to the auctions. The costs included feed for cattle and horses, a crier, clerks, food, rum, and guards. The sheriff also paid himself for ninety days service, and keeping himself in provisions and forage, at the rate of £6 per day, or £540 total, an amount later reduced when Siegfried discovered that the state allowed him only £3 per day for his service. The total of all expenses related to the auction amounted to about £800 to £900 pounds, which left more than £2,000 to be accounted for.[30]

It must have come as a surprise to Siegfried when, in February 1780, the post brought him a letter from President Joseph Reed. "During the time you were sheriff of Northampton County you received a considerable sum of

. . . .

money arising from the sale of Bachman et al.," Reed said. "We do not find that you have paid to the state more than £3,000 on order drawn of you in favor of the paymaster of the militia. Therefore, the Council requests you to make a report to us immediately of your proceedings and pay the balance to [the state treasurer] without delay."[31] Siegfried ignored this summons. Council waited sixteen months for a response to their order, and then directed the state attorney general to make "an inquiry respecting public money, not accounted for, in the hands of John Siegfried . . . and, if necessary, prosecute [him] at common law."[32] In June 1783, the Council approved the attorney general's audit of Siegfried.[33] The former sheriff had settled the claim against him for £200.[34]

Before Siegfried could wash his hands of the Mennonites, however, he had to confront a related matter. When the inventory men appraised George Bachman's property they neglected to include an indentured male servant named William Ettinger. Siegfried had taken possession of Ettinger and sold him to a gentleman in Northampton. But the purchaser died soon after, and Siegfried repossessed the servant. Siegfried then sold the servant to a gentleman in Bucks County named Abraham Ettinger, who may have been related to the servant. The estate of the man who first purchased William Ettinger from Siegfried sued the second owner to recover the servant. The plaintiff complained to the Council that Siegfried never had authority to sell the servant and never accounted for him to the public in the first place. How, where, and over what period of time this mess played out is open to conjecture.[35]

In the aftermath of the summer of 1778, Mennonites Henry Zell and John Newcomer took the Test, doubtless to avoid further persecution by authorities.[36] A desire to placate authorities and to circumvent swearing the oath may have led Abraham and John Geisinger, George, Joseph, and John Bachman, Philip and John Newcomer, and Peter Zell—sons of the convicted Mennonites—to join Captain John Stahl's militia company.[37] (The Militia Act contained no provision for swearing allegiance to the state.) As for Eve Yoder, Esther Bachman, and the other Mennonites whose property had been sold at auction, no evidence has been found that the state carried through on its promise to compensate them for their loss of personal property. On the contrary, six months after the Assembly had promised restitution in this matter, the Mennonites sent another petition to the Assembly and prayed for relief. This petition, like those that preceded it, had been endorsed by a "large number of inhabitants," but the

. . . .

Assembly tabled it.[38] It would appear, therefore, that the Mennonites, with help from true neighbors, persevered and, over time, put their lives in order. It is possible that some persons, upon reflection, returned items purchased at auction, such as the Jacob Yoder family Bible acquired by Sheriff John Siegfried.

. . . .

AFTERWORD

. . . .

BY *M*ICHAEL ZUCKERMAN

Frank Fox probably knows how long ago we met. I have quite forgotten. He is simply a part of my life now. We correspond—real letters, not e-mail—desultorily, then at white heat for a while, then not at all for months. He turns up for lunch in Philadelphia or for a few days in Holland when I'm spending the year there. The man is an incorrigible wanderer. And gifts come, from emporia around the world, when Frank does not. The man is an incorrigible giver of gifts.

And stories come with them. Stories come when Frank comes, when he sends presents, and when he writes. The man is an irrepressible storyteller.

When he first thought to study Northampton County in the Revolution—or, at any rate, when he first approached me with that thought—he was not even thinking about a story, let alone about this extraordinary assemblage of stories. He was looking for guidance in mastering the craft of the academic historian. I was, of course, flattered that he wanted to do what I do. And I was more than willing to try to help him do it.

But as we talked, I sensed that academic history could never quite contain him. When he asked me for some exemplary scholarly works that he might read, I suggested instead Thomas Beer's *The Mauve Decade*. I had no idea what sort of a book Frank would ultimately write. I just had an idea that he should have as a model a *strange* book, a book unlike those that present-day professors—my peers—might write. I wanted him to begin with an odd, angular book that had its own unique voice.

Frank has, in fact, mastered the technics of academic history. He has published learned articles in learned journals and scholarly essays in scholarly books. But this book is the book I wished for him when I had no idea what I wished for him. This is the book that neither of us could have envisioned when he began his apprenticeship, at an age when most of those he knew sought nothing more strenuous than a golfing retirement in a gated community in Arizona.

Sweet Land of Liberty is indeed an odd book. And it does have its own voice, a voice at once tantalizing and maddening. It holds so much implicit. It is taut and resonant with the implications of the unstated. It is sturdy, even rough, yet gentle, even delicate. It sends forth dozens of tendrils, each bearing brilliantly intimative buds, a few bearing dazzling blooms.

The book is not quite biography. It is not quite a history of the Pennsylvania backcountry in the Revolution. It does not go anywhere, exactly, and it does not add up to anything, exactly. It disdains argument and thesis, though it teems with submerged arguments and theses. It is not about life. It *is*, like all great books—even great slight books—life itself.

I would say that it is a model for future studies of the Revolution, but it is not. No one will ever again spend a dozen years and more mulling over the archives of an obscure county to piece together dozens of obscure lives and bring them to life. And even if someone does, that someone will not have Frank's way with words.

Frank commands a prose that is vigorous, quick, pungent, and strewn with arresting turns of phrase. Sometimes it gallops. Sometimes it even prances. Yet it never goes so fast that there is no time for wry reflection, or shrewd insight, or deft, damning judgment. Frank keeps a constant eye cocked for the telling hypocrisy, the enlivening instance, the revealing paradox. He is a master of the one-liner, yet his phrases are more than merely zingy. They probe. They evoke. And they lay character bare with a wondrous wisdom.

Indeed, Frank's characters come off the page with a full portion of their idiosyncrasy, meanness, and humanity, and with all their unfathomable mystery as well. He is not only a scrupulous historian who has mined the sources assiduously but also an author who possesses a generous sympathy and a large experience of the world. His inferences from his sources are as fascinating and illuminating as they are plausible and powerful. It is as easy to concur as to admire when he says of John Wetzel—to take one example among a multitude—that the man never joined the militia because "he probably placed himself a cut above the sort of man who forked dung."

Frank has not simply told the story of the Revolution through a sequence of biographical sketches of those caught up in it in one backcountry county. In a very genuine sense, he has told the stories—indeed, caught the character—of those men and women themselves.

. . . .

More than that, he has done so by veritably getting inside his subjects. He has written not only a history of Northampton County but also a host of interior histories. He has entered into the perspective of each obscure participant. He has written history from the bottom up as we have never had it, given voice to the voiceless as we never dreamed it. Taking folks whom historians never even knew, let alone attended to, he has not only accorded them place and a bit of agency but also attempted to tell each one's tale as each one lived and felt it. He has truly tried to let them *speak*, animating them as a historical novelist might. He has deciphered all the events, developments, alliances, and antagonisms to which the data allow access—he has quite mastered the external history of the county—and then he has gone beyond that conventional research. He has worked and wormed his way into the minds and hearts of his characters.

At the same time, and with authentic virtuosity, he has rendered the larger frame of the Revolution. He has an uncanny ability to situate Northampton's unfamiliar Revolution within the one with which we *are* familiar. He enables us to see that Revolution anew and to become cognizant of actions at ground level as well as at the grander, more abstract levels, where we have always looked. He gives us a new and altogether more disturbing Revolution than we have been accustomed to reckoning with. He may change forever the way that we think about our national origins.

He literally gives new meaning to the Revolution as a time that "tried men's souls." He opens before us a world of suffering and viciousness and unforgivingness, a world of unblinking enmity and unbridled rapacity, a world of careers made and unmade, of lives built and blighted and rebuilt and blasted, when "suspicion and persecution of one's neighbors became a blood sport."

Indeed, this book is as much an investigation of American careerism and opportunism as an account of the Revolution itself. It traces the course of old ambitions and ancient vendettas transformed amid the temptations of wartime, not only among the leading people of the county but also among the men and women otherwise unknown to history. It tells of hopes dimmed and renewed and dimmed yet again, of dauntless spirits like Elizabeth Kurtz and her improbable resistance, of quiet courage, and of venality and the blatant abuse of power that compelled capitulation even from people of quiet courage.

Frank has captured the toll and the trauma of civil war as few who have written of the Revolution have. It is easy to say, and many have said it in

. . . .

hindsight of the French and Russian revolutions, that the American Revolution was a conservative revolution. But up close, as close as Frank takes us, it does not feel conservative at all.

Suddenly, that revolution emerges as one we would rather not know yet need to know, a world in which many were deprived of life, liberty, and property in the name of independence and many more silenced in the glorious cause of freedom.

Freedom, as Frank says, was not a common cause in Northampton (or, by implication, in Pennsylvania or America). Freedom of conscience was most assuredly not a shared faith among the Revolutionaries (not among mainstream Protestants and not even, ironically, among the peace sects). *Sweet Land of Liberty* suggests disturbing conundrums rather than stark simplicities regarding liberty and tyranny. And one of those conundrums derives from the very readiness with which the self-styled rebels drew starkly simple dichotomies of friend and foe.

Frank minces no words about all this. In one exquisite phrase, he pronounces a passel of revolutionary leaders "whiskey patriots." In another, he calls the militia that governed the county "a paramilitary political faction that also functioned as an internal police force." In another, he evokes an "undeclared state of martial law." Lest any miss the point, he makes explicit his insistence that intimidation and expropriation of the pacifists was, for many Northamptonites, much more the business and the attraction of the Revolution than fighting the British enemy.

No one who reads this work will ever again be able to speak glibly of Revolutionary Pennsylvania as the most democratic of the new states, or of its Constitution as the most radical. More to the point, no one will ever again be able to set the militia and the citizen-soldiery glibly in the tradition of Cincinnatus. George Washington may have styled himself deliberately on the Roman hero, but neither the militia rank and file nor their grass-roots leaders ever did. They were too intent on seizing power and pelf to put themselves in any readiness for meeting the British on the field of battle, an encounter for which, in any case, they swiftly lost all taste.

The immensity of Frank's achievement is that he rarely spells out much of his indictment. His narratives speak for themselves, constituting a cumulative and remarkable revision of our understanding of the Revolution at ground level. They allow us access to the Revolution as men and women lived it, in one particular place that may well have been like many other places. They remind us, irresistibly, that there was formal authority in

. . . .

Philadelphia and then there was actual authority north of the Blue Mountain, beyond the reach of Joseph Reed and his Council or even of the Continental Congress in all its assumptive majesty. There was politics and there were court proceedings, and then there was the will of the people. There was a war and there were the constitutions that fill the texts with which we try to teach our children, and then there was land speculation and looking out for oneself. Any number of these laconic narratives shows it. Honors and offices come and go. Dishonor threatens or befalls. But always the serious business of land speculating goes on and on and on, in flush times and foul, riding high and sinking low.

The Revolution was a defining event for the generation of Americans who fought it and for the two or three generations who followed. It was at least as enduring a defining event as the Civil War would be for its participants and their descendants, and a more enduring one than the Great Depression and the Vietnam War would be for theirs. But we have been guarded in our efforts to understand just what that event defined.

Frank disdains to be so politic. Insofar as he intimates that we will need dozens of other accounts as gritty as his to comprehend the cataclysm we call the Revolution, he guarantees that we will never comprehend it, because we will never have those other accounts. But insofar as this one wondrous work opens before us a vista of small people caught in the vortex of large forces that empowered other small people—mean people of petty, venal ambitions—it may invite vision. Insofar as it gives us a window on a place where arbitrary power and its abuse entailed the sore suffering of some to gratify the paltry lusts of others, it may draw us toward an understanding of ourselves despite ourselves.

ABBREVIATIONS

. . . .

APS   American Philosophical Society, Philadelphia

BCHSC   *Bucks County Historical Society Collections*, Doylestown, Pa.

Col. Records   *Colonial Records of Pennsylvania*, 16 vols. (Philadelphia and Harrisburg, 1851–53)

CWU   Claude W. Unger Collection, Historical Society of Pennsylvania, Philadelphia

Ettwein Papers   *John Ettwein Papers*, Archives of the Moravian Church, Bethlehem, Pa., microfilm

HSP   Historical Society of Pennsylvania, Philadelphia

JCC   Worthington C. Ford et al., eds., *Journals of the Continental Congress*, 34 vols. (Washington, D.C., 1904–37)

JHR   *Journals of the House of Representatives of the Commonwealth of Pennsylvania Beginning the twenty-eighth Day of November, 1776, and Ending the second Day of October, 1781, With the Proceedings of the several Committees and Conventions, Before and after the Commencement of the American Revolution* (Philadelphia, 1782), Boston Athenaeum, Boston

Minutes   Robert Traill, *Minutes of the Committee of Observation and Inspection of Northampton County, Pennsylvania*, vol. 4 of *Two Hundred Years of Life in Northampton County, Pa.* (Easton, Pa., 1976)

NCP   Northampton County Papers, Historical Society of
Pennsylvania, Philadelphia

Pa. Arch.   *Pennsylvania Archives*, 119 vols. (Philadelphia and
Harrisburg, 1852–1933)

Pa. Gazette   *Pennsylvania Gazette*

Pa. History   *Pennsylvania History*

PCC   *Papers of the Continental Congress, 1774–1789*, 204 reels
(Washington, D.C., 1959), microfilm

PGM   *Pennsylvania Genealogical Magazine*

PHMC   Pennsylvania Historical and Museum Commission

PMHB   *Pennsylvania Magazine of History and Biography*

RG 27   *Records of Pennsylvania's Revolutionary Governments*,
Record Group 27

Statutes   James T. Mitchell and Henry Flanders, comps., *The
Statutes at Large of Pennsylvania from 1682 to 1809*
(Harrisburg, Pa., 1896–1915)

Sus. Papers   Julian Boyd, ed., *The Susquehanna Company Papers,
1750–1772*, vols. 1–4 (1930–31; reprint, Ithaca, N.Y.,
1962) and Robert Taylor, ed., vols. 5–11 (Ithaca, N.Y.,
1967–71)

Votes   *Pennsylvania Archives*, 8th series

. . . .

NOTES

. . . .

PREFACE

1. John Blair Linn, *Annals of Buffalo Valley* (1877; reprint, Salem, Mass., 1997).

2. Marianne S. Wokeck, *Trade in Strangers* (University Park, Pa., 1999), 244, I.D. no. 211. The Kleckners arrived in Philadelphia on the *Edinburgh* after a sea voyage of more than eight weeks. They probably left Derschen sometime in May 1753.

3. Francis S. Fox, "Kleckners of Pennsylvania," *Pennsylvania Genealogical Magazine* (hereafter *PGM*) 34 (1985): 26–43.

4. David Spurgeon Jenkins, "The Kleckner-Fessler Families in Berks, Schuylkill, Northampton, and Lancaster Counties, Pennsylvania" (1957, typescript), New England Historic Genealogical Society, Boston, Mass.

5. From the preamble to the Constitution of Pennsylvania, 1776.

INTRODUCTION

1. In May 1751, a group of inhabitants led by William Craig presented a petition to the Assembly and requested that the upper part of Bucks County be erected into a new county. A bill was drawn and signed by Governor James Hamilton on March 11, 1752. Thomas Penn named the county Northampton to honor his wife, whose home was situated in Easton-Neston, Northamptonshire, England.

2. Stella H. Sutherland, *Population Distribution in Colonial America* (New York, 1936), 131.

3. The seventeenth 18-penny provincial tax records for Northampton County are unique in two respects. First, Robert Traill, secretary of the County Commissioners, summarized all of the data used to support the sum of money collected and delivered to the provincial treasurer. Thus, although some township records are missing for the year 1774, a complete profile of the county is on record. This profile is recorded on a foldout page and does not appear on the microfilm of the 1774 tax records, the originals of which are found at the Historical Society of Pennsylvania. Second, the Northampton commissioners apparently acted on their own volition and requested constables to collect data about acreage sown in grain, number of children per household under twenty-one years of age, and trades or occupations of the taxpayers. This data, however, is not included in Traill's summary. Mathew S. Henry summarized the additional data from now-missing constable's returns in around 1860. A copy of this summary may be found in the Northampton County

Miscellaneous Manuscripts, box 4, Historical Society of Pennsylvania, Philadelphia (hereafter HSP).

4. The eleven counties embraced about two-thirds of the present state, or some 30,000 square miles. Northumberland was the largest county.

5. The electors nominated, and the justices appointed, the constable. Other elected township officials included an assessor, an inspector of elections, a supervisor of highways, and a poundkeeper. See Wayne L. Bockelman, "Local Colonial Government in Pennsylvania," in *Town and Country*, ed. Bruce C. Daniels (Middletown, Conn., 1978), 216–37.

6. In 1758, an inventory taken by township constables recorded just 671 draft horses, 183 pack horses, and 201 wagons in Northampton. *Pennsylvania Archives*, 119 vols. (Philadelphia and Harrisburg, 1852–1933) (hereafter *Pa. Arch.*), 5th ser., 1:203–23.

7. Charles S. Gladfelder, *Pastors and People*, 2 vols. (Breinigsville, Pa., 1980), 1:341–67.

8. On the eve of the Revolution, Pennsylvania's population had reached about 300,000. Of that number, Moravians accounted for a fraction of one percent, or 2,295 men, women, and children, of which half lived in Northampton County, 555 of them in Bethlehem. Kenneth Gardner Hamilton, *John Ettwein and the Moravian Church During the Revolutionary Period* (Bethlehem, Pa., 1940), 7 n. 14.

9. James Burd to Edward Shippen III, Tinian, January 16, 1772, *Burd-Shippen-Hubley Papers*, HSP, quoted in Randolph Klein, *Portrait of an Early American Family* (Philadelphia, 1975), 147; A. D. Chidsey Jr., *A Frontier Village: Pre-Revolutionary Easton* (Easton, Pa., 1940), 234–65.

10. Philadelphia, Chester, and Bucks Counties each had eight representatives.

11. Between 1764 and 1774, the Assembly tabled seven petitions for additional representation in Northampton.

12. *Pennsylvania Gazette* (hereafter *Pa. Gazette*), December 12, 1765; February 6, 1766; March 27, 1766.

13. Robert Levers to John Arndt, November 6, 1781, *Records of Pennsylvania's Revolutionary Governments, 1775–1790*, Record Group 27 (hereafter RG 27), microfilm, 54 rolls (Harrisburg, Pa.: Pennsylvania Historical and Museum Commission (hereafter PHMC), 1978), roll 19, frame 155 (hereafter roll and frame are cited separated by a colon, as here: 19:155).

14. The rise of the resistance movement in Pennsylvania is examined in great detail by Richard Alan Ryerson, *The Revolution Is Now Begun: The Radical Committees of Philadelphia, 1765–1776* (Philadelphia, 1978).

15. General John Cadwalader and other officers to the Council of Safety, Morristown, N.J., January 14, 1777, *Pa. Arch.*, 1st ser., 5:186–88. Northampton men were bivouacked at Morristown.

16. Joseph Reed to Colonels of Northampton County, August 3, 1779, *Pa. Arch.*, 1st ser., 7:616.

17. Sheriff Jonas Hartzell to Lieutenant Jacob Shoemaker, August 20, 1779, *Pa. Arch.*, 1st ser., 7:655.

18. Joseph Reed to Nicholas Depui, John Chambers, and Jacob Stroud, May 1, 1781, *Pa. Arch.*, 1st ser., 9:113–14.

19. This explanation simplifies the actual course of events. The topic may be pursued beginning with the election returns found in *Pa. Arch.*, 6th ser., 11:257–70.

. . . .

20. John Boyd and John Armstrong Jr. to John Dickinson, August 7, 1784, *Pa. Arch.*, 1st ser., 10:630–32.

21. Petition from inhabitants of Northampton County to President Benjamin Franklin, March 20, 1786, RG 27, 22:862–65.

22. The Militia Act of 1780, which replaced the act of 1777, was repealed in 1793.

CHAPTER 1

1. International Genealogical Index, Church of Jesus Christ of the Latter Day Saints, AG1404, New England Historic Genealogical Society, Boston, Mass. Walter Besant, *London in the Eighteenth Century*, 2 vols. (London, 1903), 2:621; G. W. Hill and H. W. Frere, *Memorials of Stepney Parish with Goscoyne's Map of 1703* (Guildford, England 1890–91). Evidence that Robert Levers of Stepney and the subject of this book are one and the same person is circumstantial but compelling. First, in a letter to Benjamin Franklin, Levers said that he had "now advanced in life to the age of sixty-three and upwards." Robert Levers to Benjamin Franklin, October 21, 1786, *Franklin Letters*, vol. 34, folio 156, Hays Calendar III, 321, film 54-27, American Philosophical Society (hereafter APS), Philadelphia. This date is compatible with the birth of the Robert Levers christened at St. Mary Whitechapel. Second, Levers acquired extensive experience in buying and selling imported goods prior to his arrival in Philadelphia. The docks and warehouses of Stepney would have offered an apprentice clerk this kind of training. Third, the surnames Lever and Leaver are found in numerous British counties, but the name Levers is rarely encountered. Fourth, Robert Levers's second daughter bore the name Elizabeth, which was the given name of Levers's mother. For a description of London in the first half of the eighteenth century, see Daniel Defoe, *A Tour Thro' the Whole Island of Great Britain Divided into Circuits or Journeys*, 4 vols., 5th ed. (London, 1725), 2:85–148. John Lockie, *Topography of London* (1813; reprint, London, 1994). The reprint edition contains an excellent map, which includes Stepney and surrounding parishes in East London.

2. Daniel Defoe walked this stretch of river and "counted ships *en passant*, and found about two thousand sail of all sorts, not reckoning barges, lighters, or pleasure boats, and yachts; but of vessels that really go to sea." Defoe, *Tour of Great Britain*, 141.

3. The belfry topped the courthouse at Second and High Streets. The tower above the State House and the spires above several churches were erected after 1750. Russell F. Weigley, ed., *Philadelphia: A 300-Year History* (New York, 1982), 68–69, 79. London, the world's largest city in 1725 (thirty-six miles in circumference as measured by Defoe), included 146 parishes, 131 charity schools, 8 public schools, 3 colleges, 13 hospitals, 27 public prisons, and 42 markets. Defoe's tally also includes numerous other buildings and squares. Christopher Wren designed the St. Paul's Cathedral of Levers's time. It was the fourth church built on that spot, and it survives today. The height of the tower is 365 feet.

4. Robert Levers's arrival in Philadelphia is mentioned in "A letter to a friend in England c. 1758." This letter, in which Levers described his first ten years in America, is quoted in an address given by Charles R. Roberts to the Northampton Historical Society on May 11, 1926. The address was later published as "Robert Levers, Esq., Revolutionary Patriot," *Lehigh County Historical Society Proceedings*, vol. 4 (1936), 58–61. The original let-

ter has not been found. Roberts may have used "the letter" as a literary device to gather into one essay a few known facts about Levers. George E. McCracken (see below) questions the validity of this letter, saying that the people and events in the letter can be neither proved nor disproved. This is not the case. In addition to Levers's known relationship with Brockden, Captain Randolph, commander of the ship that, according to Levers, brought him to Philadelphia, is identified along with other ships' captains in the *Pennsylvania Gazette*, December 20, 1739. Moreover, that Levers may indeed have had correspondence with someone in England is corroborated to some degree by notices in the *Pennsylvania Gazette*, January 1765 and 1766, which announced that letters awaited Levers at the post office. Levers's date of arrival in Philadelphia may also be inferred from a letter written by James Scull to Levers in 1768, wherein Scull refers to his friendship with Levers, "which had existed for twenty years past." James, the son of Surveyor General Nicholas Scull (himself a deputy surveyor), and Levers doubtless met in the land office sometime between 1748 and 1750. James Scull to Levers, October 30, 1768, Claude W. Unger Collection, HSP, (hereafter CWU). George E. McCracken, "Col. Robert Levers of Pennsylvania," *The American Genealogist* (Des Moines, Iowa), 55 (July 1979): 129–41, 220–32, has been helpful in sorting out Levers's early years in Pennsylvania, especially his land speculations.

5. Charles Brockden (1683–1769) was Philadelphia's recorder of deeds from 1717 to 1767. In 1743 he united with the Moravians, a toponym for members of the Church of the United Brethren. Brockden, together with men like attorney Lewis Weiss, a Moravian who drafted many bills for the Assembly both before and after the Revolution, numbered among those who played important roles behind the scenes in Pennsylvania's provincial and Revolutionary governments. John Clement, "Charles Brockden," *Pennsylvania Magazine of History and Biography* (hereafter *PMHB*) 12 (1888): 185–89.

6. Joseph H. Fairbanks Jr., "Richard Peters (c. 1704–76): Provincial Secretary of Pennsylvania" (Ph.D. diss., University of Arizona, 1972), 80–81, 81 n. 3.

7. Warrant sold to Richard Peters by Robert Levers, October 2, 1750, Peters Papers, vol. 3, 17, HSP.

8. The standard work on eighteenth-century German immigration to Pennsylvania is Wokeck, *Trade in Strangers*.

9. Samuel Wallis to [Abel] James and [Henry] Drinker, Bethlehem, Pa., April 5, 1756, *PMHB* 24 (1900–1901): 381. In this letter Wallis points out that Robert Levers was well acquainted with the "Shawhollock" Lands. Shaholla Creek flows past present Shaholla, Pennsylvania, and into the Lackawaxen River, which marks the present boundary between Pennsylvania and New York.

10. Levers also received unexpected notoriety in Philadelphia when, because of his skill as a penman, the Assembly called him as an expert witness in a libel trial. Details of the contest between the Assembly and Justice William Moore of Chester County are found in *Pa. Arch.*, 8th ser. (hereafter *Votes*), 4:4677–747.

11. Reverend Sven Rosen and others, William N. Schwarze and Ralf Ridgway Hillman, trans., *The Dansbury Diaries, 1748–1755*, bound with Ralf Ridgway Hillman, *Old Dansbury and the Moravian Mission* (Camden, Maine, 1994), 162, 164–65, 229. *The Dansbury Diaries* was first published in a limited edition in 1939. *Old Dansbury and the Moravian Mission* was first published in 1934.

12. "Lists of Pennsylvania Settlers Murdered, Scalped, and Taken Prisoner by Indians,

. . . .

1755–56," *PMHB* 32 (1908): 309–19. A report submitted by Captain Jacob Arndt at Fort Allen on December 16, 1757, contains the names of those killed in Northampton and is included in "Lists."

13. Henry C. Mercer, *The Bible in Iron*, 3rd ed. (Doylestown, Pa., 1961), plates 167–68, quoted in William A. Hunter, *Forts on the Pennsylvania Frontier, 1753–1758* (Harrisburg, Pa., 1960), 218. The inscription is written in German: "Dis ist das Jahr, Darin witet der Inchin Schar."

14. "A letter to a friend." See note 4.

15. Fairbanks, "Richard Peters," 767. Levers to Peters, July 18, 1754, Peters Papers, 3:103–5, HSP.

16. See note 4.

17. Robert Levers to Benjamin Franklin, October 21, 1786, *Franklin Letters*, vol. 34, folio 156, film 54-27, Hays Calendar III, 321, APS.

18. *Pa. Gazette*, March 4, 1756; May 20, 1756.

19. See McCracken, "Col. Robert Levers," 133. One of the purchasers was Joseph Galloway, Speaker of the Assembly, 1765–68; 1769–74. From 1756 to 1774, Levers acted as Galloway's agent in numerous land transactions.

20. McCracken, "Col. Robert Levers," 222ff.

21. See note 4.

22. *Pa. Gazette*, April 27, 1758.

23. Between 1756 and 1763, Levers placed twelve advertisements in the *Pennsylvania Gazette* to publicize his personal services and goods available at his store. These ads appeared on the following dates: March 4 and May 20, 1756; April 27 and November 30, 1758; September 20 and September 27, 1759; May 22 and December 18, 1760; March 19 and June 18, 1761; November 25, 1762; March 17, 1763.

24. Receipt Book of Robert Levers, 1757–79, November 1, 1759, HSP.

25. *PMHB* 32 (1908): 123.

26. The commissioners included Lynford Lardner, Joseph Galloway, and Benjamin Franklin. Leonard W. Larabee, ed., and Whitfield Bell Jr., assoc. ed., *Papers of Benjamin Franklin* (New Haven, Conn., 1966), 10:362–64; 11:221–23, 260–61. A record of money paid to Levers is found in *Votes*, 7:5652, 5666, 5914–21.

27. My interpretation of Robert Levers's activities from 1763 to 1774 is based primarily on the following letters:

Levers to Timothy Horsefield, July 26, 1763, Northampton County Papers Bethlehem and Vicinity, 89, HSP, (hereafter NCPBV).
Levers to Horsefield, August 3, 1763, NCPBV, 97.
Levers to Horsefield, August 9, 1763, NCPBV, 101.
Levers to Horsefield, August 21, 1763, NCPBV, 109.
Levers to James Scull, January 30, 1765, CWU.
Levers to James Scull, August 10, 1765, CWU.
Levers to James Scull, April 4, 1766, CWU.
Levers to James Scull, July 17, 1766, CWU.
Levers to John Scull, October 28, 1766, CWU.
Levers to John Scull, September 17, 1768, CWU.
Levers to John Scull, October 20, 1768, CWU.

John Scull to Levers, October 30, 1768, Northampton County Papers, 3:3–17, HSP, (hereafter NCP).

Levers to [Abel] James (copy), December 29, 1768, NCP, 3:29.

Levers to James Scull, March 9, 1769, CWU.

Levers to James Scull, August 29, 1769, CWU.

Levers to James Scull, September 7, 1769, CWU.

Levers to James Scull, September 20, 1769, CWU.

Levers to Peters, November 7, 1769, NCP, 3:29.

Levers to Peters, June 21, 1770, NCP, 3:29.

Levers to Peters, September 11, 1770, NCP, 3:55.

Levers to Peters, October 28, 1770, NCP, 3:67.

Levers to James Scull, November 2, 1770, CWU.

Levers to Peters, January 12, 1771, NCP, 3:71.

Thomas Asheton to Levers, NCP, box 6.

Levers to Peters, March 18, 1772, NCP, 3:89.

Richard Asheton to Levers, August 19, 1772, NCP, 3:99.

Levers to Thomas Asheton, October 17, 1772, NCP, 3:107.

Levers to James Scull, November 21, 1772, CWU.

Levers to John Lukens, December 21, 1774, Society Collection, HSP.

28. Schwarze and Hillman, *The Dansbury Diaries*, 120.

29. Levers referred to this property as the Mill Place at Hermon. In 1764 he paid £19 for two millstones. Receipt Book of Robert Levers, April 5, 1764.

30. NCP, 2:251. See also Russell Sage Nelson Jr., "Backcountry Pennsylvania (1709–1744): The Ideals of William Penn in Practice" (Ph.D. diss., University of Wisconsin, 1968), chaps. 3 and 4.

31. NCP, 2:241.

32. Native Americans sold all of the land within the present boundaries of Pennsylvania—45,045 square miles, or a little less than 29 million acres—to William Penn, his heirs, and the State of Pennsylvania in a series of thirty-three treaties executed between 1682 and 1792.

33. *Colonial Records of Pennsylvania*, 16 vols. (Philadelphia and Harrisburg, 1851–53) (hereafter *Col. Records*), 9:206, 245, 285, 333. Northampton inhabitants had a long tradition of holding public officials accountable. For example, in 1753 inhabitants complained that Sheriff William Craig held too many jobs and padded the payroll. *Votes*, 4:3547, 3561, 3567, 3570–75.

34. Levers to James Scull, October 20, 1768, CWU.

35. Lewis Gordon, Will no. 853, Register of Wills, Northampton County Courthouse, Easton, Pa.

36. Levers to Abel James, December 29, 1768, a copy of which is included in Levers to Richard Peters, November 7, 1769, NCP, 3:29.

37. Margaret Smith v. Robert Levers, July 6, 1767, NCP, 2:255.

38. Levers to James Scull, July 17, 1766, CWU.

39. Levers to John Lukens, December 21, 1774, Society Collection, HSP. In this letter Levers referred to his financial difficulties in the late 1760s.

40. Levers to James Scull, September 20, 1769, CWU.

. . . .

41. Levers's place (misspelled "Levis") is marked on "A Map of Pennsylvania . . . from the late map of W. Scull Published in 1770," *Pa. Arch.*, 3rd ser., 10.

42. Receipt Book of Robert Levers, June 13, 1770, HSP.

43. Levers to Peters, June 21, 1770, NCP, 3:68.

44. Levers to Peters, September 11, 1770, NCP, 3:55.

45. Levers to Peters, October 21, 1770, NCP, 3:67.

46. Levers to Peters, January 12, 1771, NCP, 3:71. The tumult Levers refers to in this letter is generally known as the Wyoming Controversy, which arose when New England men [from Connecticut] organized a land speculation and began to sell and settle land in Pennsylvania's Wyoming Valley, a region that embraced present Wilkes-Barre. The dispute between Connecticut and Pennsylvania broke out in 1753 and was not resolved until 1807. A brief account of this conflict is found in Philip Klein and Ari Hoogenboom, *A History of Pennsylvania* (New York, 1973), 171–72. The primary source, however, is Julian Boyd, ed., *The Susquehanna Company Papers, 1750–1772*, vols. 1–4 (1930–31; reprint, Ithaca, N.Y., 1962) and Robert Taylor, ed., vols. 5–11 (Ithaca, N.Y., 1967–71) (hereafter *Sus. Papers*).

47. Levers to Peters, March 18, 1772, NCP, 3:89.

48. Ibid.

49. The locations of stores operated by Levers and Stroud are identified as landmarks on Reading Howell's *Map of Pennsylvania* published in 1792. *Pa. Arch.*, 3rd ser., 10.

50. Levers to Thomas Asheton, October 17, 1772, NCP, 3:107.

51. Levers to John Lukens, December 21, 1774, Society Collection, HSP.

52. Mary Levers was indentured to the Grant family of Philadelphia in 1772. *PMHB* 33 (1909): 482.

53. Levers to Peters, January 12, 1771, NCP, 3:68.

54. Copies of the circular letter written by Charles Thomson, secretary of the Philadelphia Committee, and addressed to leaders in all counties are found in J. I. Mombert, *An Authentic History of Lancaster County* (Lancaster, Pa., 1869), 199–200; John Gibson, ed., *History of York County* (Chicago, 1886), 115.

55. The First Provincial Convention convened at Carpenters' Hall, July 17–22, 1774.

56. *Votes*, 8:7100–101.

57. *Pa. Gazette*, November 9, 1774.

58. Robert Traill, *Minutes of the Committee of Observation and Inspection of Northampton County, Pennsylvania*, vol. 4 of *Two Hundred Years of Life in Northampton County, Pa.* (Easton, Pa., 1976) (hereafter *Minutes*). From December 21, 1774, to August 14, 1777, the Northampton Committee met fifty-eight times. A fifty-nineth meeting of all past and present members of the executive committee was scheduled for August 21, 1777, to settle financial accounts, but this meeting, if it took place, does not appear in the minutes. Of the fifty-eight meetings for which there are minutes, the full Committee attended only ten. In the absence of the full Committee, a simple majority of an executive committee with five to nine members acted on behalf of the Committee. Minutes of the Northampton Committee are also found in *Pa. Arch.*, 2nd ser., 2:591–633. This edition, however, is not an accurate copy of the original manuscript. Mid-nineteenth century sensibilities probably led the editor of the *Pennsylvania Archives* to substitute ellipsis points for the words shit and whore. Conversely, the content of the bicentennial edition conforms in nearly every respect to the original manuscript, which is found in Skillman Library,

Lafayette College, Easton, Pennsylvania. Robert Traill recorded the minutes in an eighty-eight-page notebook with a marbleized cover, 32.5 cm high by 19.5 cm wide. Pages 2–8, 16, 24–25, 27–29, and 34 are blank for which, except in one instance, there seems to be no logical explanation. The Committee met on March 1, 1776; however, except for the date and names of those present, the page in the manuscript on which the minutes should appear (26) and three following pages (27–29) are blank. (Neither this omission nor the existence of other blank pages are indicated in any printed version of the minutes.) Curiously, the minutes of the meeting on March 1 appeared in the *Pennsylvania Gazette* on March 20, 1776. It is not likely that the punctilious Traill simply forgot to record them in the minute book. What then?

Admitted to the bar in 1777, Traill, a native of Sanday, Orkney Islands, Scotland, held public office as clerk of county commissioners (1773–79), secretary of the Northampton Committee (1774–77), Northampton sheriff (1781–83), representative in the Assembly (1785–86), member of the state's Supreme Executive Council (1787–88), and associate judge of Northampton County (1796–98). On the life of Robert Traill (1744–1816), see William Traill, *A Genealogical Account of the Traills of Orkney* (Kirkwall, Mainland, 1883); Uzal W. Condit, *The History of Easton . . . 1739–1885* (Easton, Pa., 1889), 71–76; William Henry Egle, *Notes and Queries*, 2nd ser. (Harrisburg, Pa., 1895), 2:4–5; Michael Schrader, *Bench and Bar*, vol. 5 of *Two Hundred Years of Life in Northampton County* (Easton, Pa., 1976), 63–65. In 1821 the original minutes were dedicated to the Easton Library Company (founded 1811) by a stockholder of the then-private library.

59. *John Ettwein Papers*, Archives of the Moravian Church, Bethlehem, Pa., microfilm, (hereafter *Ettwein Papers*), Articles of Association for Allen and Forks Townships, 7:1586–87. Although the language in these two documents differs slightly, it is believed that documents signed by militia in other Northampton townships in the summer of 1775 also emphasized defense and not war.

60. These events took place on April 21 and 25, May 9 and 10, June 14, 15, and 17, 1775.

61. *Pa. Gazette*, May 22, 1776.

62. The best account of events in Pennsylvania leading up to the Declaration of Independence is found in David Freeman Hawke, *In the Midst of a Revolution* (1961; reprint, Westport, Conn., 1980).

63. Peter Force, ed., *The American Archives*, 4th ser. (Washington, D.C., 1837–46), 6:521.

64. Ibid.

65. *Pa. Gazette*, June 5, 1776. On May 27, the Second Battalion assembled at Lawrence Guth's farm, and on May 29, the Fourth Battalion met at John Van Campen's north of Delaware Water Gap.

66. *Minutes*, 44–45.

67. Hamilton, *Ettwein*, 157. The outburst may be attributed to either Frederick Kuhl, a prominent Philadelphian, or Christopher Ludwig, a baker and former president of the German Society in Philadelphia, both of whom had been sent to Easton by the Philadelphia Committee to "incite such of the good people who are friends to liberty." See also Force, *The American Archives*, 6:520.

68. *Minutes*, 45.

69. *Pa. Gazette*, June 5, 1776.

70. Proceedings of the Provincial Conference of Committees, *Pa. Arch.*, 2nd ser., 3:557–82.

71. In some cases the territory of more than one battalion was included in the same election district. Hence, the twenty-three electoral districts cited in the text contained 60 percent of all Pennsylvania militia battalions, or 31 of the 53 total battalions in 1775. Although representatives from 57 battalions appeared at the Convention of Delegates from the Associated Battalions, held at Lancaster, Pennsylvania, on July 4, 1776, it appears that the Provincial Conference, June 18–25, 1776, created the new electoral districts on the basis of 53 battalions. *Pa. Arch.*, 2nd ser., 2:260–68. On June 14, 1777, the Assembly completed the task of gerrymandering the state. In a supplement to the act entitled An Act for Amending the Several Acts for Electing Members of Assembly, the Assembly completed the job started by the Provincial Conference of County Committees and subdivided Philadelphia, Bedford, Westmoreland, and Northumberland Counties for a net gain of twelve voting districts. Only the City of Philadelphia (State House) and Berks County (Reading) continued to provide just one polling place. Hence, after June 1777, Pennsylvanians cast their votes at 41 polling places, compared with 11 before the Revolution. James T. Mitchell and Henry Flanders, comps., *The Statutes at Large of Pennsylvania from 1682 to 1809* (Harrisburg, Pa., 1896–1915) (hereafter *Statutes*), 9:114–23.

72. The authors of this resolution wanted to apply the same formula throughout Pennsylvania; however, the city and county of Philadelphia, as well as the counties of Bucks, Berks, and Bedford, refused to go along. Northumberland also joined the latter group but agreed to move its polling place from Sunbury, the county seat, to a location more accessible to militia rank and file.

73. When Congress called for a resolution declaratory of independence on July 2, 1776, Pennsylvania and Delaware did not approve it. Four of seven Pennsylvania congressmen present cast negative votes. Another vote was taken the next day and this time Pennsylvania—and Delaware—approved the Declaration. Three Pennsylvania congressmen—Benjamin Franklin, James Wilson, and John Morton—cast favorable votes; Thomas Willing and Charles Humphreys opposed the resolution; John Dickinson and Robert Morris abstained. Four of the eight Pennsylvania congressmen (Willing, Humphreys, Dickinson, and Andrew Allen) whose sympathies lay with the crown were replaced by the Constitutional Convention on July 20 with five men who became signatories to the Declaration on August 2, without having been in a position to vote for it: Benjamin Rush, George Clymer, George Ross, James Smith, and George Taylor. Taylor (Northampton) and Smith (York) were the only signers from the Pennsylvania backcountry.

74. *New England Journal and Gazetteer*, July 20, 1776, in *The American Archives*, ed. Peter Force, 5th ser. (Washington, D.C., 1837–46), 1:119. On July 5, 1776, Congress ordered "Copies of the Declaration be sent to the several Assemblies, Conventions, and Councils of Safety, and to the several Commanding Officers of the Continental Troops, that it may be proclaimed in each of the United States, and at the Head of the Army." The next day Pennsylvania's Committee of Safety ordered copies of the Declaration delivered to Bucks, Chester, Lancaster, Northampton, and Berks Counties. *Col. Records*, 10:635. The first public reading of the Declaration occurred on July 8, in Philadelphia. Historians believe that this reading was followed by readings the same day at Trenton and Easton, Pennsylvania, in that order. The standard carried in the Easton parade is said to be the one

. . . .

now displayed in the foyer of the Easton public library. William J. Heller, *Historic Easton* (1911; reprint, Washington, N.J., 1984), 5–7.

75. While delegates to the Constitutional Convention met in the west wing of the State House, Congress convened in the east wing.

76. When the Twelfth Regiment was at Valley Forge, Nigel Gray was court-martialed and convicted of taking money from his troops to supplement their rations and then defrauding them both of the extra food and the money they had paid. He was cashiered, effective June 2, 1778. John B. B. Trussell Jr., *The Pennsylvania Line: Regimental Organization and Operations, 1776–1783* (Harrisburg, Pa., 1977), 133.

77. *Col. Records*, 10:737, 741, 752.

78. *Col. Records*, 11:1; Trussel, *The Pennsylvania Line*, 133–46. The Twelfth Regiment took to the field in mid-December 1776 and joined General Washington's forces for the Battle of Princeton on January 3, 1777.

79. In December 1775, a congressional committee decided "much mischief had arisen for want of regimental paymasters." Rather than trust officers incapable of keeping accounts with large sums of money, the committee recommended that each regiment employ a paymaster. The paymaster's job was a complex task in which he kept all accounts, "especially of clothing to be deducted out of the pay of soldiers." Worthington C. Ford et al., eds., *Journals of the Continental Congress*, 34 vols. (Washington, D.C., 1904–37) (hereafter *JCC*), 3:450; 4:44; 5:418–19. On June 5, 1776, Congress resolved that a civilian paymaster be appointed to each regiment, the allowance for this service to be [blank] dollars a month. In the margin of the *JCC* there appears the following notation opposite the blank: "not agreed to in committee." Congress doubtless resolved the matter of the regimental paymaster's salary, but I could find no record of it in the *JCC*. When Andrew Ledlie of Northampton became surgeon of the Twelfth Regiment in January 1777, he received "thirty-three and one-third dollars a month," compared with Levers's $12. *JCC*, 5:418.

80. General Howe's proclamation is dated November 30, 1776; Lewis Gordon resigned on December 2, 1776. There is no evidence that Gordon accepted Howe's offer of amnesty; however, the proximity of the dates leaves no doubt that the proclamation must have been a major factor in Gordon's decision to leave the Committee. I believe that because the British Army was not more than forty to fifty miles from Easton, word of Howe's intentions circulated in Easton several days before the fact. Howe's sweeping victory in New York probably persuaded men like Gordon that the end of the war was near.

81. *Pa. Arch.*, 1st ser., 5:489–90.

82. Levers to Timothy Matlack, *Pa. Arch.*, 1st ser., 5:332–33.

83. Ibid.

84. Curiously, the office of prothonotary is not mentioned in the Constitution of 1776. However, the framers diluted the prothonotary's power by providing for the establishment in each county of a register's office and an office for recording deeds with incumbents to be appointed by the Assembly. In fact, the Assembly quickly surrendered this patronage to the Supreme Executive Council.

85. Levers to Supreme Executive [Council], March 13, 1777, RG 27, 33:1444. No doubt the last line in Levers's application is a jibe at Robert Lettis Hooper Jr., who had secured an appointment as deputy quartermaster general of the Continental Army, and

who also applied for the prothonotaryship of Northampton County. Hooper, however, never had a chance to become prothonotary because he was known to oppose Pennsylvania's Constitution. Robert Lettis Hooper Jr. to the Executive Council of Pennsylvania, March 6, 1777, RG 27, 33:1217. The following law books are itemized in the appraisal of Levers's estate (see note 153): *Prothonotary's Dictionary*, 2 vols.; *Jacobs Law Dictionary*; *Ainsworth Dictionary*; *Pennsylvania's Laws*; and *Burn's Justice*, 2 vols. By contrast, Lewis Gordon had fifty-three law books in his library.

86. Levers to Supreme Executive [Council], March 13, 1777, RG 27, 33:1444.

87. Levers to Matlack, *Pa. Arch.*, 1st ser., 5:332–33.

88. Levers to President Wharton, October 8, 1777, *Pa. Arch.*, 1st ser., 5:654–55. Levers's letter contains a list of the missing documents, some dating to 1752. Except for Continuance Dockets, which are found in the archives at the Northampton County Courthouse, all court records from 1752 to 1790 have been lost.

89. Ibid. In seven counties it was necessary to issue search and seizure warrants or arrest warrants—or both—compelling colonial prothonotaries to turn over records to the Revolutionary government. Robert L. Brunhouse, *The Counter-Revolution in Pennsylvania, 1776–1790* (Harrisburg, Pa., 1971), 35–36.

90. Levers to President Wharton, October 8, 1777, *Pa. Arch.*, 1st ser., 5:654–55.

91. Ibid.

92. *Continuance Docket #11*, Northampton County Courthouse, Easton, Pa. This docket opens with the following statement: "All actions before September, 1777, are not to be brought forward." It is doubtful that Levers would have taken this action on his own initiative. On the other hand, I have has been unable to discover the source of this directive. Meyer Hart, Easton storekeeper, may have had the most to lose in this decision because he had regularly appeared in court to press for payment of bills.

93. Pennsylvania's government waited until the last minute—September 23, 1777—before it adjourned and fled to Lancaster where it remained until June 1778. Congress adjourned in Philadelphia on September 18, 1777. This body moved first to Lancaster; then, after meeting there one day, proceeded to York, where it remained until June 1778.

94. The Supreme Executive Council ordered that bells be removed from Philadelphia lest the enemy seize them and melt them to make canons and ammunition. The order was carried out in such haste that some bells were sunk in the Delaware River for safekeeping. Two Northampton farmers who had delivered produce to the city carted the State House bell to Allentown where it was hidden in Zion (now Zion Reformed) Church. Richmond E. Myers, *Northampton County in the Revolution* (Easton, Pa., 1976), 47–48.

95. The papers remained with Levers until October 3, when the Assembly doorkeeper retrieved them and carried them off to Lancaster. *Col. Records*, 11:305, 307, 309; *Pa. Arch.*, 1st ser., 5:623; Matlack to Levers, October 3, 1777, RG 27, 12:1116.

96. *Col. Records*, 11:298–99. "A Proclamation by the Supreme Executive Council of Pennsylvania," September 10, 1777.

97. On or about October 3, 1777, the Council's doorkeeper traveled from Lancaster to Easton to retrieve the state papers sent to Levers for safekeeping. No doubt Levers received a full briefing at that time on the precarious state of affairs in Pennsylvania. *Pa. Arch.*, 1st ser., 5:645.

98. Warrant to Arrest Lewis Gordon, August 6, 1777, *Pa. Arch.*, 1st ser., 5:490.

99. Thomas Affleck Sr. was one of twenty-two Quaker merchants who, because of

their refusal to swear allegiance to the new government, had been deported by the Council to Virginia in September 1777. *Col. Records*, 11:296.

100. Lewis Gordon leased the ferry from the Penn family in 1762. Peters Manuscripts, 1752–62, 117, HSP.

101. Robert Levers to President Wharton, October 8, 1777, *Pa. Arch.*, 1st ser., 5:650–52; Henry F. Marx, "Oaths of Allegiance of Northampton County Pennsylvania, 1777–1784 . . ." (1932, typescript), Marx History Room, Easton Public Library, Easton, Pa.

102. *Statutes*, 9:147–49. A Supplement to the Act, Entitled, "An Act Obliging the Male White Inhabitants . . . ," passed October 12, 1777.

103. *Col. Records*, 11:325–28. "By the Council of Safety of the Commonwealth of Pennsylvania: A Proclamation," October 17, 1777. The Council of Safety consisted of the duly elected Supreme Executive Council and nine civilian appointees. The Supreme Executive Council met separately during this period, primarily to take care of housekeeping matters. The emergency Council of Safety was dissolved shortly after the Second General Assembly convened on November 20, 1777.

104. *Col. Records*, 11:325–28.

105. *Col. Records*, 11:323–53. Minutes of the Council of Safety.

106. Levers to Matlack, November 12, 1777, RG 27, 12:1343.

107. Levers to Matlack, November 15, 1777, *Pa. Arch.*, 1st ser., 6:5–7.

108. Levers to Matlack, November 12, 1777, RG 27, 12:1343–46.

109. Levers to Matlack, November 15, 1777, RG 27, 12:1343.

110. Ibid.

111. Levers to Matlack, December 8, 1777, RG 27, 13:193; *Pa. Arch.*, 1st ser., 6:76–79.

112. Militia officers fined both men as delinquents.

113. Deposition of Alexander Sillman, January 6, 1778, NCP, 3:179.

114. Levers to Matlack, March 7, 1778, RG 27, 13:921.

115. Levers to Matlack, March 9, 1778, RG 27, 13:935–37.

116. For details of Levers's battle with John Gordon and other persons suspected of traveling into and out of Philadelphia, see Levers to Matlack, February 23, 1778, RG 27, 13:850; Levers to Matlack, March 7, 1778, RG 27, 13:921; Levers to Matlack, March 8, 1778, RG 27, 13:927.

117. Council to Levers, March 21, 1778, RG 27, 13:1041.

118. Levers to Matlack, May 20, 1778, *Pa. Arch.*, 1st ser., 6:534.

119. On July 6, 1778, news of the massacre at Wyoming reached Easton. Levers immediately informed the Council and verified the information by including a deposition from an eyewitness. On the same day, Levers also wrote to his boss, Colonel Isaac Melchoir, Barrack Master General. In the text, I have combined the contents of the two letters. Levers to George Bryan, July 6, 1778, *Pa. Arch.*, 1st ser., 6:626–27; Deposition of Captain Alexander Patterson, Twelfth Regiment, by Robert Levers, July 6, 1778, in *Papers of the Continental Congress, 1774–1789*, 204 reels (Washington, D.C., 1959–) (hereafter *PCC*), M247, r66, i53, 59, microfilm; Levers to Colonel Isaac Melchoir, Barrack Master General, July 6, 1778, *PCC*, M247, r98, i78, v14, 231. As an assistant barrack master Levers was required to file a "return every month of the wood, straw, candles, boards, etc. issued at [his] post." It was the perfect job for a former storekeeper. A more precise

. . . .

description of Levers's duties may be found under the general order of January 1, 1778, Barrack Master General's Office, *PCC*, M247, r99, i7, v15, 417.

120. Fear of Indian incursions on the frontier prompted delegates at Pennsylvania's Constitutional Convention to remind Congress of the danger, especially in Northumberland and Northampton Counties, where "farms are widely scattered and many men are now absent from their homes serving in the militia." But some men who lived in Lehigh Valley refused to serve in the militia because "they were repeatedly told the Indians would be down upon them immediately." *Journals of the House of Representatives of the Commonwealth of Pennsylvania Beginning the twenty-eighth Day of November, 1776, and Ending the second Day of October, 1781, With the Proceedings of the several Committees and Conventions, Before and after the Commencement of the American Revolution* (Philadelphia, 1782) (hereafter *JHR*), 75, Boston Athenaeum, Boston; Report of Northampton Co. Associators (Militia), Third Battalion, August 5, 1776, RG 27, 10:820–21.

121. Colonel Jacob Stroud to John Wetzel, Fort Penn, July 17, 1778, *Pa. Arch.*, 1st ser., 6:651.

122. "Count Casimir Pulaski," *PMHB* 55 (1931): 1–23.

123. Circular of Council, July 14, 1778, *Pa. Arch.*, 1st ser., 6:638–41.

124. Levers to Bryan, August 25, 1778, *Pa. Arch.*, 1st ser., 6:719–20. As Levers had correctly forecasted, Northampton was not the place for Pulaski's Legion, which pulled out in the summer of 1779 and headed for South Carolina, parading two banners made for them by Moravian women.

125. Levers to Matlack, August 25, 1778, *Pa. Arch.*, 1st ser., 6:721.

126. Levers to Council, October 17, 1778, *Pa. Arch.*, 1st ser., 7:15–16.

127. Colonel Stroud to Council, October 25, 1778, *Pa. Arch.*, 1st ser., 7:62–63.

128. In the next two and a half years Levers wrote just seven letters to the Council—compared with sixteen in the preceding ten months—most of which dealt with routine business carried on in his capacity as county prothonotary. Levers to Council, January 31, 1779, *Pa. Arch.*, 1st ser., 7:157–58; Levers to Matlack, February 23, 1979, RG 27, 14:1040–41; Levers to Matlack, August 3, 1779, RG 27, 15:205; Levers to Matlack, August 20, 1779, RG 27, 15:243; Levers to Matlack, March 8, 1780, RG 27, 15:978; Levers to Council, April 13, 1780, *Col. Records*, 12:316; Levers to Joseph Dean, May 11, 1780, RG 27, 16:10.

129. President Reed to the colonels and field officers of the Northampton militia, August 3, 1779, *Pa. Arch.*, 1st ser., 7:616.

130. Reed to Nicholas Depui, John Chambers, and Jacob Stroud, May 1, 1781, *Pa. Arch.*, 1st ser., 9:113–14.

131. Reed to Levers, June 25, 1781, *Pa. Arch.*, 1st ser., 9:227.

132. Levers to Reed, July 13, 1781, *Pa. Arch.*, 1st ser., 9:275–76.

133. Levers to Reed, July 6, 1781, *Pa. Arch.*, 2nd ser., 3:496–97.

134. Ibid.

135. Reed to Levers, July 10, 1781, *Pa. Arch.*, 1st ser., 9:268–69.

136. Levers to Reed, July 29, 1781, RG 27, 18:827–30.

137. Reed to Levers, July 30, 1781, *Pa. Arch.*, 1st ser., 9:323.

138. Levers to Reed, August 7, 1781, *Pa. Arch.*, 1st ser., 9:339–40.

. . . .

139. Reed to Levers, August 10, 1781, *Pa. Arch.*, 1st ser., 9:348–49; Reed to Levers, August 28, 1781, *Pa. Arch.*, 1st ser., 9:377–78.

140. Levers to Reed, September 10, 1781, RG 27, 18:1195.

141. Levers to Northampton sublieutenants, October 6, 1781, RG 27, 19:47–49.

142. Levers to President William Moore, May 25, 1782, RG 27, 19:757.

143. Levers to Moore, July 10, 1782, *Pa. Arch.*, 1st ser., 9:578–79.

144. Levers to President Dickinson, January 25, 1783, *Pa. Arch.*, 1st ser., 9:742–44.

145. John Armstrong to Levers, June 12, 1783, RG 27, 20:491.

146. Levers to Armstrong, June 23, 1783, RG 27, 20:559.

147. Levers to Council, June 25, 1785, RG 27, 22:259.

148. Deposition of Robert Levers before magistrate Peter Rhoads, September 21, 1785, NCP, 4:129.

149. Levers to Benjamin Franklin, October 9, 1785, *Franklin Letters*, vol. 33, folio 210, Hays Calendar III, 279, APS.

150. Levers to Franklin, October 21, 1786, *Franklin Letters*, vol. 34, folio 156, Hays Calendar III, 321, APS.

151. Levers to Peters, November 28, 1786, NCP, box 6; Robert Levers to John Lardner, March 6, 1787, Lardner Papers, HSP; Levers to Council, June 21, 1787, Society Collection, HSP; Levers to President Franklin and Council, December 9, 1787, RG 27, 46:316.

152. Robert Traill to President Franklin, May 21, 1788, *Pa. Arch.*, 1st ser., 11:289.

153. Letter of Administration issued to Mary Levers, Widow, and George Levers, August 22, 1788, on behalf of Robert Levers, #1228, Register of Wills, Northampton County Courthouse, Easton, Pa.

CHAPTER 2

1. Lewis Gordon's early years are a mystery. That he was a Scotsman is confirmed by the fact that he was a charter member of the St. Andrew's Society of Philadelphia, and society bylaws stipulated that members must be native-born or sons of native-born Scotsmen. A. D. Chidsey Jr., "Lewis Gordon, Northampton County's First Lawyer," in *A Frontier Village: Pre-Revolutionary Easton*, vol. 3 (Easton, Pa., 1940), 144–45. That Gordon was an educated man is inferred from the fact that he had a library of nearly 200 volumes, a large personal collection for that period. In addition to more than fifty law books, Gordon's library contained titles on religion, history, travel, and collections of letters. Lewis Gordon, Will no. 853, Register of Wills, Northampton County Courthouse, Easton, Pa.

2. Gordon acquired warrants for three tracts of land in Bucks County on November 1, 1745. Land Office, Harrisburg, Pa., Patent Book A-14, 519.

3. Gordon and a partner advertised in the *Pennsylvania Gazette* that they would draw "all kinds of deeds, and instruments of writing . . . at their office in Front Street . . . where dispatch and constant attendance will be given." *Pa. Gazette*, September 25, 1746.

4. William Penn and his heirs appointed members of the executive branch of Pennsylvania's colonial government. The Penns were the sole proprietors of this colony. The senior member of the Penn family held the position of governor. In practice, however, he appointed a deputy governor who resided in Philadelphia and administered the

province. Generally, the deputy governor is referred to as the governor. In its broadest application, the term proprietaries refers to the Penn family, its appointees, and its political allies.

5. Gordon married Mary Jenkins, daughter of Aaron Jenkins, on January 4, 1749. They had six children: Elizabeth (1750), Isabella (1753), John (1755), Aaron (1757), William (1760), and Alexander (1762).

6. Dr. Thomas Graeme, associate justice of the Pennsylvania Supreme Court, was the first president of the society. He was followed in 1750 by Governor James Hamilton and in 1754 by Governor Robert Hunter Morris.

7. Andrew D. Chidsey Jr., "William Parsons, Easton's First Citizen," *Pennsylvania History* (hereafter *Pa. History*) 7 (1940): 89–102; John W. Jordan, "William Parsons: Surveyor General and Founder of Easton, Pennsylvania," *PMHB* 33 (1909): 340–46.

8. Alexander Graydon, *Memoirs of His Own Times with Reminiscences of the Men and Events* (Philadelphia, 1811), 102. Because English was the official language of all court proceedings and legal business, Graydon rightly observed that the "English-speaking prothonotary of a county of German population was the most considerable personage in it."

9. The office of prothonotary is unique to Pennsylvania and Delaware. Francis S. Fox, "The Prothonotary: Linchpin of Provincial and State Government in Eighteenth-Century Pennsylvania," *Pa. History* 59 (January 1992): 41–53.

10. Michael C. Schrader, *Bench and Bar*, vol. 5 of *Two Hundred Years of Life in Northampton County, Pa.* (Easton, Pa., 1976), 23, 179.

11. *Pa. Gazette*, December 21, 1754.

12. *Pa. Arch.*, 1st ser., 2:521.

13. See *Pa. Gazette*, April 1, 1756, for the announcement by Lewis Gordon that he had left Easton and opened an office in Bordentown, New Jersey.

14. Howard N. Eavenson, *Map Maker and Indian Traders: An account of John Patten trader, arctic explorer, and map maker; Charles Swaine author, trader, public official, and arctic explorer; Theodorsus Swaine Drage clerk, trader, and Anglican priest* (Pittsburgh, 1949), 46–51, 71–84.

15. Swaine's voyage to search for the Northwest Passage is described at length in *Pa. Gazette*, November 15, 1753. In this report there is mention of Moravians who had been set ashore on Labrador in 1752. On this voyage, Swaine's ship, the *Argo*, met seven other ships within the Arctic Circle.

16. The Pennamite Wars occurred in 1769–71, 1774, and 1784.

17. *Sus. Papers*, 1:109, 169. Two men named Aaron Depui and Emanuel Gonzales bought shares on the spot. Nicholas Depui, Aaron's nephew, and Gonzales later became members of Northampton's Revolutionary committee.

18. William Parsons to Peters, December 5, 1753, Connecticut Claims, I, 6, HSP, copy in *Sus. Papers*, 1:42, 368–69; Deposition of Martin Tidd, January 30, 1784, *Pa. Arch.*, 1st ser., 10:196–97; for additional background on this incident see correspondence between President John Dickinson and Major James Moore, *Pa. Arch.*, 1st ser., 10:187–88, 197–98, 207–8.

19. Parsons to James Hamilton, February 21, 1754, Penn Papers, Official Correspondence, VI, 157, HSP, copy in *Sus. Papers*, 1:52.

20. Daniel Brodhead to James Hamilton, February 8, 1754, *Sus. Papers*, 1:54; William Allen to Brodhead, March 16, 1754, James Hamilton to Brodhead, March 17, 1754, Penn

· · · · · · · ·

Papers, Official Correspondence, VI, 167, 169, HSP, copies in *Sus. Papers*, 1:66, 68; Brodhead to Peters, November 13, 1754, *Col. Records*, 6:253–54, copy in *Sus. Papers*, 2:152–54.

21. Peters to Gordon, September 15, 1760, PHMC, Provincial Papers, XXX, 81, copy in *Sus. Papers*, 2:24.

22. Gordon to Peters, October 2, 1760, PHMC, Provincial Papers, XXX, 95, copy in *Sus. Papers*, 2:28–29.

23. Gordon and others to James Hamilton, February 17, 1761, Penn Papers, Connecticut Claims, V, 65, copy in *Sus. Papers*, 2:29–32.

24. Thomas Penn to James Hamilton, August 7, 1761, Penn Letter Book, VII, 53–59, HSP, copy in *Sus. Papers*, 2:104.

25. Governor's Proclamation, *Sus. Papers*, 2:115–16; Brodhead to James Hamilton (?), September 27, 1762, Penn Papers, Connecticut Claims, V, 63, HSP, copy in *Sus. Papers*, 2:166–70.

26. Richard Peters's Diary, May 21, 1762, HSP, copy in *Sus. Papers*, 2:134.

27. Peters to Gordon, September 1761, *Pa. Arch.*, 1st ser., 4:70–71, copy in *Sus.Papers*, 2:42–43.

28. *Pa. Gazette*, December 12, 1765; February 6, 1766; March 27, 1766.

29. See Introduction, note 3.

30. Gordon to Edmund Physic, August 14, 1769, Penn Papers, Connecticut Claims, I, 26, HSP, copy in *Sus. Papers*, 3:163–65. See also Gordon to Physic, August 7, 1769, Penn Papers, Connecticut Claims, I, 25, copy in *Sus. Papers*, 3:157–59; Physic to Thomas Penn, April 20, 1769, Penn-Physic Manuscripts, III, 9–13, copy in *Sus. Papers*, 3:100–106; a petition from the "back inhabitants" to Governor Penn, March 27, 1769, *Sus. Papers*, 3:103.

31. John Penn to Thomas Penn, January 1, 1770, Penn Manuscripts, Private Correspondence, V, 113, HSP, copy in *Sus. Papers*, 4:1–3.

32. Gordon to James Tilghman, August 11, 1771, *Col. Records*, 9:755, copy in *Sus. Papers*, 4:238–39.

33. Thomas Penn to John Penn, February 26, 1770, Penn Letter Book, X, 43–49, HSP; copy in *Sus. Papers*, 4:29–30.

34. Charles R. Roberts estimated the 1752 population of Northampton County to be 5,900 people. Roberts doubtless based his numbers on the work of J. H. Battle, published in 1887. How Battle arrived at these numbers is unknown, but he may have had access to oral historians and data now missing. See *Lehigh County Historical Society Proceedings*, 1:73; J. H. Battle, *History of Bucks County* (1887; reprint, Spartansburg, S.C., 1985), 211. Later population estimates are based on the work of Stella B. Sutherland, *Population Distribution in Colonial America* (New York, 1936), 124–43, and Evarts B. Green and Virginia D. Harrington, *American Population Before the Federal Census of 1790* (New York, 1932), 116.

35. Parliament passed four so-called coercive or "Intolerable Acts" in the first half of 1774: the Boston Port Bill, March 31; the Massachusetts Government Act, May 20; the Administration of Justice Act, May 20; the Quartering Act, June 2. The first three acts were directed at Massachusetts, the fourth applied to all North American Colonies.

36. The most comprehensive account of Pennsylvania's resistance movement is Ryerson, *Revolution*.

37. Copies of the circular letter written by Charles Thomson, secretary of the

. . . .

Philadelphia Committee, addressed to leaders in all counties are found in J. I. Mombert, *An Authentic History of Lancaster County* (Lancaster, 1869), 199–200; John Gibson, ed., *History of York County* (Chicago, 1886), 115. The author assumes that a copy was ear- marked for Taylor, and possibly Gordon, although there is no evidence that either man received this important call for action from the Philadelphia Committee.

38. In the period 1752 to 1775, I have found only two references to Philadelphia politicians who visited Northampton County on professional business. During the early years of the French and Indian War, Benjamin Franklin traveled to the county to establish a line of defense. In 1774, after radicals learned that Northampton had elected a commit- tee of correspondence and declared in favor of Pennsylvania's resistance movement, John Dickinson, Thomas Mifflin, and Charles Thomson, leaders of the Philadelphia Committee—accompanied by their wives and, in Thomson's case, his fiancée—toured Northampton and Berks Counties "under colour of an excursion of pleasure" to win sup- port for the resistance movement. The "tourists" visited Bethlehem on June 27. Since two members of the Northampton Committee were Moravians, it is likely that Bethlehem facilitated a meeting between the Northampton Committee and the trio from Philadelphia. It is also certain that the men involved had known each other for years. *Bethlehem Diary*, June 27, 1774, 487, in The Archives of the Moravian Church, Bethlehem, Pa.; Mrs. Deborah Logan to ?, n.d., in Charles J. Stille, *Life and Times of John Dickinson* (Philadelphia, 1891), 311–15; Charles Thomson to David Ramsay, November 4, 1786, The Charles Thomson Papers, *Collections of the New York Historical Society* XI (1878), 279.

39. See *Pa. Gazette*, June 29, 1774, for proceedings of the meeting in the Easton courthouse on June 21, 1774.

40. The six men appointed to the committee were well known in the county. Their ages ranged from forty-nine to sixty-six. All but one was a justice of the peace. All of them had lived many years in the region but none was born in America. The names of the com- mitteemen, their ages, and places of birth are as follows: Lewis Gordon, fifty-four, Scotland (?); George Taylor, fifty-eight, England or Ireland (his origin is disputed); Peter Kachlein, fifty-two, Germany; Jacob Arndt, forty-nine, Germany; William Edmunds, sixty-six, England; John Okely, fifty-three, England. On Lewis Gordon, see note 1. On George Taylor, see Charles Laubach, "George Taylor—The Signer," *Bucks County Historical Society Collections* (hereafter *BCHSC*) 1 (1908), 332, Doylestown, Pa.; B. F. Fackenthal, "The Durham Ironworks in Durham Township (Bucks County)," *BCHSC* 7 (1937), 59–94; Mildred Rowe Trexler, *George Taylor, Esquire* (Allentown, Pa., 1968); Spencer Lodge Windle, *A History of Warwick Furnace* (1945; reprint, West Chester, Pa., 1975). On Peter Kachlein, county commissioner (1760–62) and sheriff (1764–66, 1770–73), see E. Gordon Alderfer, *Northampton Heritage* (Easton, Pa., 1953), 108–9; Richmond E. Meyers, *Northampton County in the American Revolution* (Easton, Pa., 1976), 69–71. On Jacob Arndt, see John Stover Arndt, *The Story of the Arndt Family* (Philadelphia, 1922); William Henry Egle, "The Constitutional Convention of 1776," *PMHB* 3 (1878): 99; The Arndt Family Bible in William Henry Egle, *Notes and Queries*, Annual Volume, 1897 (Harrisburg, Pa., 1898), 170–74. On William Edmunds, see Joseph Levering, *A History of Bethlehem, Pennsylvania, 1741–1892* (Bethlehem, Pa., 1903), index of persons; William C. Reichel, *Memorials of the Moravian Church* (Philadelphia, 1870), 244n; Egle, *Notes and Queries*, 3rd ser. (Harrisburg, Pa., 1896), 3:202–3, 537–40, 542–44. On John Okely, see Levering, *Bethlehem*, 124 and index of persons; Reichel, *Memorials*,

187; Kenneth G. Hamilton, trans. and ed., *The Bethlehem Diary, 1742–1744* (Bethlehem, Pa., 1971), index; Isaac E. Wade, ed., *Okely: A Pedigree and Family History* (Pittsburgh, 1899), 14–16.

41. Lewis Gordon, Will no. 853, Register of Wills, Northampton County Courthouse, Easton, Pa. Gordon apparently had no idea who in Boston should receive the money so he held the funds in trust.

42. *Pa. Gazette*, June 29, 1774; *Pennsylvanischer Staatsbote*, July 5, 1774.

43. *JCC*, 1:74–80. Congress proclaimed the embargo in a paper entitled "The Continental Association." Guidelines for electing committees and operating them are found in Article 11. Congress directed that elections for committees of observation and inspection be conducted in the same manner as "regular" elections. Because of the season of the year and the great distance that separated most inhabitants from the polling place in Easton, probably no more than 10 or 15 percent of Northampton's estimated 1,200 eligible voters cast ballots for the committee. Every colony but Georgia had formed committees and joined in the boycott by April 1775. To preserve its rice trade with Great Britain while maintaining good relations with the other twelve colonies, Georgia later adopted a modified version of the boycott. An excellent discussion of government by county committee is found in David Ammerman, *In the Common Cause: America's Response to the Coercive Acts of 1774* (Charlottesville, Va., 1974), 103–24.

44. Walter H. Conser Jr. et al., eds., *Resistance, Politics, and the American Struggle for Independence, 1765–1775* (Boulder, Colo., 1976), 510.

45. As to the presence of Emanuel Gonzales in Northampton one guess is as good as another. Emanuel Gonzales may have been a sailor who was captured by the British. Handed over to authorities in Philadelphia about 1746, Gonzales escaped and somehow made his way north to the frontier. *Col. Records*, 5:123, 125, 131, 232, 238, 281. Gonzales was elected justice of the peace in 1777. On April 13, 1780, Indians and Tories attacked and destroyed his home and mill. Gonzales and a hired man were seized and taken away, but his wife and other women and children were spared. The fate of the captives is unknown. *Pa. Arch.*, 1st ser., 8:188–89, 551.

46. Committee minutes list 30 rather than 29 members. This can be explained by the fact that George Taylor resigned sometime in February or March and John Hays Jr. was named to replace him. The secretary, perhaps mistakenly, recorded both men as being present at the first meeting.

47. William Darlington, comp., "Pennsylvania Weather Records, 1644–1835," *PMHB* 15 (1891): 109–12. Twelve days earlier "a great fall of snow" caused the cancellation of a meeting of the Bucks County Committee. *Pa. Gazette*, January 4, 1775.

48. Force, *American Archives*, 4th ser., 1:1180. A wether is a male sheep castrated before sexual maturity. Article 7 of the Association resolves to improve the breed of sheep, to increase their number, and to kill them as seldom as possible.

49. Convention minutes are found in *Pa. Arch.*, 2nd ser., 3:625–31. For general accounts of the convention, see Ryerson, *Revolution*, 100–102; Theodore Thayer, *Pennsylvania Politics and the Growth of Democracy: 1750–1776* (Harrisburg, Pa., 1953), 163–64; Helen E. Royer, "The Role of the Continental Congress in the Prosecution of the American Revolution in Pennsylvania" (Ph.D. diss., The Pennsylvania State University, 1960), 42–46.

50. The letter was dated April 18, 1775, but neither the original letter nor a copy

has been found. There is little doubt, however, that Gordon received such a letter. The reconstruction of the letter in the text is based on the action taken by the Northampton Committee on May 6, 1775. See *Minutes*, 38. This communication, doubtless a circular letter addressed to all county committees, probably resulted in the mobilization of militia in Berks and Bedford Counties before April 26, when news of the Battle of Lexington and Concord reached Philadelphia. The quotation is found in the articles of association drawn up and signed by the associators of Allen Township, Northampton County, May 20, 1775. The men of Forks Township made a similar pledge about the same time. *Ettwein Papers*, 7:1586–87. A catalog of the *Ettwein Papers* is found in Hamilton, *Ettwein*, 298–338.

51. On Robert Towers and the Philadelphia Committee, see *PMHB* 54 (1930): 125. In July 1775, Pennsylvania's Committee appointed Towers general agent for military stores.

52. *Minutes*, 36, 78.

53. *Pennsylvania Evening Post*, June 10, 1775.

54. *Minutes*, 36–41. In 1775, a company in the continental line consisted of 68 privates, 4 sergeants, 4 corporals, 4 officers, and a drummer. The 43 officers and 755 enlisted men of the Pennsylvania Rifle Battalion (Northampton men were designated company F), under the command of Colonel William Thompson of Carlisle, Pennsylvania, saw its first action on August 27, 1775, when the British attacked the American line at Ploughed Hill, Cambridge, Massachusetts. Trussell, *Pennsylvania Line*, 21–31. Names of the men in the Northampton Company are found in *Pa. Arch.*, 5th ser., 2:35–36.

55. Lewis Gordon and Peter Kachlein to Honorable Delegates [in Congress] for the Province of Pennsylvania, July 13, 1775, Gratz Collection, case 4, box 20, HSP.

56. *Col. Records*, 10:543–44. The Committee of Safety included thirteen assemblymen and twelve laypersons. The nineteen subcommittees included those for powder and arms, accounts, fire raft, floating battery, pikes and entrenching tools, powder house, firelocks, barracks, and further defense.

57. *Col. Records*, 10:441, 456, 465, 520. Gordon to Committee of Safety, February 9, 1776, RG 27, 10:270–72.

58. *Pa. Arch.*, 2nd ser., 1:592. In this letter Gordon passes on "stand ready" orders from the Committee of Safety dated March 19 and 23, 1776. Copies of these letters, which were sent to all county committees, are found in the minutes of the Bucks County Committee. *Pa. Arch.*, 2nd ser., 15:357; see also *Col. Records*, 10:522.

59. RG 27, 10:270–72.

60. *Minutes*, 55.

61. The Constitutional Convention appointed a Council of Safety (July 23, 1776, to March 17, 1777) with twenty-five members to replace the Committee of Safety and govern the state until a new government was formed. See Ryerson, *Revolution*, 235, 241–43.

62. The Committee functioned like a tribunal and met forty-three times between June 1776 and May 1777. The *Minutes* contain numerous examples of the Committee's reliance on hearsay evidence.

63. *Minutes*, 58, "The State of Pennsylvania vs. Joseph and Robert Stackhouse."

64. *Minutes*, 59.

65. *JHR*, 75.

66. Ibid.

. . . .

67. See Andrew Ledlie's petition for remission of a fine for an assault and battery, December 13, 1790, RG 27, 41:1218–22.

68. Pennsylvania's Constitutional Convention of 1776 met in the west wing of Philadelphia's State House from July 15 to September 28.

69. John W. Jordan, "Bethlehem During the Revolution," *PMHB* 12 (1888): 390–91. Nineteen militia companies from Berks County and the section of Lancaster known as Lebanon (that part of the county nearest to Blue Mountain) passed through Bethlehem in August 1776.

70. Levering, *Bethlehem*, 450.

71. In February 1777, Captain John Arndt, who had lost an arm in battle, successfully petitioned the Assembly for the new position of county recorder of deeds. In the colonial government, this work had been performed by the county prothonotary.

72. See Chapter 1, note 80.

73. *Pa. Arch.*, 1st ser., 5:489–90. Lewis Gordon was the only prothonotary arrested by Pennsylvania's Revolutionary government. See Fox, "The Prothonotary," *Pa. History* 59 (January 1992): 41–53. That Gordon was a charter subscriber to James Burgh's *Political Disquisitions* may reveal something of the prothonotary's tormented state of mind on the eve of the Revolution. James Burgh, *Political Disquisitions*, 3 vols. (London, vols. 1 and 2, 1774; vol. 3, October 1775; and Philadelphia, vols. 1 and 2, June 1775; vol. 3, October 1775). Burgh's works "received their most sympathetic response from disgruntled colonists, in particular from the future leaders of the new American nation." James O. Baylen and Norbert J. Gossman, eds., *Biographical Dictionary of Modern British Radicals* (Atlantic Highlands, N.J., 1979), 1:72–76. Not surprisingly, the Burgh volumes do not appear in the inventory of Gordon's extensive library that was taken shortly after his death in 1778. Steve Smith called to my attention that Gordon numbered among the subscribers to Bell's edition of James Burgh's work.

74. An Act for the Further Security of the Government, April 1, 1778, required persons who would enjoy the rights of citizenship in the Commonwealth of Pennsylvania to take the oath, or have their property confiscated and be subject to banishment from the state. *Statutes*, 10:238–45.

75. *Pa. Arch.*, 1st ser., 6:534.

CHAPTER 3

1. This account is drawn from details found in *Minutes*, 63–67. All quotations are found within the pages indicated.

2. *Minutes*, 67. Long's companions, Christopher Bowman and Frederick Garres, also secured their freedom by posting a bond. To simplify the narrative, I have excluded them from the account in this text. The Committee also required Captain Mack to post a bond, perhaps because he refused to arrest Long and bring him to Easton.

3. *Statutes*, 10:201–15.

4. Edward Long, not Elias Long, is named in the proclamation dated June 15, 1778. *Col. Records*, 11:515. A clerk may have erred and recorded Edward for Elias, or perhaps Elias had a brother named Edward who also defected. Either way, there is no doubt that Elias Long defected to the enemy because the seizure of his property is a matter of record. I am grateful to Anne M. Ousterhout for sharing notes gleaned in the course of her

. . . .

research for "The Forgotten Antagonists: The Pennsylvania Loyalists" (Ph.D. diss., Michigan State University, 1972). Her list of disaffected men in Pennsylvania includes 72 from Northampton, of whom 25, including Elias Long, hailed from Mount Bethel. Since it is generally believed that most Scots-Irish supported the Revolution, Ms. Ousterhout and I question why so many Scots-Irish in Mount Bethel were disaffected. Except for the geographical remoteness of the township, there seems to be no plausible answer. For a broad discussion of opposition to the Revolution in Pennsylvania, see Anne M. Ousterhout, *A State Divided: Opposition in Pennsylvania to the American Revolution* (Westport, Conn., 1987).

5. *Pa. Arch.*, 6th ser., 12:368. This entry contains the inventory of Long's possessions.

6. Ibid.

7. Ibid., 12:232, 464–65, 13:235. The wives cited are Mary Thomas and Margaret Pugh.

8. A Petition from a Committee of Northampton County to Jacob Arndt, Jonas Hartzell, Jacob Stroud, Robert Lattimore, and Peter Kohler, Esquires, August 20, 1783, Society Collection, HSP. All of the signers of this petition viewed themselves as "virtuous, honest Whigs," none more so than Chairman Henry Geiger who, on more than one occasion, had rallied Northampton inhabitants to support a cause. David Hartley, Benjamin Franklin, John Adams, and John Jay—the men who negotiated and signed the provisional treaty in November 1782—signed the definitive treaty in September 1783. Congress ratified the Treaty of Paris in January 1784. A copy of the treaty is found in William Macdonald, *Select Documents Illustrative of the History of the United States, 1776–1861* (New York, 1911), 15–21.

9. Ibid.

10. Northampton County Tax List, 1781, 1782, 1787, 1788, 1793, 1794, 1808–15. Church of Jesus Christ of the Latter Day Saints, microfilm, New England Historic Genealogical Society, Boston, Mass.

CHAPTER 4

1. William H. Hinke, *Pennsylvania German Pioneers: A Publication of the Original Lists of Arrivals in the Port of Philadelphia from 1727–1808*, ed. Ralph Beaver Strassburger, 3 vols. (1934; reprint, Baltimore, Md., 1966), 1:242, 2:440. Geiger arrived on the ship *Priscilla* on September 11, 1749.

2. Jacob Geiger, Henry's brother, lived in present Montgomery County. This is confirmed by notice of the marriage of Elizabeth Geiger, Jacob's daughter, to Jacob Arndt in 1745. Jacob Geiger and Jacob Arndt Sr., the groom's father, were members of Christ Reformed Church at Indian Creek, Franconia Township, present Montgomery County. See Arndt Family Bible in Egle, *Notes and Queries, Annual Volume, 1897*, 170–74; Arndt, *Arndt Family;* International Genealogical Index, Church of Jesus Christ of the Latter Day Saints, P0753, New England Historic Genealogical Society, Boston, Mass.

3. *Pa. Arch.*, 5th ser., 1:63. On Geiger as a German soldier, see John W. Jordan, "Bethlehem and the Revolution," *PMHB* 12 (1888): 398.

4. Hunter, *Forts*, 289.

5. William Parsons to Robert Hunter Morris, August 21, 1756, Horsefield Papers, II, APS, quoted in Hunter, *Forts*, 276.

6. Henry Geiger to Timothy Horsefield, May 14, 1756, NCPBV, 33. Translated from the original manuscript by Marianne S. Wokeck. See also Hunter, *Forts*, 276. Geiger and a few men were stationed at a blockhouse that guarded the trails across Blue Mountain at Wind Gap. The blockhouse was known variously as Dietz's, Teet's, and other corruptions of Teed, the name of the man who owned the land and building. Born in 1708 in Liverpool, England, Timothy Horsefield immigrated to America in 1725 and settled on Long Island. He converted to the Moravian Church and moved to Bethlehem in 1745. When Northampton County was organized in 1752, Horsefield was commissioned a justice of the peace. At the outset of the French and Indian War, he was commissioned a colonel with administrative responsibility for two provincial regiments on the Northampton frontier. Horsefield resigned both offices at the conclusion of the war in 1763 and died ten years later in Bethlehem. For a detailed account of the French and Indian War in Northampton County, see Roberts, *Lehigh County*, 1:75–99.

7. For example see the report written by another Northampton officer named Jacob Arndt. Jacob Arndt to Governor William Denny, July 8, 1757, *Pa. Arch.*, 1st ser., 3:209–10. Also see note 2. I am indebted to Marianne S. Wokeck for sharing her knowledge of how German immigrants in Pennsylvania learned to speak and write English.

8. Because of Henry Geiger's distinctive handwriting, I happened across the following letter: "John Shmitt and Jacob Wanermacher to the Hounourable President and Executive Councill for the State of Pennsyilvania now Siting at Philadelphia," November 15, 1778, RG 27, 14:803–5. Geiger not only wrote this letter, he used it to "get at" his enemies. To make certain the Council did not question the veracity of his story, Geiger had the letter notarized.

9. *Pa. Arch.*, 5th ser., 1:179; Hunter, *Forts*, 276.

10. Henry Geiger to Henry Bouquet, November 29, 1759, in Louis M. Waddell et al., eds., *The Papers of Henry Bouquet*, 5 vols. (Harrisburg, Pa., 1972–84), 4:337–38. The "New Governour" was James Hamilton (c. 1710–83), who, during his lifetime, was a lawyer, a member of the Pennsylvania Assembly (1734–39), mayor of Philadelphia (1745), and lieutenant governor (1748–54, reappointed 1759–63). Geiger's "Several Officers" probably were a group of officers who, after a decade of lobbying, received large grants of land on both sides of the west branch of the Susquehanna River as a reward for their military service. The so-called officer's survey included land whose acquisition from Indian tribes was negotiated at Fort Stanwix in 1768.

11. Geiger to Bouquet, June 24, 1760, in Waddell, *Bouquet*, 4:607–8.

12. Geiger was naturalized March 23, 1761. M. S. Giuseppe, FSA, ed., *Naturalization of Foreign Protestants in the American and West Indian Colonies* (Baltimore, Md., 1979). Later the same year he was commissioned a justice of the peace. *Pa. Arch.*, 1st ser., 3:227–28.

13. Geiger to Timothy Horsefield, September 5, 1763, NCPBV, 115. See also Geiger to Horsefield, September 10(?), 1763, NCPBV, 125.

14. An account of the massacre is found in Roberts, *Lehigh County*, 1:100–113.

15. Asher Clayton to Provincial Commissioners, November 26, 1763, *Pa. Arch.*, 1st ser., 4:142.

16. James H. Hutson, "The Campaign to Make Pennsylvania a Royal Province 1764–1770," *PMHB* 94 (1970): 427–63; *PMHB* 95 (1971): 28–49.

17. Geiger to Benjamin Franklin, October 24, 1785, Benjamin Franklin Papers, APS.

. . . .

18. Lewis Gordon to Joseph Shippen, May 19, 1764, *Pa. Arch.*, 1st ser., 4:175.

19. Hutson, "Campaign," *PMHB* 95 (1971): 452.

20. Gordon to Shippen, December 4, 1764, *Records of the Provincial Council 1682–1776*, Record Group 21 (Harrisburg, Pa., 1966), B11:1461.

21. Northampton County Provincial Tax 1767–68, XR699, 700, HSP, microfilm.

22. *Pa. Gazette*, June 5, 1776.

23. Henry Geiger to Council of Safety, October 29, 1776, RG 27, 11:715–16. Geiger drafted this letter but hired a scribe to write it.

24. Lieutenant Colonel Stephen Balliet to President Joseph Reed, September 20, 1780, *Pa. Arch.*, 1st ser., 8:564–65.

25. On April 6, 1776, the Pennsylvania Assembly levied a tax of £3.10 on men who refused to join the militia. On September 14, 1776, the Constitutional Convention passed an ordinance that levied an even heavier fine on noncombatants.

26. In the Constitution of 1776 the Declaration of Rights guarantees freedom of speech, writing, and publishing; therefore, "freedom of the press ought not to be restrained." Geiger may have had in mind an ordinance passed by the Constitutional Convention on September 12, 1776: "If any person within this state shall, by advisedly speaking or writing, obstruct or oppose . . . the measures carrying on by the United States of America in defense and support of the freedom and independence of the said states, such person or persons, upon complaint and proof made on oath or affirmation before a justice of the peace . . . shall give security, for his or her behavior such sums of money as the justice may think necessary." *Statutes*, 8:18–21.

27. Geiger to Council of Safety, November 6, 1776, Gratz Collection, case 4, box 19, HSP; *Pa. Arch.*, 2nd ser., 1:642–43.

28. Agreement between residents of Lynn and Penn Townships, Northampton County, December 16, 1776, RG 27, 11:499–500, 730–31.

29. Resolution of Council of Safety, December 17, 1776, *Col. Records*, 11:54.

30. Geiger to Council of Safety, December 23, 1776, RG 27, 11:579–80.

31. Balliet also captured Tories that night. See note 51.

32. George Washington to Lewis Gordon, December 22, 1776, in *Letters of George Washington*, ed. John C. Fitzpatrick, 32 vols. (Washington, D.C., 1932), 6:423–25. Washington wrote to Gordon and asked him to distribute letters to the county colonels because Washington did not know them by name. Since Gordon had resigned, the letter must have been distributed by chairman Abraham Berlin.

33. *Col. Records*, 11:89. A return of the men under Geiger's command is found in *Pa. Arch.*, 5th ser., 8:101.

34. Council of Safety to Geiger, January 31, 1777, RG 27, 11:1154–55.

35. Council of Safety to George Washington, January 31, 1777, RG 27, 11:1153–54.

36. *Pa. Arch.*, 1st ser., 5:253–54.

37. *Minutes*, 71–73.

38. Geiger to Board of War, May 21, 1777, RG 27, 35:701–2.

39. Geiger to Board of War, April 24, 1777, RG 27, 35:622–23.

40. Geiger to Board of War, May 21, 1777, RG 27, 35:701–2.

41. Colonel George Breinig, Lieutenant Colonel Stephen Balliet, and Major Frederick Limbach were longtime residents of the region. All of them held important elected or appointed positions in Northampton County at various times during and after

the Revolution. I have found no evidence to support Geiger's claim that the army cashiered Breinig. On this matter, Geiger's imagination may have run away with him. However, it appears that the new officers and Wetzel enjoyed a close relationship.

42. Election Return, Northampton County, RG 27, 46:152–54.

43. The Sugar Loaf Massacre took place on September 11, 1780, at a place named Nescopec, near the Susquehanna River. Samuel Rea to President Reed, October 24, 1780, *Pa. Arch.*, 1st ser., 8:592.

44. Geiger to Reed, May 21, 1781, RG 27, 18:167–69.

45. Reed to Geiger, July 24, 1781, RG 27, 18:287–88.

46. Geiger to Reed, July 31(?), 1781, RG 27, 19:355–57.

47. Geiger to Reed, September 12, 1781, Dreer Collection, Soldiers of the Revolution II, HSP; *Pa. Arch.*, 1st ser., 9:396. Geiger to William Moore, July 19, 1782, RG 27, 19:883–85.

48. "Meeting of the Committee of Northampton County at the house of Conrad Kreider; Col. Henry Geiger in the Chair to Jacob Arndt, Jonas Hartzell, Jacob Stroud, Robert Lattimore, and Peter Kohler Esquires," August 23, 1783, Society Collection, HSP.

49. RG 27, 46:192; *Col. Records*, 14:174.

50. Geiger to President William Moore, October 14, 1782, RG 27, 19:1072–74. Geiger's adversary in this matter was John Balliet, whose brother, Colonel Stephen Balliet, represented Northampton on the Council.

51. See note 19.

52. Geiger to Levers, October 25, 1785, RG 27, 46:249–50; *Col. Records*, 14:638.

53. Thomas Mifflin to Valentine Upp [*sic*], May 9, 1788, Society Collection, HSP.

CHAPTER 5

1. Roberts, *Lehigh County*, 1:717–23; 3:971–72. Michael Ohl was naturalized in April 1760. M. S. Giuseppe, FSA, ed., *Naturalization of Foreign Protestants in the American and West Indian Colonies* (Baltimore, Md., 1979), 59.

2. *Minutes*, 36–38.

3. Roberts, *Lehigh County*, 1:117.

4. *Minutes*, 45.

5. Ibid., 46.

6. Ibid., 47–48.

7. *Pa. Gazette*, July 10, 1776.

8. *Col. Records*, 11:54. On calling out the militia, see George Washington to Lewis Gordon, December 22, 1776, in *Writings of George Washington*, ed. John C. Fitzpatrick, 32 vols. (Washington, D.C., 1932), 6:423–25.

9. Geiger to Council of Safety, December 23, 1776, RG 27, 11:579–80.

10. *Minutes*, 71–73.

11. On August 25, 1777, Michael Ohl took the oath of allegiance required of all men in the state. That he took the oath by affirmation rather than by swearing may have been a matter of principle; however, Ohl may have converted to one of the pacifist sects, possibly Moravian. Extant lists provide the names of 4,148 Northampton men who appeared before a magistrate and took the oath of allegiance. Of that number, only 66 took the oath by affirmation. Henry F. Marx, ed., "Oaths of All of Northampton County, Pennsylvania,

. . . .

1777–1784 from Original Lists of John Arndt, Recorder of Deeds, 1777–1800" (1932, typescript), Easton Public Library, Easton, Pa.

12. Commonwealth v. Michael Ohl, February 4, 1778, Manuscript Group 8: no. 884, PHMC, Harrisburg, Pa.

13. The single best source on the ratification of the Federal Constitution in Pennsylvania is Owen S. Ireland, *Religion, Ethnicity, and Politics: Ratifying the Constitution in Pennsylvania* (University Park, Pa., 1995). See also Robert L. Brunhouse, *The Counter-Revolution in Pennsylvania, 1776–1790* (Harrisburg, Pa., 1971).

CHAPTER 6

1. The *Unitas Fratrum*, or the Unity of the Brethren, originated in 1457 among the followers of Jan Hus, a Bohemian religious reformer who was burned at the stake in 1415. The *Unitas* spread from Bohemia and Moravia to Poland, but the Thirty Years War (1618–1648) brought an abrupt end to Protestantism in these countries. Members of the *Unitas*, most of them Moravians, eventually made their way to Saxony, where Count Nicholas Ludwig von Zinzendorf gave them refuge on his estate. Zinzendorf organized the Renewed Moravian Church, but the missionary zeal of church members angered other denominations. As a result, Zinzendorf decided to establish Moravian settlements in America to carry out the church's mission of propagating the gospel. Georgia was the site of the first Moravian settlement in mainland America in 1735. Citing a dispensation granted them by trustees of the colony, Moravians refused to bear arms in the war between English and Spaniard inhabitants of the Florida Territory. Remnants of this band joined Zinzendorf at Bethlehem. Prior to the settlement in Georgia, Moravian missions were established in St. Thomas (1732), Greenland (1733), St. Croix (1734), and Lapland (1734). Levering, *Bethlehem*, 7–30, 40. See also Roberts, *Lehigh County*, 1:641–42.

2. Preston A. Barba, *They Came to Emmaus* (Bethlehem, Pa., 1960), 85. After their conversion to the Moravian Church, Conrad Wetzel, who was reared a Lutheran, and Catherine Wetzel, who was raised in the Reformed faith, numbered among the thirty-four original members of the Macungie congregation.

3. John Ettwein, "A Short Account of the Disturbances in America and of the Brethren's Conduct and Suffering in this Connection," in Hamilton, *Ettwein*, 192. Grace Shaw Woldt, "Garrett, Haines, and Wetzel Family Data" (n.d., typescript), Library of the Lehigh County Historical Society, Allentown, Pa. In addition to John, who was born on December 14, 1730, the children of Conrad Wetzel (1697–1753) and Catherine Bayer Wetzel (1709–64) are as follows: Catherine (1733), Conrad (July 11, 1735), Henry (July 17, 1737), Maria Magdalena (June 22, 1741), Gertrude Benigna (April 25, 1743), Maria (1744), Jacob (April 8, 1746). International Genealogical Index, Church of Jesus Christ of the Latter Day Saints, N0589, New England Historic Genealogical Society, Boston, Mass. Conrad Wetzel and four other converts formed the nucleus of the Moravian Congregation at Emmaus, which gained official recognition by church authorities in 1747.

4. Levering, *Bethlehem*, 208. Levering quotes another authority but does not name the source. See also Hamilton, *Ettwein*, 52, 92.

5. Hamilton, *Ettwein*, 192.

6. Wetzel doubtless spoke "Dutch-English"; however, no evidence of his ability to read or write English has been found. Due to the lack of schools and teachers, many first-

generation Germans born in America were less educated than their parents, some of whom had attended church schools before emigrating from Germany.

7. Levering, *Bethlehem*, 461.

8. As noted in the *Evening Post*, June 10, 1775, three townships failed to respond to the Committee's call to arms. Although the townships are not identified, it is likely that, in addition to Bethlehem, the other two were Penn and Lynn, which bracketed Blue Mountain in the extreme northeast corner of the county. It later turned out that numerous inhabitants in these townships opposed the Revolution.

9. *Minutes*, 37.

10. Ibid.

11. Hamilton, *Ettwein*, 36.

12. Ibid., 18.

13. Ibid., 35.

14. Nathaniel Seidel to Benjamin Franklin, *Ettwein Papers*, 7:1556. There is no date on this letter, but Franklin must have received it after his return to Philadelphia from London in May 1775. "Letter from Franklin to Moravians, June 2, 1775," *PMHB* 12 (1888): 491–92.

15. *Ettwein Papers*, June 17, 1775, 7:1588. The Brethren may have thought this letter was too testy to send to the Committee. In the bottom margin of the letter is written in Ettwein's hand: "was *not* given to the Committee" (emphasis in original).

16. Levering, *Bethlehem*, 217–22; Hamilton, *Ettwein*, 133.

17. Hamilton, *Ettwein*, 135.

18. *Votes*, 8:7247. Congress urged those who could not bear arms because of religious principles to contribute liberally to the relief of their distressed brethren in the several colonies. *Col. Records*, 10:293–95.

19. Hamilton, *Ettwein*, 150.

20. *Minutes*, 38.

21. Hamilton, *Ettwein*, 152.

22. The Committee of Safety (July 3, 1755–July 22, 1776) and its successors, the Council of Safety (July 25, 1775–March 17, 1777), Supreme Executive Council (March 4, 1777–October 16, 1777), (Second) Council of Safety (October 17, 1777–December 4, 1777), and Supreme Executive Council (October 17, 1777–December 20, 1790) functioned as the executive branch of government in Revolutionary Pennsylvania.

23. *Col. Records*, 10:279–82.

24. Levers to John Arndt, November 6, 1781, RG 27, 19:155.

25. *Col. Records*, 10:349.

26. Ibid., 10:357.

27. On the subject of the Committee of Privates and the chain of events that preceded the fall of the Pennsylvania Assembly, the following sources are essential: David Hawke, *In the Midst of a Revolution* (Philadelphia, 1961), 87–110; Steven Rosswurm, *Arms, Country, and Class: The Philadelphia Militia and "Lower Sort" During the American Revolution* (New Brunswick, N.J., 1987), 56–81; Ryerson, *Revolution*, 138–75.

28. The number of militiamen is my estimate, based on the fact that fifty-three militia battalions had been organized by the end of 1775. Testimony given by Richard Penn, son of former governor Richard Penn, to the House of Lords in November 1775 tends to support this estimate.

. . . .

Q: What force has the Province of Pennsylvania raised?

A: When I left Pennsylvania [last summer] they had 20,000 men in arms and 4,500 since raised.

Q: How many men fit to bear arms is it supposed there are in Pennsylvania?

A: Sixty thousand.

Q: What proportion of these 60,000 men do you believe would willing come forth, if necessary, in the present contest?

A: All, I believe.

"Richard Penn's Estimate of the Strength of the Pennsylvania Associators [Militia] in 1775," *PMHB* 25 (1901): 137–38.

29. *Pa. Gazette*, February 7, 1776.

30. *Votes*, 8:7443. The Northampton petition was read in the Assembly on March 12, 1776. For other petitions, see Ryerson, *Revolution*, 161 n. 39.

31. Hamilton, *Ettwein*, 155; *Ettwein Papers*, 6:1169A.

32. Hamilton, *Ettwein*, 192.

33. Ibid., 158. At this juncture the Committee had forty members. Ettwein noted that there "were not 20 men who sent them." Hamilton, *Ettwein*, n. 157. The wording of the Committee Minutes gives the impression that all members were present. *Minutes*, 44.

34. The Address of the Deputies, from the Committees of Pennsylvania Assembled in Provincial Conference, June 22, 1776, "To The People of Pennsylvania," *Pa. Arch.*, 2nd ser., 3:575.

35. The Address of the Deputies Of the Committees of Pennsylvania, Assembled in Provincial Conference at Philadelphia, June 25, 1776, "To The Associators [Militia] of Pennsylvania," *Pa. Arch.*, 2nd ser., 3:581–82.

36. Ibid.

37. Hamilton, *Ettwein*, 156–59, n. 22.

38. Congress nudged the Pennsylvania Assembly to seize guns from the disaffected. As a result, gun collectors were chosen at special township elections held throughout the province on April 25, 1776. The three collectors in Macungie Township were very active. *JCC*, 4:19, January 2, 1776; 4:205, March 14, 1776; *Votes*, 8:7505–7, April 5, 1776.

39. *Minutes*, 51.

40. Ibid., 36.

41. Congress appears to have done everything in its power to put the Declaration in the hands of the people on the same day they would elect delegates to the Constitutional Convention.

42. Jacob Arndt, Simon Driesbach, Peter Rhoads, Peter Burkhalter, Nigel Gray, John Ralston, Abraham Miller, and Jacob Stroud represented Northampton County at Pennsylvania's Constitutional Convention. At the time of their election in July 1776, all of these men were militia officers. While only one was a member of the current County Committee, the other seven had previously served on this body.

43. Hamilton, *Ettwein*, 161–62.

44. Levering, *Bethlehem*, 448.

45. Ibid.

46. Barba, *Emmaus*, 116; Hamilton, *Ettwein*, 163; John R. Weinlick, "The Moravians and the American Revolution," *Transactions of the Moravian Historical Society* 2 (1977): 1–16.

47. Barba, *Emmaus*, 119.

48. Northampton County Board of County Commissioners, Minutes and Accounts, October 14, 1776, HSP, microfilm.

49. In one of its final acts, the provincial Assembly advised nonresisters that they did not have to pay this fine. It was this action that gave Ettwein hope that the "new" assembly would revise the law. Hamilton, *Ettwein*, 163; *Votes*, 8:7586.

50. "To the Commissioners of Northampton County," October 19, 1776, *Ettwein Papers*, 7:1598; "Reasons for putting off the payment of a Tax laid on [Non-Militia]," October 19, 1776, *Ettwein Papers*, 7:1589A; Hamilton, *Ettwein*, 163. Ettwein did not sign the letter to the commissioners, but he doubtless composed the letter. Ettwein frequently laid out his arguments in the form of a personal memorandum. For example, see Ettwein's thoughts on the radicals' plan to overthrow Pennsylvania's colonial government, *Ettwein Papers*, 6:1282, and note 43.

51. Hamilton, *Ettwein*, 163.

52. Ibid.

53. Ibid.

54. Pennsylvania's Constitution of 1776 is found in numerous sources, but the most accessible may be Theodore Thayer, *Pennsylvania Politics and the Growth of Democracy* (Harrisburg, Pa., 1953), 211–27. The Pennsylvania Assembly also chose congressional delegates. Here, too, term limits applied. "Any delegate may be superseded at any time, by the general assembly appointing another in his stead. No man shall sit in congress longer than two years successively, nor be capable of reelection for three years afterwards; and no person who holds any office in the gift of congress shall hereafter be elected to represent this commonwealth in congress." See Constitution of 1776, Section the Seventh, Section the Eighth.

55. *JHR*, 98, November 29, 1776.

56. William H. Egle, *An Illustrated History of the Commonwealth of Pennsylvania* (Philadelphia, 1880), 167.

57. Jacob Arndt held office as a Councillor; that is, a member of the Supreme Executive Council (1777–80), and as an assemblyman (1782–84). On Jacob Arndt, see Egle, "Constitutional Convention," 99; and Arndt, *Arndt Family*.

58. To conduct business, Assembly rules required that a minimum of two-thirds of the members be present. In 1776 there were 72 assemblymen, 6 for each of eleven counties and the City of Philadelphia. The first Assembly did not attain a quorum until November 28, 1776. It was not possible to raise a quorum either on December 6, 7, and 9, 1776, or between December 14, 1776, and January 13, 1777.

59. The Assembly debated the militia bill during one or both sessions over a period of fourteen days: February 12, 14, 18, 19, 20, 21, 25, and March 1, 4, 6, 7, 8, 10, 11. On several daily entries, the secretary appended the notation: "considerable time spent on the militia bill." As late as March 10 several new clauses were brought in along with motions for others. The debate ended on March 11, and 1,500 copies of the bill were printed both in English and German. On March 12, the Assembly nominated the lieutenants and sub-lieutenants for each county.

60. An Act to Regulate the Militia of the Commonwealth of Pennsylvania, *Statutes*, 9:75–94. The position of county lieutenant has ancient roots. At the start of the seventeenth century, the sheriff and the lord-lieutenant—a position like that of the Anglo-

. . . .

Saxon Earl—headed the English counties. The lord-lieutenant's principle duty was to supervise the local militia when it was called into service to suppress riots and maintain public order. Following this model, the Virginia Colony was divided into eight counties in 1634 to be governed with lieutenants and sheriffs appointed by the governor. The lieutenant commanded the militia of the county, presided at courts-martial, and had considerable dictatorial power in time of war. On the eve of the Revolution the office of county lieutenant still existed in Virginia, but it appears that no other colony or state employed county lieutenants until 1777, when the Pennsylvania Assembly created the position to enforce the provisions of the Militia Act. John A. Fairlie and Charles M. Kneier, *County Government and Administration* (New York, 1930), 8–18; Edward Channing, "Town and Country Government in the English Colonies of North America," in *Johns Hopkins University Studies in Historical and Political Science*, ed. Herbert B. Adams, vol. 2 (Baltimore, Md., 1884), 42–53.

61. The militia elected battalion officers (a colonel, lieutenant colonel, and major) and officers for each company (one captain, two lieutenants, one ensign, and two court-martial men). In turn, battalion officers appointed a quartermaster, an adjutant, a sergeant major, and a drum-and-fife major, while each company captain appointed four sergeants, four corporals, a fifer, a drummer, and a clerk. When the voting was complete, more than 750 men, or seven times the number of civil authorities in the county, held three-year terms as officers in the Northampton militia. "Exercise days" not only accelerated the institutionalization of the militia but also served as a political caucus for Pennsylvania's radicals. At each of ten company and two battalion days scheduled annually, militia hoisted flags, shouldered arms, and drilled to the martial sound of fifes and drums. They shot mark for prizes and engaged in heavy, convivial drinking. They made new friends outside the tight circles of family, church, and local tavern. For most men, camaraderie under arms was a novel experience. When they turned out to exercise, they anticipated having a good time and rubbing shoulders with militia officers whom they had elected to serve in the state Assembly.

62. In what appears to have been the only official declaration of martial law in Pennsylvania during the War of the Revolution, President Joseph Reed declared a state of emergency on June 9, 1780. I have been unable to determine when Reed's order was lifted. *Pa. Arch.*, 4th ser., 3:764; *Col. Records*, 12:382–84.

63. The practice of utilizing substitutes was not a new one. In eighteenth-century Great Britain, for example, militia laws permitted substitutes. However, at least one person frowned upon the custom and cautioned that "those who send substitutes to defend their sweethearts, their wives and families, deserve richly, that my pretty countrywomen should find substitutes to serve for them in a more pleasing way." Colonel Sir Charles Harvey, Bart., comp., *The History of the 4th Battalion Norfolk Regiment (Late East Norfolk Militia)* (London, 1899), 23. For this information I am indebted to Bob Godfrey of Norwich, United Kingdom, and a chance meeting at Skiathos, Greece, in 1993. In Pennsylvania, a substitute clause is found first in the Act for Regulating Militia passed by the provincial Assembly in April 1776.

64. Hamilton, *Ettwein*, 67; Lewis Weiss to John Ettwein, October 20, 1778, *Ettwein Papers*, 3:645.

65. Hamilton, *Ettwein*, 178.

66. Memorandum on the militia law, *Ettwein Papers*, late 1777(?), 6:1297.

67. Hamilton, *Ettwein*, 179.

68. Ibid., 135.

69. John R. Weinlick, "The Moravians and the American Revolution," *Transactions of the Moravian Historical Society* 2 (1977): 5–6.

70. "John Ettwein to John Wetzel, Lt. of the County of Northampton, John Arndt and Thomas Sillyman, Justices of the Peace," March 31, 1778, *Ettwein Papers*, 7:1607–8. The names of the Brethren against whom Wetzel sought a judgment appear on frame 1608.

71. Hamilton, *Ettwein*, 67; Lewis Weiss to John Ettwein, October 20, 1778, *Ettwein Papers*, 3:645.

72. I have assembled more than thirty letters addressed to county lieutenants in the period 1777–83. Many of these communications were circular letters; that is, they were addressed and delivered to all lieutenants simultaneously. The number of letters from county lieutenants to the president varies with each county. Only two such letters with John Wetzel's signature have been found.

73. An Act Obliging the Male Inhabitants of this State to Give Assurances of Allegiance to the Same and for other Purposes Therein Mentioned, *Statutes*, 9:110–14.

74. Ibid.

75. The misadventure of George Kriebel has been constructed from "George Kriebel's Declaration, 1777, the substance of what has passed between John Wetzel and Frederick Limbach and George Kriebel, when they tendered the Oath of Allegiance unto him." *Pa. Arch.*, 1st ser., 5:432–33. See also RG 27, 12:567–68.

76. Roberts, *Lehigh County*, 1:768. Between 1735 and 1740 most Schwenkfelders settled in present Montgomery County, Pennsylvania. However, a small band of this sect spilled over into the southwest corner of Northampton County. Kriebel may have been targeted because Limbach had his eyes on property adjoining his owned by the Schwenkfelder.

77. The amount of the fine does not tally with the fine of five shillings prescribed for missing a drill. No doubt the amount of the fine included "costs" to be pocketed by the constable and the magistrate.

78. RG 27, 12:569.

79. "Statement of Henry Funk—The substance of what has passed between me, Henry Funk, and Philip Walter and John Laub, when they took [me] up on the 6th of August, 1777." *Pa. Arch.*, 1st ser., 5:495–96, 508–9. See also RG 27, 36:250–52.

80. "To his Excellency the President and Council of the State of Pennsylvania—The Petition of Henry Funk of ye Society of Christians called Mennonists and George Kriebel belonging to the Society of Christians called Schwenkfelders and Inhabitants of the County of Northampton in the State afsd. humbly sheweth. . . ." RG 27, 36:253–54. Christopher Schultz, a Schwenkfelder minister and cousin of George Kriebel, conceived and drafted the petition. Despite his position as a sectarian religious leader, Schultz served on the Berks County Committee in 1774. As a result, he had earned the mantle of a patriot, a fact that doubtless caused the Council to give the Funk/Kriebel petition their immediate attention. The speed with which this matter was processed is remarkable. Funk was jailed on August 9, 1777. The Council received the petition dated August 12 on August 15. Council took action the same day and directed the secretary to write to Limbach. Richard K. MacMaster, Samuel L. Horst, and Robert F. Ulle, *Conscience in Crisis: Studies*

. . . .

in Anabaptist and Mennonite History (Scottdale, Pa., 1979), 416. This book is essential for students of the Revolution in the mid-Atlantic states.

81. *Pa. Arch.*, 1st ser., 5:524–25. The underlining appears in the secretary's original draft of the letter, which is found in RG 27, 12:790–91. No doubt the person who first transcribed the handwritten version of the letter confused strikeouts—of which there are many—with underlining.

82. *Pa. Arch.*, 1st ser., 5:365, 379, 523, 556, 615. From September to December 1777, some 438 Northampton militiamen were at the front. Had all members of the classes called up in this period turned out for duty, Northampton would have mustered more than 1,700 men. For a summary of the details, see Hannah Benner Roach, "The Pennsylvania Militia in 1777," *PGM* 23 (1964): 3.

83. *Col. Records*, 11:222, 257, 278.

84. An Act for the Attainder of Divers Traitors if They Render not Themselves by a Certain Day, and for Vesting Their Estates in this Commonwealth, and for More Effectually Discovering the Lawful Debt and Claims Thereupon, March 6, 1778, *Statutes*, 9:201–15. An Act for the Further Security of the Government, April 1, 1778, *Statutes*, 9:238–45.

85. Levering, *Bethlehem*, 498–99; Barba, *Emmaus*, 122.

86. Hamilton, *Ettwein*, 192.

87. Ibid., 193.

88. Ibid.

89. Barba, *Emmaus*, 124. Barba has translated this scene directly from the *Diary of the Emmaus Congregation.*

90. Ibid. See Levers to John Ettwein, May 27, 1778, *Ettwein Papers*, 2:366. Levers said that Wetzel asked for a warrant because Giering "had behaved in a very unbecoming manner."

91. Andreas Giering to Chief Judge Thomas McKean, June 1, 1778, *Ettwein Papers*, 7:1603–5. In this copy of Giering's letter, Ettwein said: "Wetzel fell into a great passion, saying: if he had a sword, he would run Giering through." Lewis Weiss to John Ettwein, July 9, 1778, *Ettwein Papers*, 3:644–45. Lewis Weiss argued Giering's petition before Chief Judge Thomas McKean. Weiss, a Philadelphia attorney, was an ordained minister and member of the Church of the United Brethren. Leaders of all factions in Pennsylvania's colonial and Revolutionary governments recognized his ability to draft legislation, a skill for which he received handsome remuneration. "Lewis Weiss, of Philadelphia, Conveyancer, Lawyer, and Judge," *PMHB* 15 (1891–92): 361–65.

92. Hamilton, *Ettwein*, 194.

93. Vice President George Bryan to Colonel John Wetzel, May 22, 1778, *Pa. Arch.*, 1st ser., 6:541.

94. Bryan to Levers, May 25, 1778, *Ettwein Papers*, 7:1520.

95. Levers to John Ettwein, May 27, 1778, *Ettwein Papers*, 2:366–67.

96. Lieutenant John Wetzel to President Wharton, May 25, 1778, *Pa. Arch.*, 1st ser., 6:551–52; RG 27, 14:126. On May 22, Bryan advised Wetzel that President Wharton was very sick. On May 25, when Wetzel replied to his superior, President Wharton, he did not know that Wharton had died that same day.

97. RG 27, 14:120–21, 202–3, 204.

98. Wetzel to Vice President Bryan, July 8, 1778, *Pa. Arch.*, 1st ser., 6:629.

99. Hamilton, *Ettwein*, 213–19. An edited and embellished account of Ettwein's description of events in September 1778 is found in Levering, *Bethlehem*, 501–5.

100. Like George Bryan, Speaker John Bayard was well aware that overly zealous radicals could pose a serious threat to the government. See Hamilton, *Ettwein*, 207–8. On September 10, 1778, the Assembly did indeed amend the Test Act, but, contrary to the hopes of some, this amendment merely closed loopholes in the law. The amendment reprieved men who had been unable to take the oath because they had been held as prisoners of war, required Pennsylvania's congressional delegates to take the oath, and required every person who cast a vote to show proof that he had taken the oath.

101. John Van Campen to Henry Limbach, September 7, 1778, *Ettwein Papers*, 7:1521.

102. Jacob Arndt to Jacob Morey and Frederick Limbach, Esqs., September 8, 1778, *Ettwein Papers*, 7:1518.

103. On September 11, the committee requested the advice of the Council on a "case the House conceives to be of great importance." *Col. Records*, 11:574.

104. Hamilton, *Ettwein*, 214.

105. Matlack to Ettwein, September 11, 1778, *Ettwein Papers*, 2:399. Although Matlack, the Council secretary, penned this letter to Ettwein, the content is obviously the work of skilled lawyers who examined Limbach's warrant.

106. Hamilton, *Ettwein*, 216.

107. Ibid., 218.

108. *Statutes*, 10:303–8.

109. Hamilton, *Ettwein*, 223.

110. *Statutes*, 12:178–81. The Assembly did not repeal all laws that required sworn allegiance to the state until 1789, sixteen months after Pennsylvania had ratified the U.S. Constitution, and one month before George Washington entered the presidency. *Statutes*, 13:222–24.

111. 1741–1839, NCPBV, 203. August 5, 1786.

112. Hamilton, *Ettwein*, 19 n. 5. Ettwein said that because he had traveled much, one might call him "the pilgrim." In his lifetime he undertook 12 sea voyages, 3 of them between England and America; 11 journeys on foot in Europe totaling about 3,000 miles; and 67 journeys on land in America totaling 20,000 miles, 1,500 of them on foot.

113. Hamilton, *Ettwein*, 67–72, 78.

114. On February 5, the Assembly referred three petitions against Wetzel to the grievances committee. One of them had been carried over from August 1778. (Only one petition has been found. Petition of the Fourth Battalion of Militia, February 3, 1779, RG 27, 14:990.) The grievances committee reviewed the petitions and sent them to the Council. (One of the petitions was lost in transit.) On February 22, the Council ordered Wetzel to appear the next day. Wetzel denied the allegations of malfeasance and submitted documents defending himself. *Col. Records*, 11:705–6. On March 9, two Northampton militia officers sent a petition to the Assembly in which they absolved Wetzel of wrongdoing and fixed the blame instead on John Van Campen, a sublieutenant who had resigned his post in order to retain his seat in Assembly. Colonel John Siegfried and Major James Boyd on behalf of the Fourth Battalion, March 19, 1779, RG

27, 14:1100–101. John Van Campen was the legislator who informed Ettwein in September 1778 that the Assembly hoped to revise the Test Act.

115. *Pa. Arch.*, 3rd ser., 6:721–26.

116. *JHR*, September 15, 1785, December 17, 1785.

117. *Pa. Arch.*, 6th ser., 11:257–68.

118. NCP, box 1.

119. The first number appeared July 27, 1810, two years before the formation of Lehigh County. Roberts, *Lehigh County*, 1:277.

CHAPTER 7

1. A. D. Chidsey, *Penn Patents at the Forks of the Delaware* (Easton, Pa., 1937); Nelson, "Backcountry Pennsylvania," 102; William Parsons to Richard Peters, "Respecting Easton," December 8, 1752, *Pa. Arch.*, 1st ser., 2:95–98; "The Drylands of Northampton County," *PMHB* 21 (1897–98): 502–3; William Parsons to Peters, May 10, 1755, *Pa. Arch.*, 1st ser., 305–6; Levers to William Moore, March 2, 1782, RG 27, 19:523; Levers to John Armstrong, July 23, 1783, RG 27, 20:532; Geiger to Supreme Executive Council, November 17, 1783, RG 27, 20:938–40. Penn had first offered the Fermor tract to the Moravians but they bought land in North Carolina because of the prejudice against them in Northampton. Parsons loathed Moravians because he believed that his wife's conversion by the Brethren had ruined his marriage. Parsons not only wanted to sell parcels in the manor for the reason cited in this text, but he also wanted to keep Moravians in Northampton County from expanding from Bethlehem toward Easton.

2. Levers to John Armstrong, June 23, 1783, RG 27, 20:532. The secretary of the land office assigned deputy surveyor James Scull, Northampton County's justice John Moore, sheriff Peter Kachlein, and prothonotary Lewis Gordon to handle this matter.

3. Court order for Elizabeth Kurtz, NCP, 2:235.

4. Geiger to Supreme Executive Council, November 17, 1783, RG 27, 20:928.

5. Levers to Armstrong, June 23, 1783, RG 27, 20:532. Levers's memory regarding the Kurtzes' contact with John and Richard Penn is buttressed by the guest list found in "From the Waste Books of the Sun Inn," *PMHB* 39 (1915): 470.

6. Levers to Armstrong, June 23, 1783, RG 27, 20:523.

7. See note 5.

8. *JCC*, 5:877, 7:302–3.

9. Constitution of Pennsylvania of 1776, A Declaration of Rights . . . , Section IV.

10. "A Memorial from Christopher Kurtz and his wife, Elizabeth . . . ," Second General Assembly, Second Session, March 1, 1778, Clifford K. Shipton and James E. Mooney, *National Index of American Imprints Through 1800: The Short-Title Evans*, 2 vols. (Worcester, Mass., 1969), microcard 15973.

11. Levers to President William Moore, March 2, 1782, RG 27, 19:523.

12. Theodore G. Tappert and John W. Doberstein, trans., *The Journals of Henry Melchoir Muhlenberg*, 3 vols. (Philadelphia, 1955), 2:450–51.

13. Levers to Moore, March 2, 1782, RG 27, 19:523.

14. Ibid.

15. Council to Aaron Depui, April 22, 1782, RG 27, 19:681.

16. Elizabeth Kurtz to John Dickinson, April 3, 1783, RG 27, 20:329.

17. Kurtz to Dickinson, May 6, 1783, RG 27, 20:387.

18. Levers to Armstrong, June 23, 1783, RG 27, 20:532.

19. Kurtz to Dickinson, August 4, 1783, RG 27, 20:608.

20. Geiger to Supreme Executive Council, November 17, 1783, RG 27, 20:928–30.

21. Ninth General Assembly, Third Session, September 7 and 13, 1785, *Evans*, microcard 18684.

22. Kurtz to President Benjamin Franklin, May 22, 1786, RG 27, 22:1056–57.

23. Eleventh General Assembly, Third Session, August 29, September 1 and 18, 1786, *Evans*, microcard 45130.

24. Twelfth General Assembly, First Session, November 7, 11, and 23, 1787, *Evans*, microcard 20632.

25. Thomas Mifflin to Valentine Upp [*sic*], May 9, 1788, Society Collection, HSP.

26. Twelfth General Assembly, Third Session, September 13 and 20, and October 2, 1788, *Evans*, microcard 45329.

CHAPTER 8

1. *Votes*, 8:7505–7. The Continental Congress prodded the Pennsylvania Assembly to pass this legislation. *JCC*, 4:19, January 2, 1776; 4:205, March 14, 1776.

2. In 1776, Macungie Township had about 180 eligible voters. Roberts, *Lehigh County*, 2:39, Jacob Behr; 2:483, Peter Haas; 3:1282, Jacob Stephen.

3. Quoted sections in this narrative are found in *Minutes*, 46–50.

4. Raymond E. Hollenbach, trans., "Records of the Emmaus Moravian Congregation, 1754–1869," (n.d., typescript), Lehigh Valley Historical Society, Allentown, Pa.; Roberts, *Lehigh County*, 1:754, 3:1068–78.

5. The *Minutes* read: "not Christian."

6. Entry in the diary of the Moravian congregation at Emmaus dated May 25, 1776, in Barba, *Emmaus*, 115. The minutes of the Committee make no mention of the militia's foray against the Romigs, but they verify that the Macungie militia did, in fact, exercise on May 25.

7. I have edited the recantation, which appears in full in *Minutes*, 50.

8. An Act to Regulate the Militia of the Commonwealth of Pennsylvania, March 17, 1777, *Statutes*, 9:75–94; An Act Obliging the Male Inhabitants of this State to Give Assurances of Allegiance to the Same and for Other Purposes Therein Mentioned, June 13, 1777, *Statutes*, 9:110–14.

9. An Act for the Attainder of Divers Traitors if They Render not Themselves by a Certain Day, and for Vesting Their Estates in this Commonwealth, and for More Effectually Discovering the Lawful Debt and Claims Thereupon, March 6, 1778, *Statutes*, 9:201–15. The legislative progress from ordinance to law is described in Anne M. Ousterhout, "Pennsylvania Land Confiscations During the Revolution," *PMHB* 102 (1978): 328–43. The ordinance is found in *Col. Records*, 11:329–31.

10. This quotation is found in a document that is included in a genealogy of the Romig family in Roberts, *Lehigh County*, 3:1068–78. After reciting a few facts about Joseph Romig, the compiler writes: "The following document, found among the Romig family papers, shows Joseph Romig's situation in the Revolutionary period." The docu-

ment is headed: "Memorandum—Concerning the Case of Joseph Romig." The memorandum recounts Joseph Romig's clash with John Wetzel, the subsequent seizure of his personal property and land, and his attempt to reverse the "court's" decision. The author of this memorandum, stamped Macungie, July 15, 1790, is not revealed. I believe Joseph Romig either wrote the memo or had a hand in framing it.

    11. *Pa. Arch.*, 5th ser., 8:548–49.

    12. *Col. Records*, 11:493–95.

    13. *Records of the Comptroller General,* Record Group 4, PHMC, Harrisburg, Pa.

    14. Ibid.

    15. *Pa. Arch.*, 6th ser., 13:223–24, 454, 467.

    16. RG 27, 43:329. Personal property retained by Mrs. Romig. I found nothing in the Attainder Law that permits the wife of an accused traitor to retain for her own use any personal property confiscated by the state. It appears that Commissioner Stephen Balliet extended this courtesy to Mrs. Romig, as well as to the wives of Joshua Thomas, John Custard, and Samuel Custard, who joined the British Army. In addition, wives of the latter two men bought back some of their own property at auction. Moreover, it appears that all four women selected the property they desired to retain before the appraisers inventoried their estates. *Pa. Arch.*, 6th ser., 13:467.

    17. *Pa. Arch.*, 6th ser., 13:223–24.

    18. Ibid., 13:458.

    19. Here the narrative follows the sequence of events described in the memorandum cited in note 10.

    20. *Pa. Arch.*, 6th ser., 13:459.

    21. Ibid., 13:471–72.

CHAPTER 9

    1. Jacob Stroud was born in 1735 in Hunterdon County, New Jersey. His parents, Bernard and Keziah Stroud, immigrated to Pennsylvania from England early in the eighteenth century. About 1745 the Stroud family moved from Hunterdon County to Lower Smithfield Township in Northampton County. Elizabeth Stroud Colbert, "Stroud Record: Including the Ancestry and Brief History of Colonel Jacob Stroud and Elizabeth McDowell, His Wife, and Their Children" (1926, typescript), 22, Northampton County Historical and Genealogical Society, Easton, Pa.

    2. Stroud's place is identified on the Reading Howell map published in 1792.

    3. Colbert, "Stroud," 30, 31. The descriptions of Stroud by Reverend Henry Boehm and Judge George M. Stroud, Jacob Stroud's grandson, are the only eyewitness descriptions of any of the characters in this book.

    4. Jacob Stroud to the Committee of Safety, June 13, 1776, RG 27, 10:624.

    5. J. Paul Selsam, *The Pennsylvania Constitution of 1776* (Philadelphia, 1936), 176.

    6. *Minutes of the Proceedings of the Convention of the State of Pennsylvania*, August 1, 7, 10, 16, 20, and September 14, 1776. See also "Petition from the Inhabitants of Delaware and Upper Smithfield Townships in Northampton County," RG 27, 10:829–32.

    7. Jacob Stroud to John Wetzel, July 17, 1778, *Pa. Arch.*, 1st ser., 6:651. Cochecton lies on the New York side of the Delaware River opposite present Damascus, Pennsylvania, itself situated about thirty miles north of Milford, Pennsylvania. Because of the terrain,

eighteenth-century settlers on the New York side of the narrow upper valley of the Delaware River found it convenient to cross into Pennsylvania to conduct business. Stroud sent a copy of his letter to Wetzel to John Nicholson, who was at the time a clerk to the Board of Treasury of the Continental Congress. By 1787 Nicholson had become the "fiscal dictator" of Pennsylvania. Why Stroud sent a copy of this particular letter to Nicholson begs the imagination. Perhaps Nicholson, with Stroud's help, had already begun land speculation north of Blue Mountain. If so, the Stroud-Wetzel letter would have let Nicholson know that the enemy was encroaching on his land. In 1800, Nicholson's speculations landed him in jail along with Robert Morris. "Guide to the Microfilm of the John Nicholson Papers" (Harrisburg, Pa., 1967), 1–8, PHMC.

8. Jacob Stroud to Council, October 25, 1778, *Pa. Arch.*, 1st ser., 7:63–64. Like Stroud, the colonel of Northampton's Third Battalion had little faith that Lieutenant Wetzel would come to his aid. Therefore, the colonel sought relief from the Constitutional Society, a Philadelphia-based political organization that had organized a cell within at least one of Northampton's militia battalions. Local members of this Society advised the colonel to station guards at critical points along the trails, and to lay his plan before the Council. More important, the Society promised that "their brethren in Philadelphia" would personally deliver the petition to the Council. The membership of the Constitutional Society included judges, generals, colonels, and prominent civic leaders: Thomas McKean, George Bryan, Timothy Matlack, William Moore, and Jonathan Bayard Smith, to name a few. Still to be determined is who organized this Society, which is said to have operated as the secret political wing of the Sons of Tammany, and how it gained a foothold in Northampton County. See Petition of Inhabitants of Northampton County, May 1, 1779, *Pa. Arch.*, 1st ser., 7:360–61; Captain Matthew McHenry to Captain Charles Wilson Peale, May 10, 1779, *Pa. Arch.*, 1st ser., 7:384. Charles Wilson Peale, famous portraitist of George Washington, was the patriarch of a dynasty of painters. According to Francis Von A. Cabeen, the Constitutional Society was "either our Sons of Saint Tammany under another name, or that it was the nucleus around which the Saint Tammany Society gathered on great occasions. Most likely the members of the Constitutional Society were the real active political workers of the larger Tammany organization." Francis Von A. Cabeen, "The Society of the Sons of Saint Tammany of Philadelphia," *PMHB* 26 (1902): 21–22, 346–47.

9. President Reed to Jacob Stroud, August 3, 1779, *Pa. Arch.*, 1st ser., 7:613.

10. Wetzel to Reed, August 4, 1779, *Col. Records*, 12:65.

11. Reed to Arndt, August 6, 1779, *Pa. Arch.*, 7:625.

12. *Col. Records*, 12:100–101, September 10, 1779.

13. John Van Campen to Reed, December 12, 1780, RG 27, 17:163.

14. Levers to Arndt, November 8, 1781, RG 27, 19:155.

15. Levers to Reed, June 30, 1781, Northampton County Miscellaneous Papers, box 1, HSP; Levers to Reed, July 8, 1781, *Pa. Arch.*, 1st ser., 8:275–76; Reed to Levers, July 10, 1781, *Pa. Arch.*, 1st ser., 8:268–69; Levers to Reed, July 29, 1781, RG 27, 18:826–30; Levers to Reed, August 7, 1781, *Pa. Arch.*, 1st ser., 8:339–40; Reed to Levers, August 10, 1781, *Pa. Arch.*, 1st ser., 8:348–49; Levers to Reed, August 23, 1781, *Pa. Arch.*, 2nd ser., 3:522–24; Reed to Levers, August 28, 1781, *Pa. Arch.*, 1st ser., 8:377–78; Isaac Van Campen and John Rosenkranz to President Reed, September 17, 1781, RG 27, 18:1271–72.

. . . .

16. Northampton County Election Returns, 1781, 1782, 1783, *Pa. Arch.*, 6th ser., 11: 254, 255, 256.

17. *Sus. Papers*, 6:292, 413. Stroud's father-in-law, John McDowell, almost certainly befriended the settlers from Connecticut.

18. *Sus. Papers*, 7:xv–xxxix, 316–18, 352–53, 356–57, 368–69; Brunhouse, *Counter-Revolution in Pennsylvania*, 129–30, 164. Stroud served as a Northampton County commissioner between 1791 and 1793.

19. Colbert, "Stroud," 29, from the Journal of Samuel Preston, Surveyor.

20. Ibid., 32–33. The advertisement appeared in the *American Eagle*, October 17, 1799, published in Easton, Pennsylvania.

21. Reverend Henry Boehm, *Historical and Biographical, of Sixty-four Years in the Ministry* (New York, 1865), quoted in Colbert, "Stroud," 31.

22. George W. Stroud, "Colonel Jacob Stroud," pamphlet, n.d., 14, Monroe County Historical Society.

CHAPTER 10

1. The following sources have been useful in sorting out the career of George Taylor: Mildred Rowe Trexler, *George Taylor, Esq.* (Allentown, Pa. 1968); Warren S. Ely, "George Taylor, Signer of the Declaration of Independence," *BCHSC* 5 (1925), 101–12; B. F. Fackenthal Jr., "The Homes of George Taylor, Signer of the Declaration of Independence," *BCHSC* 5 (1925), 113–33; B. F. Fackenthal Jr., "The Durham Iron Works in Durham Township," *BCHSC* 5 (1925), 59–93; Charles Laubach, "The Durham Iron Works," *BCHSC* 1 (1908), 220–49; Charles Laubach, "George Taylor—The Signer," *BCHSC* 1 (1908), 326–33.

2. *Pa. Gazette*, January 19, 1748. In Europe, King George's war was known as the War of the Austrian Succession.

3. An account of the formation of the Association, Pennsylvania's first volunteer militia, is found in Barbara A. Gannon, "The Lord Is a Man of War, the God of Love and Peace: The Associate Debate, Philadelphia 1747–1748," *Pa. History* 65 (1998): 46–61. See also Esmond Wright, *Franklin of Philadelphia* (Cambridge, Mass., 1986), 77–81; Theodore Thayer, *Pennsylvania Politics and the Growth of Democracy, 1740–1776* (Harrisburg, Pa., 1953), 20–23; Provincial Council to the Proprietaries, July 30, 1748, *Col. Records*, 5:319–23.

4. Durham Iron Company was formed in 1726 as a partnership by twelve men. In addition to William Allen, the partners included Jeremiah Langhorne, Anthony Morris, James Logan, Charles Read, Robert Ellis, George Fitzwater, Clement Plumstead, Andrew Bradford, John Hopkins, Thomas Lindley, and Joseph Turner. The proprietary party was comprised of men who championed the best interests of the king and the Penn family.

5. *Votes*, 7:6135–39.

6. *Pa. Gazette*, August 23, 1770.

7. *Votes*, 7:5542–47, 5580, 5583, 5597–99, 5608, 5610, 5626, 5636, 5641.

8. Ibid., 7:5572, 5774, 6103, 6111, 6118.

9. Ibid., 7:6476, 6487, 6489, 6491, 6496, 6502–3, 6524. One authority suggests that the amendment was added to render representation in the back counties more difficult by "preventing the western counties from choosing a member from the east who, with less inconvenience, could be present at all times in the Assembly." Charles H. Lincoln,

"Representation in the Pennsylvania Assembly Prior to the Revolution," *PMHB* 23 (1899–1900): 33.

10. *Votes*, 8:6737, 6806, 6976, 7020, 7103–4, 7159, 7164, 7168–69, 7171, 7182.

11. See Ryerson, *Revolution*, 52–55. With support from backcounty leaders like George Taylor, Philadelphia radicals went on to pave the way for the Revolution in Pennsylvania. Had the back counties, which held two-thirds of the population, refused to support the radicals, it is likely that the Revolution in Pennsylvania would have floundered, thereby changing the course of American history.

12. An advertisement in which Joseph Galloway offered to lease Durham Iron Company appeared in the *Pa. Gazette*, June 30, 1773. Galloway probably became the principal owner of the works by buying shares on a timely basis from the original partners.

13. Bucks County Court Records, September Term, 1765. Cited in B. F. Fackenthal Jr., "The Durham Ironworks in Durham Township," *BCHSC* 5 (1925), 72 n. 14.

14. *Col. Records*, 10:297–98, 315, 331, 339, 382. Weekly capacity of Durham Furnace in 1775 probably did not exceed twenty tons at full blast. Arthur C. Bining, *Pennsylvania Iron Manufacture in the Eighteenth Century* (Harrisburg, Pa., 1979), 65–68. Durham shallow-draft boats were constructed to carry iron from Durham to Philadelphia. These boats were also pressed into service to transport troops across the Delaware on the eve of the Battle of Trenton.

15. Peter Kachlein, longtime resident of Northampton and former sheriff, was also elected at this time.

16. See Chapter 1, note 73.

17. George Taylor to Matlack, May 24, 1777, original in HSP, quoted in Warren S. Ely, "George Taylor, Signer of the Declaration of Independence," *BCHSC* 5 (1925), 107.

18. Taylor to Supreme Executive Council, July (?), 1778, quoted in Warren S. Ely, "George Taylor, Signer of the Declaration of Independence," *BCHSC* 5 (1925), 110.

19. Taylor to Levers, October 23, 1780, Gratz Collection, case 1, box 11, HSP. An Act for the Gradual Abolition of Slavery, March 1, 1780, *Statutes*, 10:67–73. Under the law, slaves not registered by November 1, 1780, would have been eligible for their freedom.

20. Taylor's son, James, who married Lewis Gordon's daughter, died in 1775, leaving her with five children. Taylor doubtless contributed to the support of his son's children and provided as well for his five children born out of wedlock.

21. Samuel William of Greenwich Forge, New Jersey, to Richard Backhouse at Durham, February 22, 1781, quoted in B. F. Fackenthal Jr., "The Homes of George Taylor, Signer of the Declaration of Independence," *BCHSC* 5 (1925), 132; original in Bucks County Historical Society, Doylestown, Pa. Greenwich Forge was part of the Durham operation.

22. Charles Laubach, "George Taylor—The Signer," *BCHSC* 1 (1908), 332.

CHAPTER II

1. The bill to abolish slavery in Pennsylvania passed by a vote of 34 to 21. In this session of the Assembly, Northampton was represented by John Ralston, John Van Campen, Simon Driesbach, Peter Rhoads, and Christopher Waggoner. The delegation split its votes, but not along discernible lines. Ralston and Van Campen each owned one slave, the others owned none. Ralston voted for the bill; Van Campen opposed it. Rhodes also voted for the bill, while Driesbach and Waggoner opposed it.

. . . .

2. Joseph S. Foster, *In Pursuit of Equal Liberty: George Bryan and the Revolution in Pennsylvania* (University Park, Pa., 1994), 109–15.

3. Gary B. Nash and Jean Soderlund, *Freedom by Degrees: Emancipation in Pennsylvania and Its Aftermath* (New York, 1991), 111.

4. William S. Henry, *History of Lehigh Valley* (Easton, Pa., 1860), 96–97.

5. Edward R. Turner, *The Negro in Pennsylvania* (Washington, D.C., 1911), 38–88. The American Historical Association awarded Turner's essay the Justin Winsor Prize in American History in 1901.

6. The Federal Census for 1790 lists one servant in the Hart household. Tax records for 1793 indicate that Michael Hart possessed "one bound servant." Northampton County Tax List, 1781, 1782, 1787, 1788, 1793, 1808–15, Church of Jesus Christ of the Latter Day Saints, microfilm, New England Historic Genealogical Society, Boston, Mass.

7. "xxxxx" in original.

8. Deposition of Phillis, a Negro slave, November 6, 1783, 1778–97, NCP, 54. The original deposition has almost no punctuation.

CHAPTER 12

1. In late 1779, Moses Hazen, for one, still hoped that Canada would become the fourteenth state: "It is hoped and really wished that the period may not be far off when this regiment may be adopted by their own—a fourteenth state in America." The Memorial of Colonel Moses Hazen to General Washington, November 30, 1779, *Pa. Arch.*, 1st ser., 8:17–20.

2. *Pa. Arch.*, 5th ser., 5:765–66; Fred Anderson Berg, *Encyclopedia of Continental Army Units* (Harrisburg, Pa., 1972), 16–17; John B. B. Trussell Jr., *The Pennsylvania Line* (Harrisburg, Pa., 1977), 221–22; George F. Scheer and Hugh F. Rankin, *Rebels and Redcoats* (New York, 1957), 129–45; Don Higginbotham, *The War of American Independence* (1971; reprint, Boston, 1983), 106–15; Dumas Malone, ed., *Dictionary of American Biography*, vol. 8 (New York, 1932), 477–78.

3. Scheer and Rankin, *Rebels and Redcoats*, 251–60.

4. Deposition of Mathew and Mary Myler by Robert Levers, January 9, 1778, NCP, box 6.

5. Mary Myler probably invented the name of Sergeant O'Brian, for none of the O'Brians—and variations of that name—found in the *Pennsylvania Archives* matches the rank, time, and place of the Sergeant O'Brian in Mary's story.

6. A fulling mill increased the weight and bulk of cloth by shrinking and beating or pressing.

7. *Pa. Arch.*, 5th ser., 2:622. An account of the First Regiment in action at the Battle of Brandywine specifically mentions the injury suffered by Captain Grier.

8. Mathew Myler to Major Johnson, October 1777, quoted in John W. Jordan, "The Military Hospitals of Bethlehem and Lititz During the Revolution," *PMHB* 20 (1896): 147.

CHAPTER 13

1. Hanau, a small principality in the Duchy of Hesse, is located on the outskirts of Frankfurt. Stade lies east of Hamburg.

. . . .

2. William L. Stone, *Memoirs, and Letters and Journals of Major General Riedesel During His Residence in America*, 2 vols. (Albany, 1868), 1:17–39.

3. Bernard Knollenberg, *Washington and the Revolution: A Reappraisal* (1940; reprint, New York, 1968), 145. For a brief account of events both before and after the Battle of Saratoga, see Higginbotham, *War of American Independence*, 188–98.

4. Details of this episode are found in William M. Dabney, *After Saratoga: The Story of the Convention Army* (Albuquerque, N.Mex., 1954).

5. This account of Isaac Klinkerfuss is based on material found in the following sources: "Examination of Isaac Clingafoose by Robert Levers," March 7, 1782, RG 27, 19:609; Deposition of Valentine Beidleman by Robert Levers, Sussex County, N.J., March 25, 1782, RG 27, 19:607; Deposition of Abraham H. Haines by Robert Levers, Sussex County, N.J., March 25, 1782, RG 27, 19:613. Even though Klinkerfuss's signature at the bottom of the deposition is remarkably clear, Robert Levers never got it right. In various documents he spelled it Clingafoose, Clinkafoose, Clinkerfoos, Clingafoos, Clinkerfoosen, Klinkerfoos, Clinkerfoose, Clinkerfus, and Clinkerfuss—but not Klinkerfuss, the spelling used here.

6. Issued from 1723 to 1835, the johannes was a Portuguese gold coin worth about £1.10. The coin circulated widely and was well known in the American colonies, where it was called half-joe, the joe being the dobra or double johannes.

7. Andrew Ledlie, Deputy Commissioner of Prisoners, to Robert Levers, March 26, 1782, RG 27, 19:605.

8. Levers to Secretary Benjamin Lincoln, Board of War, March 30, 1782, RG 27, 19:629.

9. Andrew Ledlie to Board of War, April 9, 1782, *Pa. Arch.*, 1st ser., 9:527.

10. Robert Levers to President William Moore, April 19, 1782, Society Collection, HSP.

11. William J. Heller, *Historic Easton From the Window of a Trolley-Car* (1911; reprint, Washington, N.J., 1984), 146.

CHAPTER 14

1. Robert Levers, June 21, 1778, Dead Soldier Deposition, NCP, 3:211. Because this document is written in Levers's hand, it would appear that he went before the court for "direction" and wrote his own ticket. Thomas Sillyman, president of the court, signed the document.

2. Major General John de Kalb, General Frederick von Steuben, and the Marquis de La Fayette, who recuperated at Bethlehem from wounds suffered at the Battle of Brandywine, were among other foreign officers whose mission brought them to the Moravian town for varying periods of time during the Revolution.

3. *Pa. Arch.*, 5th ser., 3:885.

4. Levering, *Bethlehem*, 885–88.

5. Board of War to Brigadier General Count Pulaski, March 9, 1779, *Pa. Arch.*, 1st ser., 6:233–34; General George Washington to President Joseph Reed, April 27, 1779, *Pa. Arch.*, 1st ser., 6:353; President Reed to General Washington, May 8, 1779, *Pa. Arch.*, 1st ser., 6:378. A brief biography of Pulaski is found in Benson J. Lossing, *The Pictorial Field-Book of the Revolution*, vol. 2 (New York, 1860), 529.

. . . .

6. Northampton County Commissioners Cash Book, 1754–70. Arthur Lattimore, Coroner, 1762. Church of Jesus Christ of the Latter Day Saints, HSP, microfilm.

7. Levers to Bryan, July 6, 1778, *Pa. Arch.*, 1st ser., 6:626–27.

CHAPTER 15

1. An Act For The Attainder of Divers Traitors If They Render Not Themselves By A Certain Day, And For Vesting Their Estates In This Commonwealth, And For More Effectually Discovering The Same And For Ascertaining And Satisfying The Lawful Debts And Claims Thereupon, March 6, 1778, *Statutes*, 9:201–15.

2. An Act For The Further Security Of The Government, April 1, 1778, *Statutes*, 9:238–45. Pennsylvania first required all white men to swear loyalty to the state in An Act Obliging The Male White Inhabitants Of This State To Give Assurances Of Allegiance To The Same And For Other Purposes Therein Mentioned, June 13, 1777, Ibid., 9:110–14. The act was repealed on March 13, 1789. Ibid., 13:222–24.

3. Each of these laws had different rules and procedures that governed the forfeiture of real estate. Simply stated, under the Attainder Act the state confiscated personal property and real estate as soon as it had been determined that a person had defected to the British. Under the Security Act, the state seized personal property upon refusal to take the oath of allegiance, but real estate passed to the next male in the family line on condition that he take the oath. If he refused, the real estate passed to the next in line, and so on. Hence, under the Attainder Act loss of property was automatic, while under the Security Act loss of real estate was threatened, but I have found no example of it being enforced.

4. George Bryan to Colonel John Wetzel, May 22, 1978, *Pa. Arch.*, 1st ser., 6:541. Bryan's biographer explains why the vice president attempted to restrain ultraradicals like John Wetzel. "[Bryan] was nearly always highly supportive of many of the controversial features of the Constitutionalists [Pennsylvania's radical faction], but at the same time he appeared to exert a moderating influence among his peers. . . . This enigmatic aspect of his personality was almost schizophrenic, for he perceived himself as being able to maintain both unbridled zeal and reasoned compromise—to be, in effect, the outspoken partisan and the quiet negotiator." Foster, *In Pursuit of Equal Liberty*, 91–95.

5. John Wetzel to President Wharton, May 25, 1778, *Pa. Arch.*, 1st ser., 6:551. Unaware that President Wharton had died on May 23, Wetzel's letter was doubtless forwarded to Vice President Bryan.

6. The eleven Mennonites were John Geisinger, Abraham Geisinger, Henry Geisinger, Jacob Yoder, Caper Yoder, Abraham Yoder, Henry Zell, Peter Zell, John Newcomer, George Bachman, and Christian Young.

7. Some Northampton militiamen and the companies who fought in these battles are identified in Hannah Bender Roach, "The Pennsylvania Militia in 1777," *PGM* 23 (1964): 182, 188, 195–96.

8. Records of the inventory and sale of Mennonite property are found in *Pa. Arch.*, 6th ser., 12: Abraham Geisinger, inventory, 347, sale, 433; John Geisinger, 351, 437; Henry Geisinger, 350, 440; Casper Yoder, 363, 430; Jacob Yoder, 365, 442; Abraham Yoder, 361, 445; George Bachman, 340, 429; Henry and Peter Zell, 374, 435; John Newcomer, 369, 444; Christian Young, 396, 446.

. . . .

9. A muster roll dated June 27, 1778, contains the names of the men called out for this detail, days served, and the money owed them. *Pa. Arch.*, 6th ser., 12:478.

10. A few of the surnames of those who purchased items at the auction are found only in the tax records of Bucks and Berks Counties.

11. *Col. Records*, 11:525.

12. Timothy Matlack to Agents for Forfeited Estates in Northampton County, July 1, 1778, RG 27, 14:334.

13. Instructions to the Sheriff, July 1, 1778, *Pa. Arch.*, 1st ser., 6:621–22.

14. Roberts, *Lehigh County*, 3:1229–30.

15. Bond posted by Jacob Arndt, *Col. Records*, 11:525.

16. Referring to the conviction of eleven men on June 17, John Ettwein said, "nine Mennonites and two others were harshly dealt with." Hamilton, *Ettwein*, 296. I believe Ettwein erred in this matter, because a subsequent petition identifies all eleven men as Mennonites. Although eleven Mennonites were tried and had forfeited their property, the petition, dated July 4, 1778, was signed by twelve Mennonites. Philip Geisinger, who had neither been convicted nor forfeited his property, provided the extra signature. How this discrepancy came about, I have been unable to determine.

17. The petition was signed July 4, its appendage on July 5, 1778. The full petition is found in Richard K. MacMaster with Samuel L. Horst and Robert F. Ulle, *Conscience in Crisis: Studies in Anabaptist and Mennonite History* (Kitchener, Ontario, 1979), 429–30. These authors note: "The entire petition is in the handwriting of Dr. Felix Lynn . . . except for the signatures of the other petitioners." A copy of the original petition is also found in RG 27, 36:436–37.

18. It is likely that Limbach's knowledge of the law was based on hearsay and rumor. Even had this not been so, it would not have altered the sentence handed down by Limbach. Clearly, both the justice and Wetzel had foul intentions.

19. That Council minutes do not record receipt of the Mennonite petition may be indicative of the uproar in Philadelphia caused by news of Indian troubles on the frontier.

20. Council received Jacob Bachman's petition on July 7, 1778. *Col. Records*, 11:527. Signers in addition to those cited in the text were John Newcomer, one of the eleven convicted Mennonites, or possibly his son, and John Beaver, who, in fact, may have been the Jacob Beaver who served under Captain Stahl. If not that, John and Jacob were related. A copy of the original petition is found in RG 27, 43:3. A less than perfect copy is found in *Pa. Arch.*, 6th ser., 13:222.

21. MacMaster, *Conscience*, 441. This petition also appeared in the *Pennsylvania Evening Post*, August 22, 1778.

22. Before the sale, Anthony Kleckner doubtless knew that, like himself, Henry Geisinger was a blacksmith. Kleckner lived in Lower Saucon from 1760 to 1774. Francis S. Fox, "The Kleckners of Pennsylvania," *PGM* 34 (1985): 26–43.

23. A shallow cup or bowl with a handle.

24. One authority on this matter states that the sales brought £6,455.7.5. See MacMaster, *Conscience*, 399.

25. I have been unable to determine who wrote the petition signed by Eve Yoder and Esther Bachman. However, the unaffected style of the petition and its focus on keeping families together strongly supports the scenario given in this text.

26. The full petition, dated September 9, 1778, and the extract from the minutes of

. . . .

the General Assembly that is appended to it, are found in MacMaster, *Conscience*, 441–42. A copy of the original petition and the appendage is found in RG 27, 43:517–24. Although eleven Mennonites were summoned and sentenced by Justice Limbach, only ten are mentioned in the Yoder-Bachman petition. (Peter Sell's name is missing.) I have no explanation for the discrepancy.

27. Ibid.

28. George Bryan to John Ralston, Peter Rhoads, Esq., and Doctor Lynn, September 17, 1778, MacMaster, *Conscience*, 442–43; see also RG 27, 36:522–23.

29. John Ralston, Peter Rhoads, and Felix Lynn to George Bryan, October 2, 1778, MacMaster, *Conscience*, 443–44; *Pa. Arch.*, 1st ser., 6:772.

30. *Pa. Arch.*, 6th ser., 13:461–62.

31. President Reed to John Siegfried, February 28, 1780, RG 27, 15:953.

32. *Col. Records*, 12:775.

33. Ibid., 13:592.

34. *Pa. Arch.*, 3rd ser., 5:285.

35. *Pa. Arch.*, 6th ser., 13:221–22.

36. Marx, *Oaths of Allegiance*, 1932; Henry Zell, November 24, 1778; John Newcomer, January 6, 1779.

37. *Pa. Arch.*, 5th ser., 8:359, 360, 366.

38. A Memorial from a number of Mennonites in the County of Northampton, February 9, 1779, *JHR*.

INDEX

· ·

. . . .

. . . .